THE OVERSTREET®
GUIDE TO GRADING COMICS

By Robert M. Overstreet

Grant Adey, Jon Berk, Dr. Arnold T. Blumberg,
Steve Borock, Gary M. Carter, William M. Cole,
Tom Gordon III, Paul Litch, Caitlin McGurk,
Amanda Sheriff, J.C. Vaughn and Carrie Wood
CONTRIBUTING WRITERS

Mark Huesman
LAYOUT & DESIGN

Mark Huesman
Amanda Sheriff
J.C. Vaughn
Carrie Wood
EDITORS

Grant Adey, Jon Berk, Steve Borock,
William M. Cole, Stephen Fishler, Douglas Gillock,
Tom Gordon III, Mark Haspel, Paul Litch,
Josh Nathanson, James Payette, Barry Sandoval,
West Stephan and Vincent Zurzolo
SPECIAL ADVISORS TO THIS EDITION

SEE A FULL LIST OF OVERSTREET ADVISORS ON PAGES 376-379

GEMSTONE PUBLISHING • TIMONIUM, MARYLAND
WWW.GEMSTONEPUB.COM

Why A New Grading Guide?

Accurate grading of comic books has never been more important because the stakes have never been higher. While most of us don't dwell in the rarified atmosphere of selling or buying CGC-certified 9.0 copies of *Action Comics* #1 for $3.2 million, everyone out there seeking the best possible copy of his or her favorite comic knows that condition is king.

And if we acknowledge the importance of condition, it follows that understanding how a grade is determined can offer a major insight into how we can and should collect.

If you grade your own comics, you need to know what you're doing.

If you use third party, independent grading services, the same is still true – the grading services have been a great addition to our market, but one should approach them with reasonable, informed expectations when submitting. The only way to do that is to understand grading in the first place.

The original edition of *The Overstreet Comic Book Grading Guide*, this book's predecessor, appeared in 1992. The refinement of its 100-point grading system into the 10-point scale was published in the 2003 edition (as well as *The Overstreet Comic Book Price Guide*), with a subsequent edition in 2006.

As industry experts and our Overstreet Advisors have debated and addressed the art and science of comic book grading over the decades, it has been much more common for the changes in grading to be nuanced rather than revolutionary. There are indeed changes in this new book. While we believe they are relatively minor, they are nonetheless important to correctly forming an understanding of the grades assigned to comics.

The Overstreet Guide To Grading Comics, like any effort that tries to walk the line between definitive science and subjective art, represents the best thinking of the experts in our industry and hobby. And like all of our books, we welcome your feedback on it.

Sincerely,

Robert M. Overstreet
Publisher
feedback@gemstonepub.com

GEMSTONE PUBLISHING

STEPHEN A. GEPPI
PRESIDENT AND CHIEF EXECUTIVE OFFICER

ROBERT M. OVERSTREET
PUBLISHER

J.C. VAUGHN
VICE-PRESIDENT OF PUBLISHING

MARK HUESMAN
CREATIVE DIRECTOR

AMANDA SHERIFF
ASSOCIATE EDITOR

CARRIE WOOD
ASSISTANT EDITOR

WWW.GEMSTONEPUB.COM

GEPPI'S ENTERTAINMENT MUSEUM

STEPHEN A. GEPPI
FOUNDER AND CHIEF EXECUTIVE OFFICER

MELISSA BOWERSOX
PRESIDENT

WWW.GEPPISMUSEUM.COM

THE OVERSTREET GUIDE TO GRADING COMICS. NOVEMBER 2014. ISBN: 978-1-60360-167-2 PUBLISHED BY GEMSTONE PUBLISHING, INC., 1940 GREENSPRING DRIVE, SUITE I, TIMONIUM, MD 21093.
©2014 GEMSTONE PUBLISHING, INC. AND RESPECTIVE COPYRIGHT HOLDERS.
COVER: BATMAN AND SUPERMAN ©2014 DC COMICS. SPIDER-MAN ©2014 MARVEL CHARACTERS, INC.
THE WALKING DEAD ©ROBERT KIRKMAN.
OVERSTREET® IS A REGISTERED TRADEMARK OF GEMSTONE PUBLISHING, INC. ALL RIGHTS RESERVED. PRINTED IN CANADA.

TABLE OF CONTENTS

Important Notice: All of the information in this book, including that which concerns defects, has been compiled from the most reliable sources, and every effort has been made to eliminate errors and questionable data. Nevertheless, the possibility of error always exists in a work of such immense scope. The publisher will not be held responsible for losses which may occur in the purchase, sale, or other transaction of items because of information contained herein. Readers who feel they have discovered errors are invited to inform us so that the errors may be corrected in subsequent editions.

PASSION for COLLECTING...

When it comes to passion for collecting, dedication to the hobby, and amassing high-grade, award winning runs... few measure up to Pedigree Comics' CEO and President, Doug Schmell, who sold his personal collection of Silver Age Marvels in 2012 for over 3.94 Million Dollars (a record price for a comic book collection).

So, who is best qualified to help you build your collection and find you the books and upgrades you need?

Over the past 20 plus years, I have amassed over fifteen thousand Marvel comic books, most of which are in very high grade condition. When CGC was in the process of forming in March, 1999, I was one of a handful of collectors asked to attend their start-up meeting and provide input to the creation of this third party grading service. When the CGC commenced operations later that year and began encapsulating and grading comic books for the public, I began submitting my runs of Marvel titles. Now, known as "Captain Tripps" on the CGC Registry and chat boards, I have come to be recognized as one of the leading collectors of Marvel Silver and Bronze Age comics, with many of my books being the highest graded copies in existence. In fact, I received the coveted Achievement in Comics Collecting 2006, awarded by the CGC Comics Registry, in honor of the outstanding runs of Marvel comics I had registered since November, 2003, including the highest graded set of virtually every Marvel Silver Age and Bronze Age title.

Although I sold the majority of my Bronze Age titles when I moved to Florida in 2004, I kept and continued to add to my Silver Age sets, looking for upgrades on any individual issue whenever possible. The formation of this collection, which has been painstakingly pared down to around 700 books, took an incredible amount of effort, time, expense, and patience. The stories I could tell of meeting at diners, post offices in Northern New Jersey, law offices, street corners in New York City, dealers' tables, and comic stores around the country in order to obtain that missing issue or coveted upgrade, would blow your mind. My decision to sell the collection was based on my feeling that I had reached a sort of collector's Nirvana, that I had finally obtained every sought after pedigreed issue or top of the CGC census book I could possibly find. The long journey has taken me to this point in time and I couldn't be any happier.

**Let me help you find the same fulfillment I have!
Email me at dougschmell@pedigreecomics.com
or call me today at 1-561-422-1120.**

PedigreeComics.com

ACKNOWLEDGEMENTS

As we go to press, *The Overstreet Guide To Grading Comics* is the latest in our growing "how to" line of books, all of which are dedicated to informing newcomers and reenergizing experienced participants in their respective subject fields. We hope it will become a valuable tool in your collecting arsenal.

Although there have been so many changes since *The Overstreet Comic Book Grading Guide* first appeared in 1992, we all owe a mountain of gratitude to Gary M. Carter, who put his heart and soul into that early edition. While so much has changed since then, our desire to understand how to better describe the grades our comics receive has not. Likewise, credit is due to everyone who contributed to that one, as well as to Dr. Arnold T. Blumberg and the entire team who contributed to the second and third editions.

It would be a huge oversight if I failed to mention contributions over the years from such stalwart Overstreet Advisors as Stephen Fishler, Steve Borock, Douglas Gillock, Tom Gordon III, the late Bruce Hamilton, Mark Haspel, Paul Litch, Joe Mannarino, Josh Nathanson, Matt Nelson, Jim Payette, Barry Sandoval, John K. Snyder, Jr., West Stephan, John Verzyl, Mark Zaid, and Vincent Zurzolo.

I also know that there are *many* others who should be named here but aren't, and for that they have our heartfelt thanks and apologies. As I've said before, this kind of book simply can't be made in a vacuum.

Without the guidance and support of many informed individuals throughout the comic book collecting community who lent their time and expertise over the years and during the production of this book, we would never have been able to complete the volume you now hold in your hands.

This book is a tribute to the cohesive efforts of everyone involved, including our fine team at Gemstone Publishing: Mark Huesman (Creative Director), Amanda Sheriff (Associate Editor), Carrie Wood (Assistant Editor), and J.C. Vaughn (Vice-President of Publishing).

I would also like to single out the support of CGC, CBCS and Metropolis Collectibles for this new edition, as well as our many advertisers, who make projects such as this possible in the first place, and I believe that everyone who loves this hobby owes thanks to Steve Geppi, President of Gemstone Publishing.

As always, I would also like to thank my wife, Caroline, for always supporting and encouraging our Gemstone projects, and to you, our reader, for purchasing this book.

–RMO

New Grading Issues

When we were working on the 2006 edition of this guide, pressing was a major area of conflict. It is still an area of concern for many veterans, while others have taken the attitude that if they can't detect it, it's not a problem. While significantly less combative an issue than it was previously – and while it has been accepted by an overwhelming percentage of the market – we are mindful of the concerns raised about it.

Heritage Auctions' Barry Sandoval, one of our Overstreet Advisors, dropped us a line, saying, "One thing in the last grading guide that the hobby at large seems to disagree with is that a comic with a missing centerfold can still be Fair. I would say almost all collectors would say a book with this defect has to be Poor."

This produced a number of strong reactions. CGC and CBCS would both rank in 0.5 Poor.

"We would grade it a Poor. If it was nice enough otherwise, we might consider a Qualified grade," said CGC's Paul Litch. "Most of the time it would be a Universal 0.5 (Poor)."

"Poor. It's incomplete and usually affects story. What's the difference if it's a centerfold or two random pages or seven panels cut out?" said CBCS's Steve Borock.

Those taking the other side of the equation leaned more to Qualified grades.

"If a book has the centerfold out then to me it is incomplete. I would grade the book as it looks if complete, then mention what is missing. For example if a book was VG with a centerfold missing I would grade it VG and mention the missing centerfold. I would more than likely price the book half of Good or as a Fair. It all depends on the book," said veteran Overstreet Advisor and dealer Jim Payette.

"A missing centerfold is a topic that lies outside of the grade. The book is simply incomplete. Good or Fair or Poor does not do the job," said Stephen Fishler of Metropolis Collectibles.

"I've had really nice books that were missing the centerfold. Books that are otherwise VF or NM that have a centerfold out are not that uncommon. I don't see them as being the same as a Poor. They are definitely Incomplete, though. CGC seems to sort of ride the fence on this issue. I see 0.5 incompletes and Qualified grade incompletes," said ComicLink's Douglas Gillock. "I personally feel like it is more accurate to market to qualify a grade on a book missing the centerfold,"

While it is very hard to argue with the points raised by Litch and Borock, the practices of dealers and collectors over the year have weight as well. At some point, however, a consensus must be reached on this issue.

If you would like to weigh in on this matter – or any other issue in the realm of grading – we would greatly appreciate hearing from you. Please drop us a line via email at feedback@gemstonepub.com or by regular mail at Gemstone Publishing, 1940 Greenspring Drive, Suite I, Timonium, MD 21093. We value all serious input on such topics, whether you're an Overstreet Advisor or not.

What such discussions remind us of is that while we as an industry have done a fantastic job codifying our grading standards, there are still points that arise which are perhaps still too subjective. Grading has its solid rules, but like building a collection it's still a journey at this point.

Again, I urge you to get as much experience grading as you can. Develop your opinions and reputation carefully. Participate in the hobby. Make your voice heard.

Happy collecting!

THE EVOLUTION OF GRADING

The grading of comic books has never been a static enterprise. As the years have gone by and the hobby has matured, both the methods and standards of grading comic books have undergone a gradual, but undeniable evolution. While some of the most dramatic changes in grading have taken place in the last several years alone, there has always been a slow but steady development in existing standards and the ways in which comic book enthusiasts look at the many factors involved in grading comics.

After all these years, the current comic book grading scale and the related nomenclature still bears the mark of its progenitors in two other major collectible disciplines: coins and stamps. In fact, even though stamps shared some similarities with comics when it comes to determining condition – i.e. they are both composed of paper – it was the grading system used by coin collectors, many of whom took up comic book collecting as well, that was adapted for use by our hobby. As a result, comic book grading still labors under the weight of coin-based terminology that, while not wholly appropriate when applied to comics, has nevertheless long since passed into common usage and will not be debated further in these pages.

While the grading standards for comics grew out of a similar system for coins, both have undergone changes as their respective hobbies have evolved. Additions and adjustments to the existing scales speak to a need for ever more detailed evaluation of the collectibles in question. Some might wonder why we clamor for such intense scrutiny, but then one need look no further than the educational system to see where our understanding of and later appreciation for detailed evaluation was first born.

When one attends some traditional nursery schools, only two grades are required to describe student performance:

S   Satisfactory
U   Unsatisfactory

As the child progresses to kindergarten, this system expands:

+   Above Average
   Average
-   Below Average

By elementary school, a far more familiar 5-point system has taken shape:

A   Excellent
B   Above Average
C   Average
D   Below Average
F   Failing

Eventually, even that scale expands to fit the needs of older children and adults, resulting in the full and all too familiar grading system that almost all of us know very well:

A+ Superb
A   Excellent
A- Excellent Minus
B+ Above Average Plus
B   Above Average
B- Above Average Minus
C+ Average Plus
C   Average
C- Average Minus
D+ Below Average Plus
D   Below Average
D- Below Average Minus
F   Failing

Of course, letter grades and the related nomenclature are only part of the story. Most of us are also very familiar with the numerical 100-point system for evaluating academic work. Employed as is or in a percentage format, the 100-point numerical grading system can be matched to the letter scale, but with a far greater range of accuracy and detail than what is possible with the letter scale alone. Just as our experience with an evolving system of educational evaluation has introduced us to nomenclature and a 100-point grading scale, so too did the coin and comic book hobbies employ similar systems as their need for more advanced grading criteria intensified.

In the 1932 edition of *The Star Rare Coin Encyclopedia*, compiled and published by the Numismatic Company of Texas and B. Max Mehl – the foremost numismatics authority of his time – a system for grading coins was detailed that parallels the standards adopted by the fledgling comic book hobby about twenty years later. At the time of the *Encyclopedia*, the scale for grading coins was fairly simple:

Proof
Uncirculated or As Minted
Fine
Good
Fair
Poor

This 6-point system evolved, with two new grades inserted into the scale to enable coin collectors to grade with a higher degree of accuracy and detail:

Proof
Uncirculated
Extra Fine or Extremely Fine
Very Fine
Fine
Good
Fair
Poor

Later, the coin hobby settled on a 70-point scale still in use by coin collectors and coin grading services. But for the relatively newborn comic book collecting hobby, the original coin grading scale – with the Proof grade dropped – served as a somewhat ill-fitting but convenient way to begin the process of developing a comic book grading system. By the mid- to late 1950s, the 5-point scale adopted from the coin world was in common use for comics:

Mint
Fine
Good
Fair
Poor

Interestingly, many comic book dealers balked at adopting any kind of grading system, rigidly adhering to a bizarre "no grading" policy. Mail order ads of the time would often include statements like "Please do not make inquiries about condition" or "Inquiries about condition will not be answered." Comic book collectors today would no doubt cringe to see such declarations and give those dealers a wide berth; indeed, it was pressure from collectors of the day who demanded grading information prior to purchase that forced the issue and resulted in the adoption of the first comic book grading scale. Ads then frequently featured statements like "All comics guaranteed to be in good or better condition" or the gloriously vague "All books are in Good to Mint condition unless otherwise noted."

At any rate, the 5-point system soon gained two middle grades, creating a 7-point scale:

Mint
Very Fine
Fine
Very Good
Good
Fair
Poor

It was at this point that mail order dealers, discovering that the mere use of the word Mint resulted in better sales, decided to create new grades that enabled them to keep the word Mint in play even when the comic in question didn't warrant the grade. As phrases like "Nearly Mint" proliferated in advertising, a new middle grade shortened to Near Mint made its debut and became common by the early 1960s. The comic book grading scale now settled into its most familiar 8-point incarnation:

Mint
Near Mint
Very Fine
Fine
Very Good
Good
Fair
Poor

It's also worth noting that for a while, the Very Fine and Very Good grades were not considered "full grades" on par with the others on the scale, but were instead known as "half grades" that rested halfway between the adjacent grades. The adoption of Near Mint therefore caused a bit of a stir, resting between Mint and the "half grade" of Very Fine, Near Mint was a difficult grade to pin down. Was Very Fine now 1/3 of the way to Mint while Near Mint was 2/3, or was Very Fine still a "half grade," with Near Mint 3/4 of the way to Mint? While the matter was eventually settled in 1989 with *The Official Overstreet Comic Book Price Guide*, these three middle or "in between" grades soon gained "full grade" status and today occupy an equal place on the scale with the other grades.

With the release of the first *The Official Overstreet Comic Book Grading Guide* in 1992, a new 100-point scale was applied to the existing grading nomenclature in the interests of even greater accuracy and a heightened level of descriptive detail:

98-100	Mint
90-97	Near Mint
75-89	Very Fine
55-74	Fine
35-54	Very Good
15-34	Good
5-14	Fair
1-4	Poor

This became known as The ONE – The Overstreet Numerical Equivalent – and in concert with the new paper quality grading scale, dubbed The Overstreet Whiteness Level, or The OWL, a new era in comic book grading began.

By the end of the '90s, however, it was clear that further refinement was needed. The 100-point system, while more accurate – perhaps – and descriptive, was a bit too complex, often leading to confusion as to exactly where within a particular sub-range a specific comic fell. In attempting to enhance the descriptive potential of the comic book grading scale, the 100-point system had introduced an intense level of detail that jarred some users of the scale.

In addition, even newer middle grades had come into use throughout the hobby over the years. Most were employed by dealers and collectors on a colloquial basis to try to express condition with more specificity than the current system could not provide, while others came into being when unscrupulous types tried to convince buyers that a comic in a particular condition was actually in better shape by using the terminology of the next higher grade in concert with the real grade. By the end of the '90s, the hobby was replete with "middle grades," "plus/minus grades," and "split grades." Clearly, order had to be made of chaos.

By 1999, through the participation of many of the hobby's most prominent dealers, collectors and enthusiasts, a new 10-point version of the scale was created that essentially moved the decimal place in the 100-point system while introducing a few minor tweaks as to the placement of certain grades along the scale. The new system also incorporated the most widely used "plus/minus" and "split" grades, rigorously anchoring them to the scale and establishing their positions with regards to the other grades. The result was the 10-point scale that debuted in the 30th edition of *The Official Overstreet Comic Book Price Guide* in 2000.

Apart from a minor modification to the nomenclature for 10.0, which now becomes Gem Mint (GM) as of this new edition of the *Grading Guide*, the system remains the same as it did when it first appeared in the 2000 *The Official Overstreet Comic Book Price Guide*. Note, however, that calling it the "10-point" system is a bit misleading – while it does indeed use a numerical scale from 0 to 10, the scale actually features 25 distinct grades and their numerical equivalents.

The comic book grading scale has certainly evolved over the last fifty years, and there's no reason why we shouldn't expect that evolution to continue as the hobby itself grows and develops with time. For now, however, this Grading Guide will provide you with as much information as possible concerning the current scale and its usage. We hope that this book will enhance your understanding of comic book grading and enable you to utilize the 10-point system to evaluate your own comic books with a greater degree of accuracy and satisfaction.

USING THE 10-POINT GRADING SCALE

The following grade descriptions use both the traditional nomenclature and grade abbreviations – with the exception of the newly designated Incomplete (INC) – as well as the numerical equivalent on The Overstreet 10-Point Comic Book Grading Scale.

Please note that we have tried to be as exhaustive as possible within the space available when listing the many defects that can occur within the various grades. This does *not* mean that all listed defects are allowed within each grade *simultaneously*. Each grade will likely exhibit some combination of the allowable defects, and the final grade depends on the number of defects present and their relative severity. For example, some defects may be more extreme for a particular grade as long as other acceptable listed defects are almost non-existent.

Policy on Plus/Minus Grades

All of the grades on the 10-Point scale have been given their own section, with explanatory notes and a table of allowable defects, *except for the plus/minus grades from VF+ and below*. Comic books that are graded with either a plus or a minus grade fit all of the criteria for the primary grade in question, with one specific defect or small accumulation of defects – or a comparable number of virtues – that, respectively, limit or heighten the book's value beyond that of the major grade. In almost all such cases, it is the cumulative effect on the eye appeal of the book that determines whether or not a comic shifts from a primary grade (for example, Very Fine) to a plus or minus grade (either Very Fine + or Very Fine -).

Number of Allowable Defects

The accompanying chart provides some idea of the estimated number of accumulated defects allowed for each grade. Please remember that quantity of defects is only part of the story. For example, a book with two or three minor defects may grade significantly higher than a book with one very severe defect.

On Generalized Terminology

Throughout the grade descriptions and tables of allowable defects, the Grading Guide employs a number of modifying adjectives like "minor," "moderate" and "severe" to describe a wide range of comic book conditions. Given the subjective nature of comic book grading, we do not wish to set all such determining factors in stone – nor, indeed, could we if we wanted to – but we do want to give all comic book graders a generalized sense of what is allowable in any given grade.

We do understand that such vague terms could be frustrating, so to further clarify the use of such terminology, we offer a brief guide on the page following the allowable defects chart to the kinds of mea-

10 Point Grading Scale		
10.0	GM	Gem Mint
9.9	MT	Mint
9.8	NM/MT	Near Mint/Mint
9.6	NM+	Near Mint+
9.4	NM	Near Mint
9.2	NM-	Near Mint-
9.0	VF/NM	Very Fine/Near Mint
8.5	VF+	Very Fine+
8.0	VF	Very Fine
7.5	VF-	Very Fine-
7.0	FN/VF	Fine/Very Fine
6.5	FN+	Fine+
6.0	FN	Fine
5.5	FN-	Fine-
5.0	VG/FN	Very Good/Fine
4.5	VG+	Very Good+
4.0	VG	Very Good
3.5	VG-	Very Good-
3.0	GD/VG	Good/Very Good
2.5	GD+	Good+
2.0	GD	Good
1.8	GD-	Good-
1.5	FR/GD	Fair/Good
1.0	FR	Fair
0.5	PR	Poor
0.3	INC	Incomplete
0.1	INC	Incomplete

Suggested Number of Allowable Defects per Grade

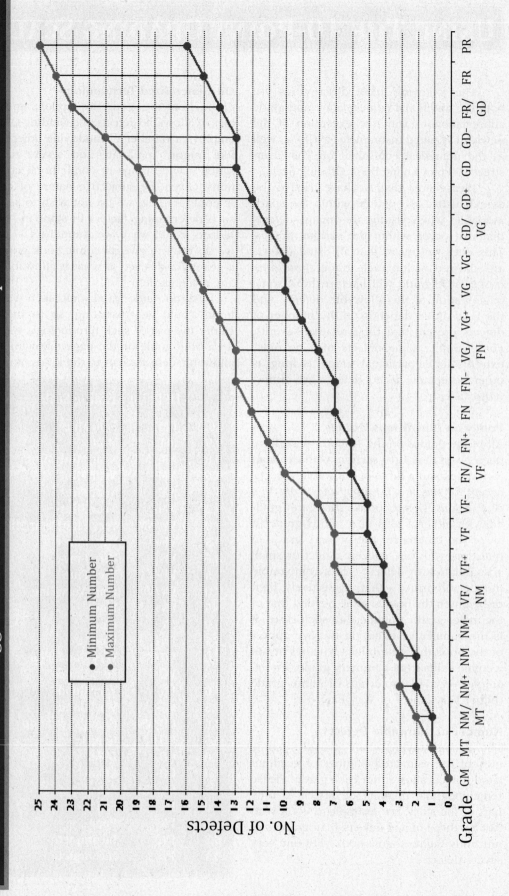

surements and/or quantities that may be implied by these terms. Please note that as with all such material in this volume, these are only guidelines and do not necessarily apply to all cases.

Obviously, combinations of these generalized terms are also used to describe certain aspects of a grade, and in those cases, you might consult this list to see what measurement and quantity ranges might apply. For example, a comic book in Fine/ Very Fine 7.0 is allowed "some accumulation of minor defects" under the category "Bindery/Printing Defects." Consulting the ranges below, this could mean that such a comic might have 4-6 related defects of no more than 1/4" in size or length. This could include an 1/8" white area on the front cover near the spine (where the back cover has wrapped around to the front), a diagonal miscut of the cover, a vertical miscut that has resulted in 1/16" of the front cover removed from the bottom, and/or a 1/8" bindery tear in the top right corner.

Paper Quality – What is "White?"

While we continue to use the familiar terminology scale in describing interior paper quality – "white," "off-white," "cream," and so on – we must qualify our use of these terms. Due to the wildly diverse paper stocks employed by the various comic book publishers over the years, the freshest possible quality of the paper in any given comic book may differ markedly in color and tone from that of another comic from another company or era. In fact, some Golden Age examples can differ drastically from one copy of the same issue number

to another, and even within the pages of a single issue, varying paper stocks were sometimes used, resulting in a patchwork of initial tones and hues. Obviously this poses a significant challenge when trying to determine a base "white" level with which to grade a given book's paper quality.

Therefore, we use the term "white" loosely in all cases to refer to the freshest and brightest color and tone of the dominant paper stock used in any given comic regardless of the actual color(s) and tone(s) that may be evident. Subsequent descriptions of "off-white," "cream," "tan" and others should then be interpreted in relation to the "white" starting point of the comic described.

Pedigree Books

As many collectors already know, there are a group of special comic books, usually referred to as "pedigrees," that represent the most exceptional examples of an issue or title - in fact, many agree that a book from one of these collections could very well be one of, if not the only, best surviving copies of a given book. Pedigree books have high cover gloss, brilliant cover inks and white, fresh, supple pages that place them far above other books that might receive the same technical grade. Books from these pedigree collections, therefore, actually transcend their technical grade. Of these, many collectors and dealers agree that the most important collections are the Mile High (Edgar Church) collection, the San Francisco (Reilly) collection, and the Gaines file copies, but there are of course many others. The striking difference between a regular copy of a particular

	TERM	INDIV. DEFECT	QTY OF DEFECTS
	slight, subtle	1/32" to 1/16"	1
	small	1/16" to 1/8"	1-2
	limited accumulation		2-4
	very minor	1/16" to 1/8"	2-5
	few		3-5
	minor, minimal	1/8" to 1/4"	3-5
	some accumulation		4-6
	moderate	1/4" to 1"	4-8
	small accumulation		4-8
	considerable, significant	1" and up	8-10
	many, accumulation		8-16
	extensive, extreme	2-3" and up	10-25

SUGGESTED RANGES OF MEASUREMENT/QUANTITY

issue and a pedigree copy becomes apparent when comparing two such examples in the same basic grade. In most cases, the pedigree book will far outshine the generic one.

Other Defects

The grade descriptions attempt to provide an overall view of the defects that can come into play throughout the scale. There are, of course, many other defects that are not mentioned specifically within those descriptions, but are just as important in determining grade. While these additional defects, such as dust shadows and pin holes, may not be discussed in the grade descriptions themselves – not for any qualitative reason but more for a simple lack of space – they are at the very least either illustrated by examples shown throughout the book or described in the glossary. In the case of creator autographs and owner signatures, we suggest that such inscriptions might not be considered a defect in any book graded Mint (9.9) and below. As for the question of transparent covers, there does not seem to be any appreciable affect on grade when

that particular defect is present according to many experts, although it has inspired some debate as to whether the impact of a transparent cover on a comic book's grade should be reevaluated in the future.

One other caveat: in many of our grade descriptions, we might say "tears are common" or "book-length creases are allowed." Many of our descriptions make use of the plural tense when referring to various individual grades. While an accumulation of a particular defect may indeed be allowed within a given grade, the use of the plural tense in describing certain defects is not necessarily indicative of the presence of multiple defects, but merely a grammatical choice indicating that a given defect is allowed in all of the comics that fall within that grade.

As you can see, while we have tried to quantify some aspects of comic book grading to aid understanding and provide a set of standards for all collectors to follow, for practical purposes we have left many areas intentionally open to interpretation. Ultimately, the grade of an individual comic book must be decided by human observers.

DIAGRAM OF A COMIC BOOK

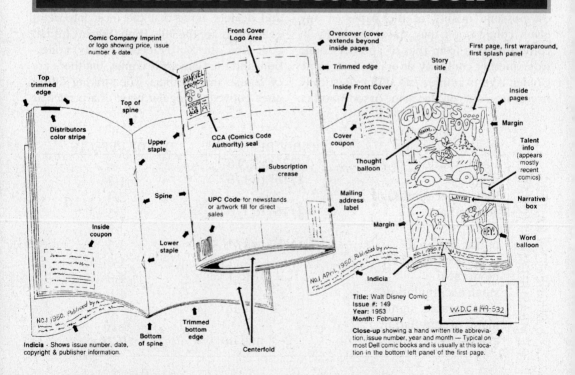

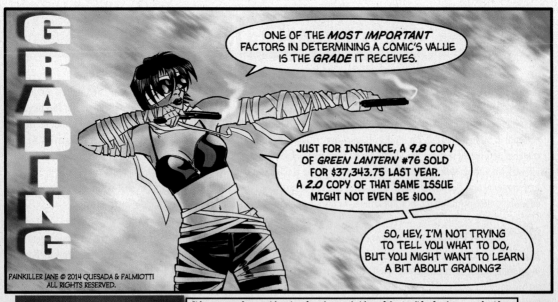

GRADING

ONE OF THE *MOST IMPORTANT* FACTORS IN DETERMINING A COMIC'S VALUE IS THE *GRADE* IT RECEIVES.

JUST FOR INSTANCE, A *9.8* COPY OF *GREEN LANTERN #76* SOLD FOR $37,343.75 LAST YEAR. A *2.0* COPY OF THAT SAME ISSUE MIGHT NOT EVEN BE $100.

SO, HEY, I'M NOT TRYING TO TELL YOU WHAT TO DO, BUT YOU MIGHT WANT TO LEARN A BIT ABOUT GRADING?

THE OVERSTREET GUIDE TO GRADING COMICS

INSIDE THE 10-POINT GRADING SCALE

THE ALL-IN-ONE GUIDEBOOK FOR BOTH NEW AND EXPERIENCED COLLECTORS

BY ROBERT M. OVERSTREET

It's a good practice to develop relationships with dealers and other collectors who prove themselves trustworthy.

MANY PEOPLE HAVE STARTED USING INDEPENDENT, THIRD-PARTY GRADING SERVICES.

HEY, SOMEONE TOOK A BITE OUT OF THIS COMIC!

OKAY, THE BASICS OF GRADING ARE PRETTY STRAIGHTFORWARD. THE TOP OF THE SCALE IS *10.0* AND THE BOTTOM IS *0.1*.

IF YOU'RE *NEW* AT THIS, DON'T EXPECT TO BE AS GOOD AS A VETERAN COLLECTOR OR DEALER RIGHT AWAY. YOU'LL GET BETTER AT IT QUICKLY, AND IT'S SOMETHING *EVERY COLLECTOR* SHOULD LEARN.

WHEN YOU'RE READY, TURN THE PAGE AND YOU'LL FIND THE DEFINITIONS OF EACH GRADE.

GRADING DEFINITIONS

10.0 **GEM MINT (GM):** This is an exceptional example of a given book - the best ever seen. The slightest bindery defects and/or printing flaws may be seen only upon very close inspection. The overall look is "as if it has never been handled or released for purchase." Only the slightest bindery or printing defects are allowed, and these would be imperceptible on first viewing. No bindery tears. Cover is flat with no surface wear. Inks are bright with high reflectivity. Well centered and firmly secured to interior pages. Corners are cut square and sharp. No creases. No dates or stamped markings allowed. No soiling, staining or other discoloration. Spine is tight and flat. No spine roll or split allowed. Staples must be original, centered and clean with no rust. No staple tears or stress lines. Paper is white, supple and fresh. No hint of acidity in the odor of the newsprint. No interior autographs or owner signatures. Centerfold is firmly secure. No interior tears.

9.9 **MINT (MT):** Near perfect in every way. Only subtle bindery or printing defects are allowed. No bindery tears. Cover is flat with no surface wear. Inks are bright with high reflectivity. Generally well centered and firmly secured to interior pages. Corners are cut square and sharp. No creases. Small, inconspicuous, lightly penciled, stamped or inked arrival dates are acceptable as long as they are in an unobtrusive location. No soiling, staining or other discoloration. Spine is tight and flat. No spine roll or split allowed. Staples must be original, generally centered and clean with no rust. No staple tears or stress lines. Paper is white, supple and fresh. No hint of acidity in the odor of the newsprint. Centerfold is firmly secure. No interior tears.

9.8 **NEAR MINT/MINT (NM/MT):** Nearly perfect in every way with only minor imperfections that keep it from the next higher grade. Only subtle bindery or printing defects are allowed. No bindery tears. Cover is flat with no surface wear. Inks are bright with high reflectivity. Generally well centered and firmly secured to interior pages. Corners are cut square and sharp. No creases. Small, inconspicuous, lightly penciled, stamped or inked arrival dates are acceptable as long as they are in an unobtrusive location. No soiling, staining or other discoloration. Spine is tight and flat. No spine roll or split allowed. Staples must be original, generally centered and clean with no rust. No staple tears or stress lines. Paper is off-white to white, supple and fresh. No hint of acidity in the odor of the newsprint. Centerfold is firmly secure. Only the slightest interior tears are allowed.

9.6 **NEAR MINT+ (NM+):** Nearly perfect with a minor additional virtue or virtues that raise it from Near Mint. The overall look is "as if it was just purchased and read once or twice." Only subtle bindery or printing defects are allowed. No bindery tears are allowed, although on Golden Age books bindery tears of up to 1/8" have been noted. Cover is flat with no surface wear. Inks are bright with high reflectivity. Well centered and firmly secured to interior pages. One corner may be almost imperceptibly blunted, but still almost sharp and cut square. Almost imperceptible indentations are permissible, but no creases, bends, or color break. Small, inconspicuous, lightly penciled, stamped or inked arrival dates are acceptable as long as they are in an unobtrusive location. No soiling, staining or other discoloration. Spine is tight and flat. No spine roll or split allowed. Staples must be original, generally centered, with only the slightest discoloration. No staple tears, stress lines, or rust migration. Paper is off-white, supple and fresh. No hint of acidity in the odor of the newsprint. Centerfold is firmly secure. Only the slightest interior tears are allowed.

9.4 **NEAR MINT (NM):** Nearly perfect with only minor imperfections that keep it from the next higher grade. The overall look is "as if it was just purchased and read once or twice." Subtle bindery defects are allowed. Bindery tears must be less than 1/16" on Silver Age and later books, although on Golden Age books bindery tears of up to 1/4" have been noted. Cover is flat with no surface wear. Inks are bright with high reflectivity. Generally well centered and secured to interior pages. Corners are cut square and sharp with ever-so-slight blunting permitted. A 1/16" bend is permitted with no color break. No creases. Small, inconspicuous, lightly penciled, stamped or inked arrival dates are acceptable as long as they are in an unobtrusive location. No soiling, staining or other discoloration apart from slight foxing. Spine is tight and flat. No spine roll or split allowed. Staples are generally centered; may have slight discoloration. No staple tears are allowed; almost no stress lines. No rust migration. In rare cases, a comic was not stapled at the bindery and therefore has a missing staple; this is not considered a defect. Any staple can be replaced on books up to Fine, but only vintage staples can be used on books from Very Fine to Near Mint. Mint books must have original staples. Paper is cream to off-white, supple and fresh. No hint of acidity in the odor of the newsprint. Centerfold is secure. Slight interior tears are allowed.

9.2 **NEAR MINT– (NM–):** Nearly perfect with only a minor additional defect or defects that keep it from Near Mint. A limited number of minor bindery defects are allowed. Cover is flat with no surface wear. Inks are bright with only the slightest dimming of reflectivity. Generally well centered and secured to interior pages. Corners are cut square and sharp with ever-so-slight blunting permitted. A 1/16"-1/8" bend is permitted with no color break. No creases. Small, inconspicuous, lightly penciled, stamped or inked arrival dates are acceptable as long as they are in an unobtrusive location. No soiling, staining or other discoloration apart from slight foxing. Spine is tight and flat. No spine roll or split allowed. Staples may show some discoloration. No staple tears are allowed; almost no stress lines. No rust migration. In rare cases, a comic was not stapled at the bindery and therefore has a missing staple; this is not considered a defect. Any staple can be replaced on books up to Fine, but only vintage staples can be used on books from Very Fine to Near Mint. Mint books must have original staples. Paper is cream to off-white, supple and fresh. No hint of acidity in the odor of the newsprint. Centerfold is secure. Slight interior tears are allowed.

9.0 **VERY FINE/NEAR MINT (VF/NM):** Nearly perfect with outstanding eye appeal. A limited number of bindery defects are allowed. Almost flat cover with almost imperceptible wear. Inks are bright with slightly diminished reflectivity. An 1/8" bend is allowed if color is not broken. Corners are cut square and sharp with ever-so-slight blunting permitted but no creases. Several lightly penciled, stamped or inked arrival dates are acceptable. No obvious soiling, staining or other discoloration, except for very minor foxing. Spine is tight and flat. No spine roll or split allowed. Staples may show some discoloration. Only the slightest staple tears are allowed. A very minor accumulation of stress lines may be present if they are nearly imperceptible. No rust migration. In rare cases, a comic was not stapled at the bindery and therefore has a missing staple; this is not considered a defect. Any staple can be replaced on books up to Fine, but only vintage staples can be used on books from Very Fine to Near Mint. Mint books must have original staples. Paper is cream to off-white and supple. No hint of acidity in the odor of the newsprint. Centerfold is secure. Very minor interior tears may be present.

8.5 **VERY FINE+ (VF+):** Fits the criteria for Very Fine but with an additional virtue or small accumulation of virtues that improves the book's appearance by a perceptible amount.

8.0 **VERY FINE (VF):** An excellent copy with outstanding eye appeal. Sharp, bright and clean with supple pages. A comic book in this grade has the appearance of having been carefully handled. A limited accumulation of minor bindery defects is allowed. Cover is relatively flat with minimal surface wear beginning to show, possibly including some minute wear at corners. Inks are generally bright with moderate to high reflectivity. A 1/4" crease is acceptable if color is not broken. Stamped or inked arrival dates may be present. No obvious soiling, staining or other discoloration, except for minor foxing. Spine is almost flat with no roll. Possible minor color break allowed. Staples may show some discoloration. Very slight staple tears and a few almost very minor to minor stress lines may be present. No rust migration. In rare cases, a comic was not stapled at the bindery and therefore has a missing staple; this is not considered a defect. Any staple can be replaced on books up to Fine, but only vintage staples can be used on books from Very Fine to Near Mint. Mint books must have original staples. Paper is tan to cream and supple. No hint of acidity in the odor of the newsprint. Centerfold is mostly secure. Minor interior tears at the margin may be present.

7.5 **VERY FINE– (VF–):** Fits the criteria for Very Fine but with an additional defect or small accumulation of defects that detracts from the book's appearance by a perceptible amount.

7.0 **FINE/VERY FINE (FN/VF):** An above-average copy that shows minor wear but is still relatively flat and clean with outstanding eye appeal. A small accumulation of minor bindery defects is allowed. Minor cover wear beginning to show with interior yellowing or tanning allowed, possibly including minor creases. Corners may be blunted or abraded. Inks are generally bright with a moderate reduction in reflectivity. Stamped or inked arrival dates may be present. No obvious soiling, staining or other discoloration, except for minor foxing. The slightest spine roll may be present, as well as a possible moderate color break. Staples may show some discoloration. Slight staple tears and a slight accumulation of light stress lines may be present. Slight rust migration. In rare cases, a comic was not stapled at the bindery and therefore has a missing staple; this is not considered a defect. Any staple can be replaced on books up to Fine, but only vintage staples can be used on books from Very Fine to Near Mint. Mint books must have original staples. Paper is tan to cream, but not brown. No hint of acidity in the odor of the newsprint. Centerfold is mostly secure. Minor interior tears at the margin may be present.

6.5 **FINE+ (FN+):** Fits the criteria for Fine but with an additional virtue or small accumulation of virtues that improves the book's appearance by a perceptible amount.

6.0 **FINE (FN):** An above-average copy that shows minor wear but is still relatively flat and clean with no significant creasing or other serious defects. Eye appeal is somewhat reduced because of slight surface wear and the accumulation of small defects, especially on the spine and edges. A FINE condition comic book appears to have been read a few times and has been handled with moderate care. Some accumulation of minor bindery defects is allowed. Minor cover wear apparent, with minor to moderate creases. Inks show a major reduction in reflectivity. Blunted or abraded corners are more common, as is minor staining, soiling, discoloration, and/or foxing. Stamped or inked arrival dates may be present. A minor spine roll is allowed. There can also be a 1/4" spine split or severe color break. Staples show minor discoloration. Minor staple tears and an accumulation of stress lines may be present, as well as minor rust migration. In rare cases, a comic was not stapled at the bindery and therefore has a missing staple; this is not considered a defect. Any staple can be replaced on books up to Fine, but only vintage staples can be used on books from Very Fine to Near Mint. Mint books must have original staples. Paper is brown to tan and fairly supple with no signs of brittleness. No hint of acidity in the odor of the newsprint. Minor interior tears at the margin may be present. Centerfold may be loose but not detached.

5.5 **FINE− (FN−):** Fits the criteria for Fine but with an additional defect or small accumulation of defects that detracts from the book's appearance by a perceptible amount.

5.0 **VERY GOOD/FINE (VG/FN):** An above-average but well-used comic book. A comic in this grade shows some moderate wear; eye appeal is somewhat reduced because of the accumulation of defects. Still a desirable copy that has been handled with some care. An accumulation of bindery defects is allowed. Minor to moderate cover wear apparent, with minor to moderate creases and/or dimples. Inks have major to extreme reduction in reflectivity. Blunted or abraded corners are increasingly common, as is minor to moderate staining, discoloration, and/or foxing. Stamped or inked arrival dates may be present. A minor to moderate spine roll is allowed. A spine split of up to 1/2" may be present. Staples show minor discoloration. A slight accumulation of minor staple tears and an accumulation of minor stress lines may also be present, as well as minor rust migration. In rare cases, a comic was not stapled at the bindery and therefore has a missing staple; this is not considered a defect. Any staple can be replaced on books up to Fine, but only vintage staples can be used on books from Very Fine to Near Mint. Mint books must have original staples. Paper is brown to tan with no signs of brittleness. May have the faintest trace of an acidic odor. Centerfold may be loose but not detached. Minor tears may also be present.

4.5 **VERY GOOD+ (VG+):** Fits the criteria for Very Good but with an additional virtue or small accumulation of virtues that improves the book's appearance by a perceptible amount.

4.0 **VERY GOOD (VG):** The average used comic book. A comic in this grade shows some significant moderate wear, but still has not accumulated enough total defects to reduce eye appeal to the point that it is not a desirable copy. Cover shows moderate to significant wear, and may be loose but not completely detached. Moderate to extreme reduction in reflectivity. Can have an accumulation of creases or dimples. Corners may be blunted or abraded. Store stamps, name stamps, arrival dates, initials, etc. have no effect on this grade. Some discoloration, fading, foxing, and even minor soiling is allowed. As much as a 1/4" triangle can be missing out of the corner or edge; a missing 1/8" square is also acceptable. Only minor unobtrusive tape and other amateur repair allowed on otherwise high grade copies. Moderate spine roll may be present and/or a 1" spine split. Staples discolored. Minor to moderate staple tears and stress lines may be present, as well as some rust migration. Paper is brown but not brittle. A minor acidic odor can be detectable. Minor to moderate tears may be present. Centerfold may be loose or detached at one staple.

3.5 **VERY GOOD− (VG−):** Fits the criteria for Very Good but with an additional defect or small accumulation of defects that detracts from the book's appearance by a perceptible amount.

3.0 **GOOD/VERY GOOD (GD/VG):** A used comic book showing some substantial wear. Cover shows significant wear, and may be loose or even detached at one staple. Cover reflectivity is very low. Can have a book-length crease and/or dimples. Corners may be blunted or even rounded. Discoloration, fading, foxing, and even minor to moderate soiling is allowed. A triangle from 1/4" to 1/2" can be missing out of the corner or edge; a missing 1/8" to 1/4" square is also acceptable. Tape and other amateur repair may be present. Moderate spine roll likely. May have a spine split of anywhere from 1" to 1-1/2". Staples may be rusted or replaced. Minor to moderate staple tears and moderate stress lines may be present, as well as some rust migration. Paper is brown but not brittle. Centerfold may be loose or detached at one staple. Minor to moderate interior tears may be present.

2.5 **GOOD+ (GD+):** Fits the criteria for Good but with an additional virtue or small accumulation of virtues that improves the book's appearance by a perceptible amount.

2.0 **GOOD (GD):** Shows substantial wear; often considered a "reading copy." Cover shows significant wear and may even be detached. Cover reflectivity is low and in some cases completely absent. Book-length creases and dimples may be present. Rounded corners are more common. Moderate soiling, staining, discoloration and foxing may be present. The largest piece allowed missing from the front or back cover is usually a 1/2" triangle or a 1/4" square, although some Silver Age books such as 1960s Marvels have had the price corner box clipped from the top left front cover and may be considered Good if they would otherwise have graded higher. Tape and other forms of amateur repair are common in Silver Age and older books. Spine roll is likely. May have up to a 2" spine split. Staples may be degraded, replaced or missing. Moderate staple tears and stress lines may be present, as well as rust migration. Paper is brown but not brittle. Centerfold may be loose or detached. Moderate interior tears may be present.

1.8 **GOOD– (GD–):** Fits the criteria for Good but with an additional defect or small accumulation of defects that detracts from the book's appearance by a perceptible amount.

1.5 **FAIR/GOOD (FR/GD):** A comic showing substantial to heavy wear. A copy in this grade still has all pages and covers, although there may be pieces missing. Books in this grade are commonly creased, scuffed, abraded, soiled, and possibly unattractive, but still generally readable. Cover shows considerable wear and may be detached. Nearly no reflectivity to no reflectivity remaining. Store stamp, name stamp, arrival date and initials are permitted. Book-length creases, tears and folds may be present. Rounded corners are increasingly common. Soiling, staining, discoloration and foxing is generally present. Up to 1/10 of the back cover may be missing. Tape and other forms of amateur repair are increasingly common in Silver Age and older books. Spine roll is common. May have a spine split between 2" and 2/3 the length of the book. Staples may be degraded, replaced or missing. Staple tears and stress lines are common, as well as rust migration. Paper is brown and may show brittleness around the edges. Acidic odor may be present. Centerfold may be loose or detached. Interior tears are common.

1.0 **FAIR (FR):** A copy in this grade shows heavy wear. Some collectors consider this the lowest collectible grade because comic books in lesser condition are usually incomplete and/or brittle. Comics in this grade are usually soiled, faded, ragged and possibly unattractive. This is the last grade in which a comic remains generally readable. Cover may be detached, and inks have lost all reflectivity. Creases, tears and/or folds are prevalent. Corners are commonly rounded or absent. Soiling and staining is present. Books in this condition generally have all pages and most of the covers, although there may be up to 1/4 of the front cover missing or no back cover, but not both. Tape and other forms of amateur repair are more common. Spine roll is more common; spine split can extend up to 2/3 the length of the book. Staples may be missing or show rust and discoloration. An accumulation of staple tears and stress lines may be present, as well as rust migration. Paper is brown and may show brittleness around the edges but not in the central portion of the pages. Acidic odor may be present. Accumulation of interior tears. Chunks may be missing. The centerfold may be missing if readability is generally preserved (although there may be difficulty). Coupons may be cut.

0.5 **POOR (PR):** Most comic books in this grade have been sufficiently degraded to the point where there is little or no collector value; they are easily identified by a complete absence of eye appeal. Comics in this grade are brittle almost to the point of turning to dust with a touch, and are usually incomplete. Extreme cover fading may render the cover almost indiscernible. May have extremely severe stains, mildew or heavy cover abrasion to the point that some cover inks are indistinct/absent. Covers may be detached with large chunks missing. Can have extremely ragged edges and extensive creasing. Corners are rounded or virtually absent. Covers may have been defaced with paints, varnishes, glues, oil, indelible markers or dyes, and may have suffered heavy water damage. Can also have extensive amateur repairs such as laminated covers. Extreme spine roll present; can have extremely ragged spines or a complete, book-length split. Staples can be missing or show extreme rust and discoloration. Extensive staple tears and stress lines may be present, as well as extreme rust migration. Paper exhibits moderate to severe brittleness (where the comic book literally falls apart when examined). Extreme acidic odor may be present. Extensive interior tears. Multiple pages, including the centerfold, may be missing that affect readability. Coupons may be cut.

0.3 **INCOMPLETE:** Books that are coverless, but are otherwise complete, or covers missing their interiors.

0.1 **INCOMPLETE:** Coverless copies that have incomplete interiors, wraps or single pages will receive a grade of .1 as will just front covers or just back covers.

COMIC BOOK RESTORATION

Restoration - the word carries with it a lot of baggage, particularly in today's comic book market. Once considered an acceptable and at times even desirable way to preserve and/or revive aging key comics to some semblance of their original glory, restoration has today become a source of considerable debate in the hobby.

When restoration of comics first began, it was a collection of crude, damaging attempts to preserve or fix comics exhibiting defects like tears or missing pieces. At first, collectors employed unsophisticated methods, using tape, glue and color pens to repair their books. Restoration soon evolved, however, and skilled professionals (and plenty of aspiring amateurs) began to utilize more advanced techniques like chemical baths and deacidification to not only repair comics but restore them to a more desirable condition.

Today, professional restorers work in a constantly evolving field using methods that have stood the test of time. Unfortunately, the value of comic book restoration itself has undergone a major reevaluation in recent years, leading to a general downturn in the opinion of most collectors as to the desirability of a restored comic.

The stigma that has attached itself to the restoration of comic books has less to do with the actual results of professional, reliable restoration methods than it does with the poor results of amateur restoration, and more alarmingly, the unethical behavior of many amateur restorers and dealers who have concealed such repairs from buyers and passed off restored books as original condition collectibles. Such behavior has severely affected the overall opinion of restoration in the comic book marketplace. In the quest for perfection, restoration now occupies a shadowy corner that has not yet been fully illuminated.

Without honest and full disclosure of restoration on a given book, and without a greater understanding of the many methods involved in preserving and/or restoring comics, restoration is likely to continue to suffer a negative reputation in the comic book market. In this section, we hope to clarify some aspects of this aspect of comic book collecting, as well as present one possible way to evaluate such restoration.

Although the term 'restoration' applies to a wide range of preservative and restorative methods, it could be argued that there are three distinctly different types of processes at work in the catch-all category of restoration:

Preservation: This type of restoration applies to comics where no materials have been substantially added to the original comic. Work has been done to preserve the comic's own paper and structure, with minor repairs to prevent further damage and deterioration. Preservation can include securing a loose staple, small tear or sealing a minor hole by refastening the folded paper flap back to the page. Traditionally, attempts to preserve a comic as well as possible without actually 'restoring' it to any degree have been known as 'conservation.' Whatever the term, it implies a decision to leave the book in its current state while preventing further decay.

Restoration: This is the middle ground, containing comics that have had minor preservative and restorative work done in order to prevent or slow further damage and decay and revive the original appearance of the existing materials. Restoration can include minor tear and hole repairs, minor color touch or removal of soil to reveal original color, and possibly staple replacement.

Reconstruction: This area includes comics that have had extensive repair work or have had significant amounts of new material added to the existing comic. Comics that have had large portions of a cover corner, chunk or interior page reconstructed and recolored or illustrated, comics that have been assembled from the pieces of several other lower grade examples, and comics that have had extensive repair work that significantly transformed the condition of the original comic can be considered reconstructions. Some might even say these comics are now not truly a legitimate representation of an actual original copy of that book but rather a newly created collectible

out of the ashes of the old, but that is a debate for another time.

Currently, Comics Guaranty LLC (CGC) employs a series of abbreviations to designate states of Extensive, Moderate, and Slight restoration as follows:

EA	**Extensive Amateur**
EP	**Extensive Professional**
MA	**Moderate Amateur**
MP	**Moderate Professional**
SA	**Slight Amateur**
SP	**Slight Professional**

CGC also uses a purple label to distinguish restored certified books from unrestored books, which are usually encapsulated with a blue label. The purple label itself has gained a certain level of notoriety due to the industry-wide stigma carried by the notion of restoration. For many, receiving a purple label from the grading company is a fate worse than death, but this attitude may yet change with time.

How to Describe a Comic Book

In the old days, mail order was the life's blood of the comic book collecting world, and while a great deal of mail order business still goes on, many readers of this book will doubtless be buying and selling comics on Internet auction sites like eBay. No matter what the venue, the principles of honesty and full disclosure still apply. Above all, you want to convey to any potential buyers all pertinent details about the comic for sale and its condition. In the case of eBay listings, for example, while you have as much space as you need to provide an exhaustive description on the item page itself, you have a limited amount of space to convey important details in the title description that will appear in any general item search. Succinct use of terminology is key in making sure that everyone knows what you mean when you offer a comic book for sale.

Below we present some guidelines for describing a comic book in a single line of text. These are merely suggestions, but remember that it's probably best to provide too much information rather than too little; informed buyers are happy buyers.

Relevant information about a comic book can be listed in the following order:

TITLE - *Detective Comics, Walking Dead, Amazing Spider-Man, Night Nurse,* etc.

ISSUE NUMBER - #5, #121, #0, V3 #4, etc.

GRADE OR GRADE ABBREVIATION - NM, VF/NM, GD+, FR, etc.

ADDITIONAL INFORMATION ON CONDITION - Short notes on interior defects, restoration specifics if necessary, etc.

SUPPLEMENTARY INFORMATION ON COMIC - Is it a pedigree, does it feature a first appearance, does it have a classic cover, etc.

PRICE - $14.95, $92, $1,500, $42 ea., etc. Traditionally, comics were usually listed for sale as follows. Note that the exact style of describing the grade has not always remained consistent:

Amazing Spider-Man V2 #36 near mint

All Star Comics #3 vg+ (small chip out lower left, minor color touch URFC, first JSA)

Fantastic Four #1 fair (severe water damage, small piece out LLFC, research copy)

Amazing Mystery Funnies V2 #7 Very Fine+ (Mile High copy, unrestored, intro Fantom of the Fair, Near Mint except for 1/2" tear LRBC, white pages)

With the advent of a simplified numerical scale, more collectors than ever before have taken to describing a comic book grade by its number rather than its nomenclature. For example, someone might now say "I have a 9.0 *Incredible Hulk* #181" rather than "I have a Very Fine/Near Mint copy of *Incredible Hulk* #181." Whether you believe the numerical grade equivalent is enough or whether you favor the nomenclature, it is best to use both when describing a comic book for sale. Today, the four comics listed above might be described as follows:

Amazing Spider-Man V2 #36 NM 9.4

All Star Comics #3 Very Good+ 4.5 (small chip out lower left, minor color touch URFC, first JSA)

Fantastic Four #1 Fair 1.0 (severe water damage, small piece out LLFC, research copy)

Amazing Mystery Funnies V2 #7 VF+ 8.5 (Mile High copy, unrestored, intro Fantom of the Fair, NM except for 1/2" tear LRBC, white pages)

How to Grade a Comic Book

While it takes time to hone grading skills and become a true expert, there is a general step-by-step process that anyone can follow to evaluate a comic and arrive at a reasonable estimation of the book's grade.

Step 1: Lay the comic down on a flat, clean surface. If it is in a plastic bag or a Mylar sleeve, carefully remove it, being sure not to snag the comic on any exposed tape or adhesive fastener on the bag flap. In some cases, it might be wiser to remove the tape entirely first, or fold it down until it adheres to the bag itself and cannot catch the cover of the comic when it slides out.

Step 2: Make sure your grading area is well-lit, moisture-free and smokeless. Do not let direct sunlight fall on the comic, and do not put the comic under any unfiltered fluorescent light which may generate ultraviolet (UV) rays - the same bleaching agent emanated by sunlight. Normal incandescent lighting is best.

Step 3: Review the general exterior look of the comic and find a comparable example in the *Grading Guide* pictorial sections. Double-check your selection by comparing the comic to pictorial examples in the nearest adjacent grades as well.

Step 4: Carefully examine the exterior of the comic from front cover to back cover, identifying all defects, such as: condition of staples; creases, folds, and tears; soiling, staining and discoloration; ink brightness and cover gloss; and the other defects detailed throughout the *Grading Guide*.

Step 5: If any defect warrants reducing the grade from your original selection, compare the comic with the next lowest grade to see if it more accurately represents the condition of the comic you are grading. Note that even the smallest flaw on the cover can be a determining factor - after all, the cover is the first thing anyone will see, and its condition is the principle concern of collectors to determine the book's grade and over all "eye appeal."

Step 6: Carefully examine the spine of the comic. Next to the cover, this is the most important area for evaluating the comic's grade. Check for rusted staples, stress lines, tears, spine roll, and other such defects.

Step 7: Examine the inside front and back covers and check for further defects like tearing, creasing, and yellowing. Pay particular attention to the area where the interior of the comic meets the covers. **NOTE:** Do not open the cover of higher grade books to more than a 45-degree angle to avoid stressing the spine.

Step 8: Confirm that the centerfold and all pages are still present and check their condition.

Step 9: Estimate the whiteness level of the interior pages. This can be very difficult, especially on older books, without a truly fresh copy of the same book or at least a comparable book of the same time period for comparison. *Refer to our discussion of paper quality on page 25.* In the past, we have recommended the use of the Overstreet Whiteness Level (OWL) card to determine the hue of a given book's paper, but we no longer recommend relying on that card as it is not up to date with current grading standards and its tonal scale is inaccurate. In this area, you just have to do the best you can, and use other comics to hone your skills.

Step 10: Locate and identify interior defects such as chipping, flaking, possible brittleness, and other flaws. In all cases, keep comparing the comic to the examples depicted in the pictorial grade section you selected to either confirm your choice or further refine your selection.

Although this is a generalized method of grading that should serve most collectors well enough, the expertise and experience required to reliably grade comic books accurately is not easy to come by. For as much as some have tried to make comic book grading a science, it remains more of an art form, and even the most seasoned graders still make the occasional error. While novices should not expect to become superb graders overnight, they may be able to avoid the common pitfalls by following the standards set down in this *Guide*. A few other suggestions:

• Get a second opinion from a veteran grader or another collector as a "reality check."

• NEVER grade a large quantity of comics at one time. You will almost certainly "burn out" - your concentration will flag and you will miss crucial details when evaluating later comics that may seriously affect your determination of grade.

• Try to keep samples of actual comic books in various grades for ready comparison.

• The middle of the 10-point scale remains the murkiest area of comic book grading. Pay special attention to all the little factors that push a comic from 9.0 (Very Fine/Near Mint) down to 8.0 (Very Fine), or from 4.0 (Very Good) up to 6.0 (Fine). Even the most experienced graders in the world can some-

times slip up on those transitions.

• When purchasing a comic, always ask to see the interior before you buy it. This protects both parties in the transaction. You can ask the seller to show you the interior rather than presume to handle the comic yourself, and this ensures that you will incur no liability should handling of the book result in further damage. This will also enable the seller to prove to you that he or she is hiding no additional defects in the interior of the comic that might detract from the over all grade. After all, a book with superb eye appeal on the outside cover may still harbor a secret or two within. Ask anyone who collected mid-'70s Marvel comics, and they'll tell you about all the Marvel Value Stamps that are missing from those letters pages. Above all, when dealing with comic book sellers, be as polite and honest as you would expect them to be.

Grading is inherently a subjective enterprise, and no matter how specific the criteria, differences of opinion can arise. Collectors on either side of the equation should respect the right of the other party to their opinion as to a comic's grade, if that opinion can be reasonably supported by the physical evidence. Discussion can sometimes result in a compromise. Ultimately, a buyer can always just walk away from a transaction if they are unsatisfied with the book or the grade.

GRADING VICTORIAN AND PLATINUM AGE BOOKS

by Tom Gordon III

The origin of comic books dates back farther than the previous conceived idea of *Funnies on Parade*. The early comics known as the Victorian and Platinum Age are the foundation for what we know as the modern comic book. These early books are historically significant and also provide insight into the entertainment of a bygone era. Early comics were printed in a variety of formats and styles. The various formats from the past are also seen today in the hobby when one examines the various comic books at a local comic retail store. Typically the comic book that most people are familiar with is the saddle stitched version. This type of comic book is the most common, but the wide variety of other formats offers a challenge when attempting to grade them. The known formats include hardbound, cardboard cover, saddle stitched, drawing, paint, coloring book format, and a variety of others.

The main difference in Victorian and Platinum Age books compared to their later counterparts is the size and multiple formats used in their production. The sizes of these books alone are a major factor in their condition and survival rate. When compared to the size of the standard Modern Age comic book it is easy to see that proper storage of these books is a long-term problem. Paper quality can also be an issue; as these books were printed with a multitude of dif-

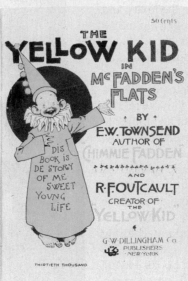

ferent paper stocks, including tracing paper, cardstock, pulp, rag paper, hemp, and others.

Below we have highlighted some of the more readily seen examples of early comic book formats to assist in understanding them better.

Hardbound Format

This format is found in both Victorian and Platinum Age comics. The Victorian Age examples are typically found in the style of antique books and are hardbound with leather or heavy stock covers. These types of comics may have gilded covers or end pages in which defects can include loss of gild and spine damage. This usually occurred when removing the book from the shelf and is unique to this style of book. The Platinum Age examples are usually found in a hardbound format, which is made of a heavy stock cardboard instead of the standard fine hardbound book, which is more often seen in Victorian Age editions.

Cardboard Cover Format

This format of the Platinum Age is usually found in several sizes, including 10x10" and 11x16". Cardboard cover books also turn up in an assortment of sizes. The 10x10" size format was used heavily by the publisher Cupples and Leon. When a person thinks of Platinum Age comics, they may envision this type of comic format. These books feature a cardboard stock cover with a thin cloth binding to the spine. The interior pages are stapled together and then glued to the inside of the spine of the cover. This format and its larger counterpart have a very common condition defect - they almost immediately receive damage when read. The covers, when opened, tend to cause a separation inside the cover near the spine. This separation occurs when the cover is opened at an angle of more than approximately 45 degrees. This defect is due to the materials and the size of the books. This separation, however, should not be confused with the cover being detached from the interior; in many cases, the cover and interior are still firmly attached. If one were to evaluate a lower grade example, this defect should be factored in to the grade as it occurs very frequently. If one has a very fine condition or better copy, this defect could lower the grade by perhaps .5 of a grade or so depending on the severity of the separation.

Saddle Stitched Format

This format is in many ways similar to that of modern comic book counterparts. These books are structurally the same as the standard saddle stitched comics with paper covers. In some cases, they may have a string binding instead of staples, as found in some Victorian Age examples; books with string binding should be graded the same as those with staples. The type of paper stock used in the manufacturing of these books will greatly affects the conditions in which these books are found. In some cases, the paper is a heavy stock that has little flexibility and cannot stand the wear and stress from usage.

Drawing, Paint, Coloring Book Formats

This format is typically found in the Platinum Age. Numerous comics of the era were more than just comics; they were also toys for children. These books are found in several formats that include both paper covers and cardboard cover formats.

As noted in the cardboard format, examples of these books with cardboard covers should be viewed in the same light as those noted above.

Typically, drawing books and coloring books are not found in high grade due to most surviving copies of the books having been used as well as read. In some cases,

these books may be found used but intact in an acceptable condition. One must take into consideration that they are drawing books or coloring books when grading them; it is fair to grade these types of books based on the overall condition of the book. If neatly drawn in, one could easily have a *Buster Brown Drawing Book* that structurally grades very fine, but actual grade is Fne+ condition due to the usage of the book. Unused examples of this type of book are very rare to locate.

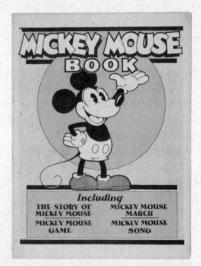

GRADING ODD FORMAT COMIC BOOKS

by J.C. Vaughn

What do you do when they don't fit in the bags, boards, and boxes?

Whether it's the thick, square-bound comics of the Platinum Age or the "Treasury Edition" size given such a wonderful revitalization by IDW Publishing, the comic books we group into "odd formats" have always provided a challenge in terms of storage and care. While several manufacturers have created Mylar sleeves and other preservation products for them, the availability at some local comic book shops has been spotty, reflecting retailers' hesitancy to display non-standard format items.

This is true of both new comics and back issue stock, making it a challenge for some collectors to take care of their comics. With the evolution in what we understand comic books to be (and to have been in the past), though, it seems prudent to acknowledge that grading of odd format titles' issues is going to become more common.

Like their regular Golden Age, Silver Age and later counterparts, the main point of successful storage of odd format comics is preserving their condition. It isn't, and hasn't been, an easy thing to do. And that doesn't even include convincing fellow collectors that not all comics look the same.

Bound volume collectors have been grabbing onto important pieces of history for years only to have them denigrated as worthless (or certainly worth less). In more common terms, they were the predecessors of the beautiful hardcover and softcover editions produced so readily by publishers today.

Spirit fans have heard for a long time from some quarters that *The Spirit* sections aren't comic books, but rather than splitting hairs it's just time to acknowledge that they are collected and that condition can be a determining factor with them just as with any modern comic book.

When we first addressed this topic in 2003's second edition of *The Overstreet*

Comic Book Grading Guide, Origins of Marvel Comics and the other books in the Fireside series have had fans for years, but recognition of their value was hard to come by. Now, though, they have many more collectors and condition is becoming a real distinguishing point.

Warren Publishing's *Vampirella*, Marvel's *Planet of the Apes*, Charlton's *Six Million Dollar Man* and others have long had enthusiastic collectors, but the respect granted to magazines – particularly black and white magazines – within the ranks of comics fandom was grudging at best before CGC started grading them.

Superman vs. The Amazing Spider-Man wasn't only the first meeting of Marvel's and DC's flagship characters, it was an oversized "Treasury Edition" production, another format slow to win acceptance from the general comics collecting audience. Yet over the last decade we've seen the Alex Ross series from DC Comics, various specials from Image Comics, almost

monthly publications from IDW Publishing.

In each successive era, the argument about "What is a comic book?" becomes increasingly difficult to settle. The debate is nothing new, however. Whether with relatively new formats such as hard cover originals and collections or with older presentations such as bound volumes, comic book collectors have been faced with the task of assessing editions that seem to defy normal evaluation.

Much of the problem for collectors may stem from the perceived difficulty of storing items of dissimilar shapes and/or obtaining collecting supplies such as bags, boards or boxes for said items. From the wonders of the Platinum Age to the original Marvel Graphic Novel line to Chris Ware's *Acme Novelty Library* series, though, most of the same things that apply to grading other comics still apply; there are just a few additional considerations to watch out for… keeping in mind that condition is still king.

Two examples of the wildly variant **Acme Novelty Library** series by Chris Ware, which ranges from digest-sized to tabloid-sized issues, along with a DC **Tarzan** treasury edition.

*Two copies of the Marvel Graphic Novel, **The Death of Captain Marvel**, that illustrate the difficulty of preserving black cover editions. Note the extreme spine wear on the copy at right.*

Bound Volumes

Some collectors want to be able to hold an individual comic book in their hands when they read it - holding a whole volume just doesn't satisfy them the same way. Others, though, have long found such volumes to be a meaningful, quick and relatively easy to collect otherwise hard-to-find items.

In a bound volume, it is frequently possible to get a complete run of a title, often with bright covers and interior pages in Fine or better with the exception of the outer edges, where browning may have occurred.

When evaluating a bound volume, there are several additional areas to assess in addition to the standard grading procedure one would utilize for a single comic book. These factors, not surprisingly, mostly have to do with the binding process used and the actual binding itself. Other areas of concern frequently include paper quality, trimming, tears, notations, the manner in which the bound volume was read, and the frequency with which it was read.

There are varying levels of professionalism evident in binding. This, along with the source of the material, can have significant impact on the desirability of a bound volume.

There are basically two types of bindings for bound volumes - those that are glued together (called "perfect bound") and those that are Smythe sewn (sewed as signatures with no glue). Theoretically, those volumes that are Smythe sewn could be un-bound and restored to single issues by cutting the threads and reinserting the staples into each issue. Most bound volumes are not hand sewn, and there would be glue used on the spines of each book, making it nearly impossible to remove them.

As a result of the binding process, many comics within bound volumes have been trimmed so as to create a uniformed appearance. The edges of those copies that are not trimmed tend to be more ragged (referring to the manner in which they line up staggered or "ragged" when viewed as a stack, not as an indication of damage).

In addition to the appearance of the volume's edges, another reason for trimming was that comics were often made to fit the hardcover material or bindery size that was available rather than finding

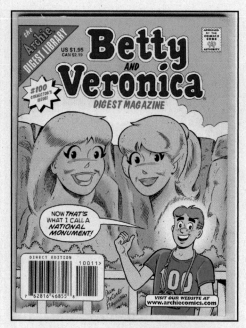

This **Betty and Veronica Digest Magazine** is an example of a small-sized comic format that has been popular for decades.

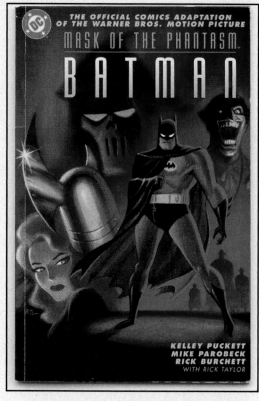

This 5" x 7-11/16" edition of **Batman: Mask of the Phantasm** was packaged with the VHS video cassette. Like many dark colored Prestige Format comics, color cracking is evident along the spine.

materials to completely fit or cover the comic book size. The most desirable format would have the hardcover edges protruding very slightly beyond the comics, or at the very least flush with the edges.

Bound Volumes Checklist
- Binding may show varying levels of wear.
- Method of binding may eliminate benefit of removing comics from binding.
- Varying degrees of professionalism in binding may affect desirability.
- Number of comics per bound volume may affect the success of the binding and therefore the desirability of the volume.
- Insect damage is common in bound volumes.
- Paper tears, sometimes depending on the frequency of reading, can be common.
- Finding pages that have been trimmed, sometimes down to – or even into – the art, is common.

An example of the cover roll that can occur on even a recent treasury edition if adverse environmental conditions, like excessive moisture in the air, are present.

*A copy of the black and white Marvel magazine, **Rampaging Hulk** #1, showing some substantial wear.*

the same as one would find on a regular comic book. Additionally, paper condition varies based on which newspaper printed the section. Two Spirit sections of the same date that would otherwise grade the same may be very different based solely on paper quality. The success of DC Comics' line of *The Spirit Archives* has bolstered interest in these sections.

The Spirit sections varied slightly in size, but the standard sections were 7-1/2" or 7-3/4" wide x 10" to 10-1/2" inches high, a bit larger than standard comic books. It's also important to note a very desirable size variant: *The Philadelphia Record/ Sunday Bulletin* published an oversize *Spirit* section measuring about 10-1/4" x 15" inches. These are gorgeous and bring premium prices.

A separate problem somewhat unique to these inserts is that some newspapers, notably *The Chicago Sun*, inserted *The Spirit* folded but uncut. The edges had a printed notice, "Cut on this line," but these were often cut irregularly and unevenly by careless consumers with scissors, and values on these would be affected accordingly.

- Trimming is frequently uneven between issues.
- Volumes from archives or collections of publishers, creators and others concerned with the production of a particular work may be considered more desirable.
- Volumes from prominent collections may be more desirable.

Spirit Sections

Beginning in June 1940, *The Spirit* sections were sized inserts in many newspapers across the country. Created by Will Eisner, these sections featured the Spirit and other strips, and they carried the local newspaper's imprint. As 16-pagers (later 8-pagers), these sections did not include a separate cover. As such, and without the traditional, more resilient cover stock to protect them, *The Spirit* sections frequently have taken a lot of physical abuse when they show up. Other than their newsprint-based predisposition to more rapidly browning paper, the defects one would typically note on one of these sections are almost

*This 5-15/16" x 8-15/16" **Nowheresville** trade paperback from Image Comics collected (and revised) a mini-series previously published in standard Modern Age comic book format by Caliber.*

Spirit Sections Checklist
- Paper is most often light brown or worse.
- Brittleness is not uncommon.
- Blunted corners are very common.

Magazines

Comics magazines generally lend themselves to the same types of evaluation as comic books. Beyond the obvious (they're just bigger), there are few other items to watch for, mostly based on the notion that the overwhelming number of these publications were sold on the newsstand and not through comic book specialty shops. As such, they're more closely related to Golden Age and Silver Age comics when evaluating them for defects.

Magazines Checklist
- Date stamps common on older books.
- Blunted corners common on covers, interior pages.
- Page tears common.
- Staple tears common.
- Rust migration is less likely because of generally superior cover stock.
- Interior page stock is generally heavier, but often cheaper and highly prone to browning.
- Bends, creases or spine stress not uncommon.
- Spine alignment on square bound copies may be in question.

Treasury Editions

With their full scale revival at IDW Publishing in recent years (ranging from Dave Stevens' *Rocketeer* to *My Little Pony*, and from *Danger Girl* to *Star Trek*), the over-sized comics generally called "Treasury Editions" (after their Marvel Comics trade name in the 1970s) have made a comeback not only in terms of new product but as collectible back issues as well.

Going back to the originals in the '70s, often these large format comics were displayed standing up like traditional

*Like dust jackets, slip covers should also be graded separately as they too can sustain the same kind of wear visible on book covers and dust jackets. Pictured is a slip cover two-book set of the Fireside editions, **Origins of Marvel Comics** and **Son of Origins of Marvel Comics**.*

*This copy of **Bring On the Bad Guys**, one of the Fireside series of softcover collections, shows severe spine wear and a complete cover split down the bottom half of the book.*

*Once a popular format of the 1970s, the treasury editions have undergone a revival thanks to projects like DC's **Shazam: Power of Hope** (above), and IDW's **The Rocketeer Jetpack Treasury Edition** (below).*

comics. This in and of itself created a set of commonly seen defects, because the Treasury Editions would frequently bend forward, sagging under their own weight. The defects generally associated with this format include spine stress, spine creases, cover creases, and blunted corners.

Alternately, many retailers displayed copies in this format flat, as on the lower magazine racks at a newsstand. This, though, came with its own set of problems. Frequently the cover ink, particularly on darker issues, would rub off on the facing covers when Treasury Editions were stacked (an excellent example of this is *Captain America's Bicentennial Battles*, on which the black ink frequently smudged onto the copy on top or below it). It should be noted that many of the modern Treasury Edition format publications are bound by staples rather than squarebound.

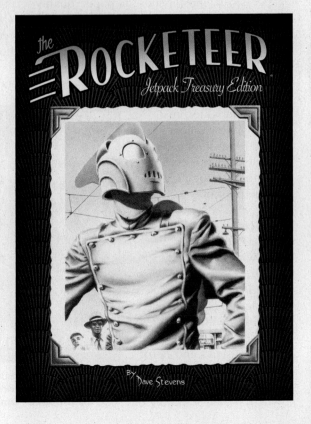

Treasury Editions Checklist
- Blunted corners common.
- Page tears common.

- On non-square bound issues, rust migration is less likely because of generally superior cover stock, though it may be present.
- Interior page stock is generally heavier, but often cheaper and highly prone to browning.
- Bends, creases or spine stress common.
- Spine alignment on square bound copies may be in question.

Graphic Novels

Many of the covers on the early *Marvel Graphic Novel* line (and on those from other publishers) featured large areas of black. As a result, many of these editions show white spine cracks ranging in size from almost undetectable to highly visible, book length marks. Various cover defects are the primary detractors for most graphic novels, with the spine being the focal point for most of them. Additionally, where they have been stacked on top of one another, ink smudging problems similar to the Treasury Editions may be found.

Since the graphic novel lines from the major publishers were generally (though not exclusively) printed on a higher-grade paper stock, most issues of paper quality are not a big concern.

Graphic Novels Checklist
- Color cracking on spine common
- Blunted corners common on covers
- On non-square bound issues, rust migration is less likely because of generally superior cover stock, though it may be present

Hardcover Collections & Trade Paperbacks

With the addition to *The Overstreet Comic Book Price Guide* about a decade ago of the Fireside (Simon & Schuster) series, books like *Origins of Marvel Comics* and *Bring on the Bad Guys* have gained in popularity with a wider selection of dealers and collectors.

These books, generally paperback but occasionally hardcover, were among the first of what is now an increasingly sought-after format - the collected edition (*The Silver Surfer* from 1978 was actually a graphic novel, featuring a new interpretation of the Surfer's origin without the Fantastic Four). Many of the character specific editions, such as *Captain America*, command premiums as well.

In the contemporary comics market, hardcovers and softcovers play an increasingly important role. DC's Archives series and Marvel's Masterworks collect early, important, or merely popular titles in a format perceived by many to be more impressive to the general public. These books, while a bit pricey, are far more affordable and accessible than the original single issues printed within.

While the market is still in a formative period, first printings of these volumes are sought in their own right by some collectors.

When evaluating a hardcover or softcover collection, many of the rules that would come into play evaluating traditional books should be added to those for grading comics. The areas for particular attention include the spine, covers, and leading edges of the book. Paper quality is frequently higher than traditional comics, though this is not always the case.

Hardcovers may also feature dust jackets when originally released, which can also suffer damage common to comic book covers and may even be absent on some copies if removed by a previous owner or lost. The condition of the dust jacket should be graded independently of the book. It's also worth noting that many of the early strip reprint comics were printed in hardcover with dust jackets.

Two relatively new additions to the marketplace are the hardcover and softcover omnibus editions. Identified by their substantial page counts and sometimes phonebook-like appearance, they range

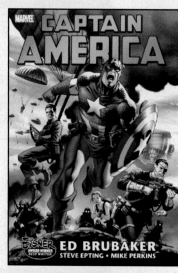

Marvel's hardcover
Captain America By Ed Brubaker Omnibus

from Marvel's hardcover *Captain America By Ed Brubaker Omnibus* to Image's *The Walking Dead Compendium* softcovers and carry price tags from $50 to $125.

Hardcover and Soft Cover Checklist
- Blunted corners common.
- On non-square bound issues, rust migration is less likely because of generally superior cover stock, though it may be present.
- Interior page stock on older soft covers is often highly prone to browning.
- Bends, creases or spine stress common.
- Some times of binding fail with age.
- In case of hardcovers with dust jackets, tearing, bending and color breaks are common.

As is the case with most new products, value drops precipitously with any type of damage. Typically damage occurs in the form of blunted corners on the covers, turn dust jackets on the hardcovers, and bent covers on the soft covers.

Another relatively new and increasingly popular sector of collecting hardcovers overlaps the markets for both comic books and original comic art. Its focus is the limited edition, large or oversized, hardcover volumes commonly artist "Artist's Editions" (named after the line name of IDW Publishing's titles; their Scott Dunbier pioneered the format).

As of press time for this edition,

the publishers that have produced such volumes are Dark Horse Comics, Dynamite Entertainment, Genesis West, Graphitti Designs, IDW Publishing, and Titan Books, with the bulk coming from IDW.

The volumes feature comic art shot at actual size directly from the black and white originals in color, so that they show every pencil line, brush stroke, paste-up, dab of whiteout, editorial notes and even the effects of aging.

For some of these volumes, some collectors have put a premium on having the cardboard shipping packaging intact if it has an image of the product stickered on the outside. Many retailers, it should be noted however, don't offer the packaging.

Damage on these hardcovers typically comes in the form of blunted corners, which usually happens during shipping.

Thanks to John K. Snyder, Jr., Russ Cochran, Denis Kitchen, and Marc Nathan, who advised on the original version of this article, and to Scott Braden, Charlie Novinskie and John K. Snyder III, who offered comments prior to this edition.

Wally Wood's EC Stories Artist's Edition, one of the recent IDW offerings: cover and interior spread shown.

THIRD PARTY PROFILE: CBCS

Company: Comic Book Certification Service

Mission Statement: Comic Book Certification Service, LLC will expertly, impartially, and consistently certify comics. Grading and restoration/conservation checks will be done by veteran hobbyists with many years of experience in the market place as trusted collectors and sellers, as well as many years of professional comic book grading. Using the highest quality materials, we will efficiently and safely certify our clients' comic books. CBCS will promote the hobby of comic collecting with integrity, transparency, and a friendly attitude: educating hobbyists, welcoming suggestions, and promoting related charities. Team members will be ready and available to provide any assistance or information requested by CBCS clients.

Certification offered for: Comic books

Established: 2014

Address: PO Box 33048
St. Petersburg, FL, 33733

Phone: (727) 803-6822
or (844) 870-2227

Website: www.cbcscomics.com

Descriptions of services offered on website: Yes

Email: CustomerService@cbcscomics.com

Fees: Varied based on services

Signature/Autograph verification offered: Both witnessed and non-witnessed signatures/autographs can be submitted for certification and authentication

Ways To Submit: Via CBCS website or at most major conventions, select stores, and member dealer websites

On-Site Grading at Conventions: Offered at select shows

Submissions Accepted at Conventions: At every convention CBCS or their representatives attend

Amazing Spider-Man #2

9.0
Off-White

Marvel, 5/1963

Cover & art: Steve Ditko
Story: Stan Lee

3rd appearance of Spider-Man.
1st appearance of Vulture (Adrian Toomes)
& Terrible Tinkerer (Phineas Mason).

Amateur Restoration Includes: Small amount of color touch on cover. Top & bottom edges trimmed.

0001761-AA-001

THIRD PARTY PROFILE: CGC

Company: Certified Guaranty Company, LLC (CGC)

Mission Statement: We are committed to enhancing the collecting experience of a growing number of collectors for decades to come. To accomplish this, CGC will work diligently toward these goals:

To build trust... by increasing the confidence of collectors and new market participants.

To build interest... in the collecting public through education and resource development. By expanding hobby knowledge, we encourage collectors of all levels to explore the hobby and increase their expertise.

To build consensus... around a CGC grading standard based on market-wide research and input from collectors and dealers nationwide.

To build transparency... by revealing the unique characteristics of each collectible we grade.

To build a better market... to provide buyers with expertly and accurately graded collectibles, so they can purchase with confidence, and to assure fair prices for sellers.

Certification offered for: Comic books, magazines, lobby cards, photos

Established: 2000

Address: P.O. Box 4738 Sarasota, FL 34230

Phone: (877) NM.COMIC (941) 360-3991

Website: www.cgccomics.com

Descriptions of services offered on website: Yes

Fees: Varied based on services

Signature/Autograph verification offered: with authorized witnesses (CGC Signature Series)

Ways To Submit: Comics may be submitted by paid members of CGC Collectors Society, through a member dealer near the collector, or through a CGC internet partner.

On-Site Grading at Conventions: Offered at select shows.

Submissions Accepted at Conventions: Offered at many shows.

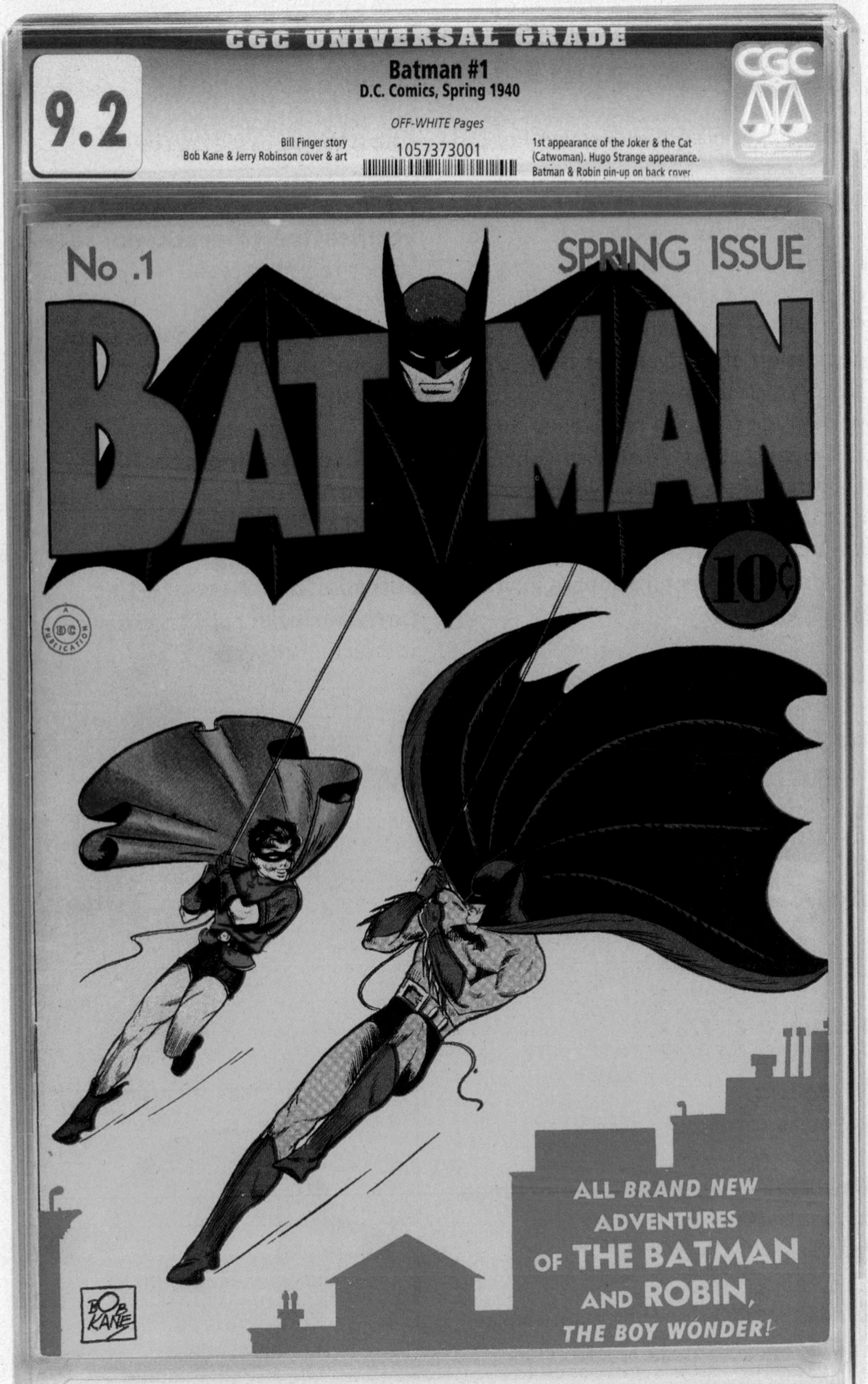
CGC UNIVERSAL GRADE
9.2
Batman #1
D.C. Comics, Spring 1940
OFF-WHITE Pages
Bill Finger story
Bob Kane & Jerry Robinson cover & art
1057373001
1st appearance of the Joker & the Cat
(Catwoman). Hugo Strange appearance.
Batman & Robin pin-up on back cover
CGC
No. 1
SPRING ISSUE
BATMAN
10¢
A DC PUBLICATION
ALL BRAND NEW
ADVENTURES
OF THE BATMAN
AND ROBIN,
THE BOY WONDER!
BOB KANE

THIRD PARTY PROFILE: HALO CERTIFICATION

Company: Halo Certification Pty Ltd.

Mission Statement: "At Halo Certification, we are *Overstreet* all the way. *The Overstreet Guide to Grading Comics* is our one and only manual that relates to grading, so collectors in possession of an *Overstreet Guide* and an OWL card can get fairly close to what grade they will receive. A change is sweeping across Australian comic collecting like a wildfire. No longer is it acceptable to say, 'Near Mint except for a half-page missing.' So it's an exciting and adventurous time for this young company."

Certification offered for: Comics, magazines, photos, toys, vintage gaming, currency, stamps, posters, and sports items

Established: 2013

Address: P.O. Box 507
Annerley, QLD 4103
Australia

Phone: 0481 176 473

Website:
www.halocertification.com.au

Descriptions of services offered on website: Not at press time (pending)

Email: info@halocertification.com.au

Fees: Varied based on services

Signature/Autograph verification offered: with authorized witnesses

Ways To Submit: Submissions accepted via authorized retailers or at select shows.

On-Site Grading at Conventions: Preliminary grades offered at select shows.

Submissions Accepted at Conventions: Submissions accepted at selected shows.

THIRD PARTY PROFILE: PGX

Company: PGX/Professional Grading eXperts

Mission Statement: "Over the past 11+ years PGX has gained a solid reputation throughout the comic book community for being reliable, consistent in grading, reasonably priced and on schedule with turnaround times. The main focus of our business continues to be providing fair and accurate grading that is a trusted benchmark in the United States comic book market and throughout the world."

Certification offered for: Comics, signatures

Established: 2003

Address: P.O. Box 25005
Eugene, OR 97402

Phone: (877) 286-1993 or
(541) 505-7581

Website: www.pgxcomics.com

Descriptions of services offered on website: Yes

Email: thecomicguys@comcast.net

Fees: Varies depending on service, starts at $13

Signature/Autograph verification offered: With or without PGX witness

Ways To Submit: Via website or at trade shows

On-Site Grading at Conventions: Offered at select shows

Submissions Accepted at Conventions: Submissions offered at select shows

P G X
5.0
WORLD
Tales To Astonish #13
VG/F 5.0
OFF-WHITE to WHITE Pages
501010368
Marvel 11/60
Jack Kirby art/cover
Steve Ditko, Don Heck art
Graded 10/10
IND.
TALES TO ASTONISH
APPROVED BY THE COMICS CODE AUTHORITY
13 NOV.
10¢
"I CHALLENGED... GROOT! THE MONSTER FROM PLANET X!"
BEHOLD! I AM GROOT, THE INVINCIBLE! WHO DARES TO DEFY ME??
I DEFY YOU, GROOT!! I SHALL DESTROY YOU BEFORE MIDNIGHT!

Company: Vault Expert Grading

Mission Statement:
(Taken from website's About page)
Vault Valuation LLC was founded in 2012 to provide professional services to art collectors, investors, and illustrative art enthusiasts. In 2014 Vault launched their comic book services division to focus on Modern, Bronze and Copper Age comic books. We grade Silver and Golden age books too.

Our organization has deep appreciation of comic, illustrative, and graphic art. The company is part of a community of investors, writers, archivists, restoration specialists, and e-commerce industrialists committed to advancing the art of illustration.

Certification offered for: Comics, art, illustrations, graphic art

Established: 2012

Address: Vault Valuation LLC
122 East 15th Street
PO Box 2746
Del Mar, CA 92014

Phone: (855) 222-5599

Website: www.vaultgrading.com

Descriptions of services offered on website: Yes

Email: contact@vaultgrading.com

Fees: Varied based on services

Signature/Autograph verification offered: None listed

Ways To Submit: Via website

On-Site Grading at Conventions: None listed

Submissions Accepted at Conventions: None listed

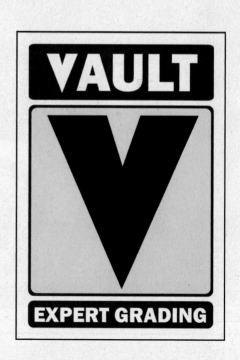

CGC: AN OVERVIEW OF COMIC BOOK RESTORATION

Repairing comic books has been around in our hobby since the first comics were sold to the public. It is natural for people to want their books to look as new as possible or to remain intact so that they can continue to be read. Early in fandom history, simple and crude repairs were performed by the owner of the comic for these reasons. For example, a couple of pieces of tape were used to hold on the cover, a dab of Dad's wood glue was used to close a tear, some crayon made the cover look better, and so on. As the hobby grew and comics became more expensive, the need to define and describe various repairs became apparent. Some repairs remained acceptable to collectors and were "grandfathered," such as tape. Most repairs, however, were defined as restoration.

Restoration can be broken down into two main types: treatments intended to prolong the existence of the comic book, and treatments done for aesthetics. Both types of restoration involve the introduction of non-original material to create or facilitate a desired effect.

CGC defines restoration as treatments intended to return the comic book to a known or assumed state through the addition of non-original material. Examples of restoration include:

- Color touch. Using pigment to hide color flecks, color flakes, and larger areas of missing color. Examples of pigments may include paint (acrylic, oil, watercolor, etc.), pencil crayon, pastel, pen, marker, white-out, etc. Color touch is sometimes called inpainting.

- Pieces added (piece replacement). Added pieces to replace areas of missing paper. Piece replacement material can be non-original paper such as wood or cotton fiber papers, married from a donor comic book, or color-copied pieces. This process is sometimes called infilling.

- Tear seals. Sealing a tear using an adhesive. An adhesive may be cellulose, chemical, or protein-based glues as well as anything that acts as an adhesive, such as saliva.

- Spine split seals. Sealing a spine split using adhesive (adhesives are described above under "tear seals").

- Reinforcement. A process by which a weak or split page or cover is reinforced with adhesive and reinforcement paper. Reinforcement papers are commonly wood or cotton fiber papers.

- Cleaned (lightened). An aqueous process to lighten the paper color or remove soluble acids, often using chemical oxidation, solvents, or water. This process is sometimes called cleaned and pressed or C&P. Common chemicals used to lighten paper include benzene, acetone, xylene, sodium hypochlorite, hydrogen peroxide, chloramine-T, chlorine dioxide, sodium borohydrate, etc.

- Re-glossed. Enhancing the cover gloss, typically through the application of canned re-glossing/art fixodent spray.

Non-additive processes such as dry cleaning (non-aqueous removal of dirt, soot, or other non-original surface material), pressing (removal or reduction of bends and creases), and tape removal, are not considered restoration by CGC. In accordance with hobby standards, the addition of tape is not considered restoration but will always be noted on the CGC label.

While we believe that tape should never be used on a comic book for any reason, our hobby has accepted that people used tape to keep comic books from falling apart. This measure was taken even before comics became collectibles. In the early days of fandom, some sellers stated that tape was not a defect and some collectors even accepted tape on mid grades. CGC will downgrade for tape, as we consider it a defect no matter why or when it was added.

Restoration has become a controversial issue in the comic book hobby because it is not always disclosed by sellers, but can dramatically affect the value of a comic book. CGC protects against this by ALWAYS disclosing detected restoration. In some cases, restoration is not readily detectible to novices or individuals lacking expertise in restoration detection. Even experienced hobbyists miss restoration when grading comic books. For this reason, CGC has made the restoration check a mandatory component of the CGC certification process.

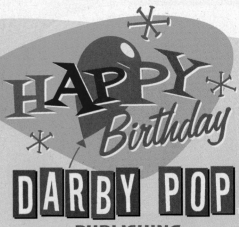

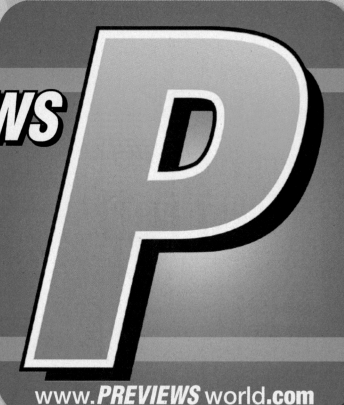

CGC RESTORATION GRADING SCALE

Quality (Aesthetic) Scale –
(Determined by materials used and visual quality of work)

A (EXCELLENT)

- Material used: rice paper, wheat paste, acrylic or water color, leafcasting

- Color match near perfect, no bleed through

- Piece fill seamless and correct thickness

- No fading, excessive whiteness, ripples, cockling, or ink smudges from cover or interior cleaning

- Book feels natural

- Near perfect staple alignment, or replaced exactly as they were

- Filled edges cut to look natural and even

- Cleaned staples or staples replaced with vintage staples

- Married cover/pages match in size and page quality. Professionally attached

B (FINE)

- Material used: pencil, crayon, chalk, re-glossing agent, piece fill from cadavers

- Piece fill obvious upon close inspection, obvious to the touch

- Color touch obvious upon close inspection, or done with materials listed above

- Cover cleaning resulting in slight color fading or excessively white

- Interior cleaning resulting in slight puffiness, cockling, excessively white

- Enlarged staple holes, obviously crooked staples, or backwards staple insertion

- Replaced staples not vintage

- Married cover/pages do not match in size and/or page quality. Professionally attached

C (POOR)

- Material used: glue, pen, marker, white out, white paper to fill missing pieces

- Piece fill obvious at arm's length

- Bad color matching, use of pen or marker. Bleed through evident

- Cover cleaning resulting in washed out/speckled colors, moderate cockling and/or ripples

- New staple holes created upon reinsertion, or non-comic book staples used

- Married cover/pages poorly attached with non-professional materials

Quantity Scale – *(Determined primarily by extent of piece fill and color touch)*

1 (SLIGHT)

- All conservation work, re-glossing, interior lightening, piece fill no more than size of two bindery chips, light color touch in small areas like spine stress, corner crease or bindery chip fill. Married cover or interior pages/wraps (if other work is present)

2 (SLIGHT/MODERATE)

- Piece fill up to the ½" x ½" and/or color touch covering up to 1" x 1". Interior piece fill up to 1" x 1"

3 (MODERATE)

- Piece fill up to the size of 1" x 1" and/or color touch covering up to 2" x 2". Interior piece fill up to 2" x 2"

4 (MODERATE/EXTENSIVE)

- Piece fill up to the size of 2" x 2" and/or color touch covering up to 4" x 4". Interior piece fill up to 4" x 4"

5 (EXTENSIVE)

- Any piece fill over 2" x 2" and/or color touch over 4" x 4". Recreated interior pages or cover

Conservation Repairs

- Tear seals
- Spine split seals
- Reinforcement
- Piece reattachment
- Some cover or interior cleaning (water or solvent)
- Staples cleaned or replaced
- Some leaf casting

Materials Used for Conservation Repairs:

- Rice paper
- Wheat glue
- Vintage staples
- Archival tape

Restoration Repairs

- Color touch
- Piece replacement
- Re-glossing
- Paper bleaching
- Married pages or cover

Materials Used for Restoration Repairs:

- White glue
- Re-glossing agent
- Acrylic or water color paint
- Pencil, crayon, chalk
- Pen, marker, correction fluid
- Leaf casting
- Cadaver piece fill
- White bleaching

CBCS RESTORATION OVERVIEW

Before a comic book is graded, it is checked for restoration and conservation by our restoration detection experts. If restoration or conservation is found, CBCS will include a list of all the work detected on the label, classifying it as either conserved or restored. CBCS has one classification level for conservation and five levels for restoration:

- Slight

- Slight/Moderate

- Moderate

- Moderate/Extensive

- Extensive

The more restoration that is detected, the higher the level becomes. Once the book has been checked for conservation and restoration, it enters the grading phase.

CBCS considers conservation anything archival safe added to the comic that helps stop its deterioration, such as sealing a spine split or a non-additive processes that helps stop deterioration, such as staple rust removal.

CBCS considers restoration to be any additive process that may enhance the aesthetics of the comic, such as color touch and pieces added. If both conservation and restoration are found, the comic will be certified as restored.

If done correctly, CBCS does not consider pressing or "dry" cleaning restoration or conservation. If not done correctly, pressing and dry cleaning can damage a book, which can result in a lower grade than the comic might have been before any pressing or dry cleaning had been done. At this point in time, the only professional pressing and dry cleaning service we can recommend is CFP. For more information on CFP and to find out if pressing is something your comic can benefit from, please visit www.cfpcomics.com. CFP is not a division of CBCS and no CBCS owner or employee has any ownership of CFP.

If a comic has been conserved, CBCS will note any conservation found on the CBCS label and it will be designated as conserved. If both restoration and conservation have been performed on a comic, the label will list both, but the comic will be designated within one of the five levels of restoration.

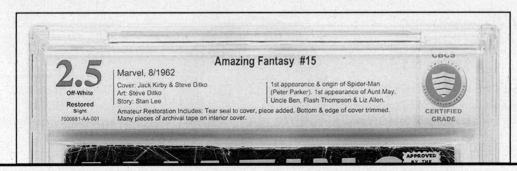

2.5
Off-White
Restored
Slight
7000881-AA-001

Amazing Fantasy #15

Marvel, 8/1962
Cover: Jack Kirby & Steve Ditko
Art: Steve Ditko
Story: Stan Lee

1st appearance & origin of Spider-Man
(Peter Parker). 1st appearance of Aunt May,
Uncle Ben, Flash Thompson & Liz Allen.

Amateur Restoration Includes: Tear seal to cover, piece added. Bottom & edge of cover trimmed.
Many pieces of archival tape on interior cover.

CBCS
CERTIFIED
GRADE

APPROVED
BY THE

EVERYONE DESERVES A
GOLDEN AGE

GIVE BACK TO THE CREATORS WHO GAVE YOU YOUR DREAMS

Support The Hero Initiative, the only charitable fund dedicated to helping yesterday's comic creators in need.

THE HERO INITIATIVE

HERO
HELPING COMIC BOOK CREATORS IN NEED

For more information or to send donation
11301 Olympic Blvd., #587
Los Angeles, CA 90064
or visit www.heroinitiative.org

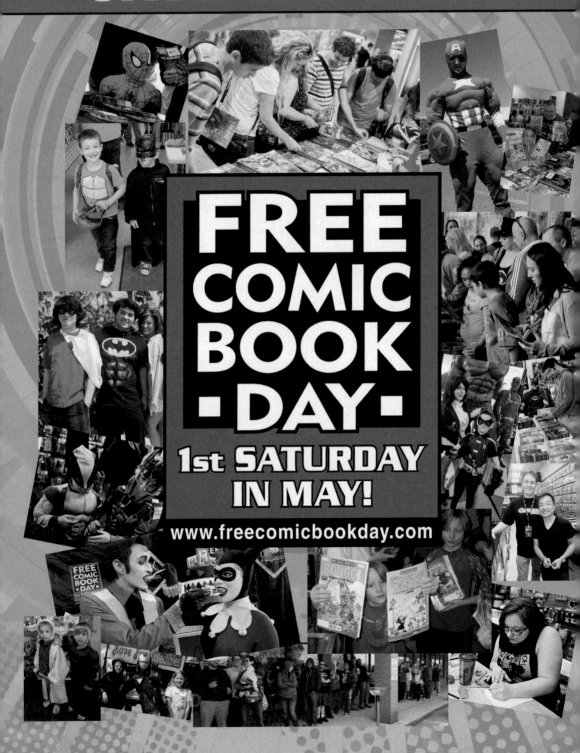

FREE COMIC BOOK DAY

1st SATURDAY IN MAY!

www.freecomicbookday.com

PRESERVATION AND STORAGE

There are a number of powerful foes waiting to strike at collectors, not least of which are the comic books themselves, or rather the effects of time on them.

Comics, after all, were not manufactured for the long haul. They were built to last just a short time, made with acidic newsprint paper, thin covers, and inconsistent inks. They weren't originally made with bags and boards, long boxes, Mylar snugs or CGC slabs. They were created, as painful as this is for a true collector to think about, to be disposable.

Is there any way to combat the ravages of time on your comics? Yes! We might not be able to keep comics in Gem Mint condition forever, but we can slow the damage with good methods of preservation and storage.

Some of the best advice for preserving a comic is simply to handle it carefully. Most dealers would prefer to remove the comic from its bag and show it to the customer themselves. In this way, if the book is damaged, it would be the dealer's responsibility and not the customer's.

When handling high-grade comics, always wash and dry your hands first, eliminating harmful oils from the skin. Lay the comic on a flat surface or in the palm of your hand and slowly turn the pages. This will minimize the stress to the staples and spine.

Careful storage is also a key element in the preservation of a cherished comic book. They must be protected from the elements, including the dangers of light, heat, and humidity. In addition to thinking about where you store your comics, you should also consider what you store them in. For years there have been arguments about what materials are acceptable.

For many years, it has been the policy of *The Overstreet Comic Book Price Guide* that in the *short term*, under good conditions, most plastic bags and boards are acceptable.

It is vital to remember that it is up to you as a collector to find out what materials are used to make your collector supplies and to understand that when combined with negative conditions, particularly heat and humidity, the safe lifespan of bags that might otherwise be fine in the short term is quickly decreased.

For long term preservation, only archivally sound materials should be used. Generally speaking, this means Mylar snugs and acid-free backing boards, but there are numerous variations on these subjects. The time you spend learning about these materials, though, will be time you don't have to spend later wondering what happened to your collection.

Even when it comes to boxes, care must be taken. Some contain chemicals that will actually help to destroy your collection rather than save it. Always be aware whether you are purchasing materials designed for long-term storage or not.

PRESERVATION AND STORAGE OF COMIC BOOKS

By William M. Cole, P. E.

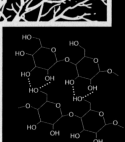

Comic Book collecting today is for both fun and profit. Yet, the comic book you thought was going to increase in value year after year has suddenly turned yellow after only three months and is now worthless. What happened? What could have been done to prevent the yellowing? This article will discuss how paper is made and what materials are best suited for long term storage and the guidelines for proper preservation.

How Paper Is Made

Paper generally has plant fibers that have been reduced to a pulp, suspended in water and then matted into sheets. The fibers in turn consist largely of cellulose, a strong, lightweight and somewhat durable material; cotton is an example of almost pure cellulose fiber. Although cotton and other kinds of fiber have been used in paper making over the years, most paper products today are made from wood pulp.

Wood pulps come in two basic varieties: groundwood and chemical wood. In the first process, whole logs are shredded and mechanically beaten. In the second, the fibers are prepared by digesting wood chips in chemical cookers. Because groundwood is the cheaper of the two, it is the primary component in such inexpensive papers as newsprint, which is used in many newspapers, comic books and paper backs. Chemically purified pulps are used in more expensive applications, such as stationery and some magazines and hardcover books.

Since groundwood pulp is made from whole wood fiber, the resulting paper does not consist of pure cellulose. As much as one third of its content may consist of non cellulose materials such as lignin, a complex woody acid. In chemical pulps, however, the lignin and other impurities are removed during the cooking process.

Deterioration Of Paper

The primary causes of paper deterioration are oxidation and acid hydrolysis. Oxidation attacks cellulose molecules with oxygen from the air, causing darkening and increased acidity. In addition, the lignin in groundwood paper breaks down quickly under the influence of oxygen and ultraviolet light. Light induced oxidation of lignin is what turns newspapers yellow after a few days' exposure to sunlight (light can also cause some printing inks to fade).

In acid hydrolysis, the cellulose fibers are cut by a reaction involving heat and acids, resulting in paper that turns brown and brittle. The sources of acidity include lignin itself, air pollution, and reaction by products from the oxidation of paper. Another major source is alum, which is often used with rosin to prepare the paper surface for accepting printing inks. Alum eventually releases sulfuric acid in paper.

Acidity and alkalinity are measured in units of pH, with 0 the most acidic and 14 the most alkaline. (Neutral pH is 7.0.) Because the scale is based on powers of 10, a pH of 4.5 is actually 200 times more acidic than a pH of 6.5. Fresh newsprint typically carries a pH of 4.5 or less, while older more deteriorated paper on the verge of crumbling, may run as low as pH 3.0. Although some modern papers are made acid free, most paper collectibles are acidic and need special treatment to lengthen their lives. Other factors which contribute to the destruction of paper include extremes of temperature and humidity, insects, rodents, mold and improper handling and storage.

Guidelines For Preservation

First and foremost, keep your paper collectibles cool, dark and dry. Store books and other items in an unheated room, if possible, and regularly monitor the humidity. Excess heat and humidity should be controlled with an air conditioner and a dehumidifier. Storage materials such as envelopes, sleeves and boxes, should be of *archival quality* only to prevent contamination of their contents.

According to the U.S. Library of Congress, the preferred material for preserving valuable documents is Polyethylene Terephthalate polyester film, such as Mylar type D or equivalent material. The film must be clear containing no plasticizers, surface coatings, UV inhibitors, or absorbents. The material must be guaranteed to be dimensionally stable, and resistant to most chemicals, moisture and abrasion.

Mylar is an exceptionally strong transparent film that does resist moisture, pollutants, oils and acids. With a life expectancy of hundreds of years, Mylar will outlast most other plastics. In addition, the brilliance and clarity of Mylar enhances the appearance of any paper collectible. (Mylar is a Registered Trademark of DuPont Teijin films.) Their brands of archival quality polyester films were and are Mylar type D and Melinex 516 of which they are exclusive manufacturers.)

Note: Mylar type D is no longer being manufactured by the Dupont Company. The use of the name Mylar is now being used generically for all material that meets the above specifications for the archival storage of paper documents.

Polyethylene And Polypropylene

For years collectors have stored their movie posters, comic books, baseball cards and other collectibles in polyethylene bags, PVC sheets and plastic wraps. Although such products may be useful in keeping away dirt, grease and vermin, many plastic sleeves contain plasticizers and other additives which can migrate into paper and cause premature aging. Both polyethylene and polypropylene contain solvents and additives in their manufacture to assure clarity and increase the flexibility in the plastic. Polyethylene when uncoated without any solvents is a good moisture barrier but has a high gas transmission rate, and eventually shrinks and loses its shape under warmer conditions.

In recent years polypropylene bags have been sold under the guise of being archivally sound. This is far from the truth. Only uncoated and untreated material is suitable for archival protection. Currently, the only way to seal polypropylene is to add a substance called PVDC (Polyvinyl Dichloride which is a relative of PVC) to allow the material to be heat sealed. Therefore, once you add the harmful additive, the sleeve now becomes non-archival and should not be used for long term storage.

Acid Free Boards And Boxes

Because ordinary cardboard is itself acidic, storage in cardboard boxes may be hazardous to your collection, and is a leading cause of premature deterioration of comic collections. For proper storage, only acid free boards that meet the US Government's *minimum* requirements are acceptable. These requirements have been defined as boards having a 3% calcium carbonate buffer throughout and a minimum pH of 8.5. Anything less will hasten your collection's destruction. While many advertisers claim that their boards are "acid free at time of manu-

facture," they are in reality only spray coated with an alkaline substance making them acid free for only a very short time. Boards termed "acid free at time of manufacture" do not offer sufficient protection or storage for anything other than short term. True acid free boards have been impregnated with a calcium buffer resulting in an acid free, alkaline pH content of 8.5 throughout.

Deacidification

Another way to extend the longevity of your collectibles is to deacidify them before storage. Deacidifying sprays and solutions are now available for home use. By impregnating the paper with an alkaline reserve, you can neutralize existing acids and inhibit oxidation, future acidity and staining due to certain fungi. However it is best left to the professionals to deacidify your comic books. Deacidification with proper storage conditions will add centuries to the lifetime of paper.

In summary, we recommend the following guidelines for the maximum protection of your collectibles: Deacidify the paper; store in Mylar sleeves with acid free boards and cartons; and keep the collection cool, dry and dark. Periodic inspections and pH and humidity tests are also recommended. By following these simple guidelines you can be assured of a comic book collection that not only will increase in value, but will also last for many years to come.

Bill Cole has been manufacturing collectors supplies for over 40 years and is the owner and CEO of Bill Cole Enterprises, Inc. in Randoph, Massachusetts. Mr. Cole is a retired Army Officer and also the author of numerous articles on preservation. Questions or comments may be directed to him at sales@bcemylar.com. Their website is www.bcemylar.com.

Comic Book Maintenance and Preservation for Archives and Special Collections

by Caitlin McGurk

From Richard Outcault's first *Yellow Kid* newspaper strip, capturing life in the tenement ghettos of New York City in the 1890s, to Peter Bagge's *Hate* series that so accurately and sarcastically depicts the Seattle grunge scene in the 1990s, it's clear that comics are doing more than telling stories - they're unwittingly documenting our cultural heritage. By combining descriptive powers similar to those of photography and novels – be it a historical event or a personal tragedy captured in a minicomic – what comics can represent about ourselves and our society is boundless. And with the wild insurgence of comic-adapted films, indie-conventions popping up in more cities than ever, and sequential art being taught in colleges worldwide, there's no arguing that now more than ever comics have become serious business. With that in mind, as librarians,

educators, and devoted lovers of the form, it's crucial that dedicated time and attention is paid toward the preservation and maintenance of comics and graphic novels in our collections to aid in resounding their enduring significance.

Before we discuss preventative methods, it's important that we understand a little bit about the deeper make-up of our materials. We're all familiar with that thin, yellowy look that pre-modern age comics wear so well, and be it aesthetically pleasing in an esoteric kind of way – that little novelty hue is the harbinger of sickness in our collection. Up until the mid-1980s when EPA regulations changed the acidity content in paper, comics, like all other "pulp" material, were printed on cheap wood pulp paper, brimming with highly photosynthetic lignin and cellulose. Just like a flower soaking up sunlight to grow, these plant compounds are by nature hungry for the elements, oxidizing with their exposure to air and light, making them a ticking time-bomb from the moment of their creation without any help from us. However, this internal war is waged mostly within the pages of Golden and Silver Age comics, as most comics produced

in the past 20 years are printed on high quality glossy paper which has been chemically de-pulped, and coated with an alkaline buffer to better protect against environmental pollutants that cause acid hydrolysis. Regardless, all paper degrades over time, and the external key factors of deterioration remain the same: light and air pollutants, handling, storage, and upkeep.

Now that we're aware of the internal menace lurking in the very fibers of our books, our only means for gaining control is preventative action! It may seem like a no-brainer that comics should not be stored within the reach of sunlight, but what not all collectors realize is that paper is affected by all kinds of light. Be it natural light, fluorescent bulbs, or even incandescent - all of these contribute some degree of UV or infrared light, quickening the process of decay. Luckily, there are a number of vendors out there offering UV protective tube guards for fluorescent lights at a fairly inexpensive cost, averaging about $7.00 per cover, and typically guaranteed to last up to 10 years.

However, if light fixture renovations aren't in your budget, simply using the right storage materials for your collection will do the trick. Sites like www.comicsupply.com, as well as Gaylord Brothers (www.Gaylordmart.com) offer acid-free storage boxes in a variety of sizes. Pay close attention while shopping around for these materials that the products you choose are in fact archival quality and acid free - those coated with a calcium carbonate buffer will maintain a steady pH content, avoiding contamination from the wood pulp in ordinary cardboard boxes. Be sure to double-check your dimensions as well, as shoving Silver Age books into boxes specified for Modern Age sizes will not only damage the material, but any obstruction of the lid is easy exposure to pollutants, let alone vermin or bugs! Boxes should be watertight, and stored vertically in cool, dry, dark environments. Silica gel packs can work long lasting wonders as well, and Gaylordmart also specializes in tiny Desiccant Canisters with color-changing indicator gel, which can be placed inside each storage box and are reusable for life by baking them in the oven once they've been saturated.

An item of frequent debate and confusion is the proper sleeves to store comics in, as polyethylene and polypropylene bags are typically the cheapest and easiest to find. In terms of longevity and superior quality though, uncoated archival quality polyester film, more commonly known as Mylar® bags, are by far the best option. These bags will outlast other plastics by hundreds of years, as polyethylene and polypropylene products are manufactured with solvents and additives that break down over time, causing premature aging in the paper. Stiff, acid free backing boards made of cotton rag or wood and cellular fiber should be inserted in each bag behind the comic as well to prevent bending and cracking. These will also have a calcium carbonate buffer, and can be purchased in bulk from any comic book supplies store. I would recommend Thin-X-Tender brand, as an inexpensive and high-quality option. You will also want to invest in tape with which to seal the flap of each sleeve, settling for nothing other than acid-free products as the off-gassing of old tape can cause serious damage to your books over time.

Now that you've gathered all of your proper storage weapons of prevention, one item worth looking into is MicroChamber interleaving paper. This product is your one sure bet for combating against the unavoidable internal-aging process occurring within the pages of your comics. MicroChamber technology uses lignin-free and sulfur-free material that actually absorbs air-borne pollutants and acidic by-products of degradation. Upon interlacing one sheet inside of the back and front covers of your comic, these sheets immediately begin working to actively soak up the hazardous toxins being released from the book, as well as preventing the ink from transferring from one page to another. MicroChamber paper only needs to be replaced every 7 years, and has been used by the CGC for every comic they grade.

Now, if the comics or graphic novels you're maintaining are receiving high circulation and handling, and these technical details are beyond consideration, the same basic principles for care of any book apply. The low-grade paper that older comics were printed on is highly susceptible to grease and oils, so always handle with clean hands and an eye for brittle pages. I've found that loosely packed rotating racks are the best for displaying comics, although they can become quickly unorganized.

Another quick and easy option for storage is three-ring binders with sealable sleeves, which can also be found in age-specific sizes made from archival materials.

Whichever route you take for maintaining your comics collection, do it economically and sensibly. If you're using MicroChamber paper, be sure to not counteract it with acidic storage boxes. There are more options on the market for these products than ever before, so shop around, be sure you're getting the best for your buck, and always acid free! Be it for business or pleasure, consider yourself a guardian of comic book history, and remember: with great power comes great responsibility!

This article was originally published by Diamond Comic Distributors on their Bookshelf *website.*

Caitlin McGurk self publishes the zine and mini-comics series Good Morning You, *and is currently finishing her MLIS degree at the Palmer School in New York City. She has worked to build and maintain the collections for Marvel Comics, The Schulz Library at The Center for Cartoon Studies, and the Bulliet Comics Collection of Columbia University. She aspires to promote the advancement of comics research by broadening their accessibility in the collections of universities and libraries worldwide.*

PEDIGREE COMIC BOOKS

What are comic book pedigrees? Why are they important?

According to the forthcoming book *The Guide To Comic Book Pedigrees*, "A pedigreed collection must have been accumulated by one individual during the time the comics were released on the newsstand. This is a critical factor because a pedigree's appeal comes from their homogenous quality and singular genesis. The books have aged together in the same environment, creating a uniform 'feel' that does not exist for comics in a collection with diverse origins."

As the book's website points out, there are three other commonly accepted stipulations for what makes a collection a pedigree collection:

- A pedigreed collection must primarily consist of high quality comic books.
- A pedigreed collection must contain a substantial number of key or rare issues, or represent a significant portion of a particular genre, company, period, or classic title/character.
- Comics Guaranty, LLC (CGC) and the collecting community must continue to recognize the pedigree name of a collection past the point of initial sale.

The first widely recognized comic book pedigree was (and is) the Edgar Church collection, which is also known as the Mile High collection, which was unveiled in the 1970s. Since it first gained notoriety, others have surfaced including the following:

Allentown	Davis Crippen ("D")	Massachusetts	Rocky Mountain
Aurora	Denver	Mohawk Valley	Salida
Bethlehem	Don & Maggie	Northford	Savannah
Big Apple	Thompson	Northland	Spokane
Billy Wright	Don Rosa	Nova Scotia	Suscha News
Boston	Edgar Church	Oakland	Tom Reilly
Bowling Green	(Mile High)	Ohio	(San Francisco)
Carson City	Gaines File	Okajima	Twilight
Central Valley	Green River	Pacific Coast	Twin Cities
Chicago	Haight-Ashbury	Palo Alto	Vancouver
Circle 8	Hawkeye	Pennsylvania	Western Penn
Cosmic Aeroplane	Kansas City	Recil Macon	White Mountain
Crowley	Lamont Larson	River City	Windy City
Curator	Lost Valley	Rockford	Winnipeg

The pedigree of a comic will be listed on the CGC label.

THE
Lamont Larson
COLLECTION

BY JON BERK

CGC UNIVERSAL GRADE

9.2

More Fun Comics #54
D.C. Comics, 4/40

WHITE Pages

Jerry Siegel story
Bart Tumey, John Lehti & Joe Sulman art
Bernard Baily cover & art

0627906019

Classic cover.

Larson

CGC

Lamont Larson

> *In the summer of 2005, unbeknownst to the majority of the attendees at Comic-Con International: San Diego a special collector was on the floor and later attended a dinner in his honor. Lamont Larson, whose comic collection is considered in the top tier of the Golden Age pedigrees by pedigree collectors, had been invited to attend. Those who had the chance to meet him knew that it was truly a once in a lifetime opportunity.*
>
> *Longtime collector and Overstreet Advisor Jon Berk details the history of the Lamont Larson Collection and the man behind it.*

I was going to start off and proclaim that "I had found Lamont Larson!" However, from the perspective of Lamont Larson, he had never been "lost". And, frankly, from my point of view, although I had often wondered about Lamont Larson, I never actively made this a crusade. I mean did I really think I could locate the man, who had amassed, as a boy, over 50 years ago, a collection of Golden Age comics which forms one of the most collectible and recognizable "pedigree" set of comic books in today's marketplace? Well, with some perseverance and a whole lot of luck I "located" Lamont Larson and have had the opportunity to speak with him as to his recollections of reading comics in the late 1930s and early 1940s.

But first, a little background. For reasons which I cannot fully articulate, I have been intrigued by collecting Golden Age comicbooks known as "Larson" books. The collection, uncovered by Joe Tricarichi in the early 1970s, comprises about 1,000 comic books. Although there are a couple of books from 1935, the bulk of the collection runs from 1936 to September 1941; the heart of the pre-Golden Age and Golden Age. (Please note, except for the "lost Larsons" described below, there are not any Larson copies covered dated after September 1941.) Although the Larson collection contains many of the early Golden Age keys, notable among the missing key issues is *Detective Comics* #27, *All Star Comics* #3 and *Flash Comics* #1. Notwithstanding these omissions, the collection contains major keys and significant runs of hard core and esoteric Golden Age. Unique to the Larson collection is that it contains several "pre-hero" comic books missing from the Church collection. The collection also contains many Big Little Books, pulps and mystery novels.

As pedigree collections go, the Larson collection contains some of the earliest books of any pedigree collection. The earliest issues for some pre-Golden Age titles are: *Famous Funnies* #10 (May 1935), *Tip Top* #2 (June 1936), *Funny Pages* #3 (July 1936), *More Fun* #15 (November 1936), *New Comics* #11 (November 1936), *Funny Picture Stories* #1 (November 1936), *Detective Picture Stories* #1 (December 1936), *King Comics* #9 (December 1936), *Detective Comics* #3 (May 1937), *New Adventure* #17 (July 1937), *Feature Fun-*

nies #9 (June 1938). Due to my interest in books from this early time period and Centaur comics, I kept on "bumping" into "Larson" books as the only specimens I could find. Eventually, as my awareness of the Larson collection grew, I took pleasure knowing that these books could be traced back to a single owner. I would search out books from this remarkable collection.

Although the condition of the books is variable (a few have been chewed by mice (see *Red Raven* #1), or have water damage or have had coupons clipped out (including *Jungle Comics* #1, *Planet Comics* #1 and *Target Comics* #1 - the coupon of these books unfortunately being on the inside of the front cover), many books are in the VF/NM range or better. Whatever the grade, most books have outstanding page quality with light to moderate "foxing" due to apparent exposure to water. Books from this collection sell for *Guide* to a premium over *Guide* for simply being a "Larson copy."

Many "Larsons" are easily identifiable by the name "Larson" prominently written in pencil on the cover. Besides the "flowing cursive" Larson signature (see *Funny Pages* V4/#1 and *Whirlwind Comics* #2), many books have a "different" Larson signature (see *Red Raven Comics* #1 and *Zip Comics* #16) or "Lamont" in a different handwriting (see *Thrilling Comics* #8 and *Top-Notch Comics* #18). In many instances, the initial buyers of these books would try to erase the name from the cover, a perceived "defect." Today that "defect" is sought out by the more avid Larson collectors. Some books just have a "number" on the cover, many books have "on" on the cover with the Larson "signature" (see *Popular Comics* #57), or without the Larson "signature" (see *Crackajack Funnies* #13); others have no markings at all. Late issues of the poorly distributed Fox Comics had an "ad" on the cover.

Some collectors have been told that books with just an "L" are Larson copies. This simply is not the case. The "signature" present or erased is always in the upper left hand quadrant of the book.

The oldest books from 1936 have "P.N." with a number (see *Detective Picture Stories* #2 and *Funny Pages* #6). Almost all the books have some degree of the distinctive foxing. Unfortunately, due to an early lack of information about these books, unless a particular book has a distinctive identifying mark, many "Larsons" have been assimilated anonymously into the comic book marketplace. (Although not absolutely definitive, the Larson list compiled by Joe Tricarichi is quite helpful. Grading of the books on the list is generally under the more liberal grading standards of the 1970s. However, Joe notes some specific defects on books, which is critical to identifying books as Larson copies if the lineage of the book is unknown.)

What draws me to "Larson" copies (beside their generally nice condition) is the knowledge that the books are part of a single identifiable collection. Although not generally of the superior virginal (i.e. "not read") quality of the Church collection, these books were read and accumulated by one person. My interest with Larson books prompted many questions. What is the meaning of the markings on the covers? Why the variation of the "signatures"? Was this the result of a father-son collaboration? What got him going on comics? How old was he? I thought these questions would never be answered. Wrong!

I had been offered a book which was a "Larson." Inquiring how the book was identified as a "Larson," I was told that it was from the coupon filled out inside the book (of *All-Star Comics* #1). Did it give an address? "Wausa, Nebraska." I called telephone information but, alas, no listing for "Lamont Larson." They did have three other listings for "Larson." What the heck, I called the first on the list, and although not a relative, she put me on the path to locate Lamont Larson in Clay Center, Nebraska. Lamont Larson was then 74 years old and a retired English teacher.

In my initial telephone conversation I spent much time convincing Mr. Larson that I had both feet planted firmly on the ground and that I was genuinely interested in events that had taken place over 50 years ago. He is totally disassociated from the world of comics and had no idea of the prominence of his comic books. After convincing him that I was not crazy, I said, "Ah, you don't know me, but I am interested in comics and, well, you collected them 50 years ago..." He interrupted me at that point and said, "I did not collect them, I read them." This was a refreshing start.

Larson was surprised at my call. He

had not given any thought to these books for many years. They were something that formed a part of his childhood, a part that he had let go as his interests turned to mystery novels and model airplanes. Understandably, Larson's recollection of the events of reading comic books as a boy is vague at best. It came as "a very big surprise" for him to learn that his books had such notoriety for comic collectors. He admitted that his initial reaction to this information was that this was all "very strange." As we talked, he warmed and found it "pleasant" as to the place his books hold in collecting circles.

Lamont Larson grew up in Wausa, Nebraska, a small farming town in northeast Nebraska about 150 miles from Omaha (Actually "Lamont" is his middle name. Growing up in the late 1930s he was not fond of the phonetic sameness of his first name "Rudolph" with a certain German leader of that time.). The town population was about 700. His family ran the local movie theater.

As a boy Larson described himself as an "avid reader." He read comics from about the age of 9 through the age of 15. As he told me, "I always liked comics in the daily and particularly in the Sunday paper. As they came up with comic books, I began to prize and enjoy them." (Remember the "modern" comic book only hit the newsstands in 1934, with original material beginning in 1935/1936.) He did not buy to "collect" comics, but rather, as Larson stated, "to read and enjoy them." He stated that he always enjoyed the comics in the newspaper. Comic books represented "a step beyond that. I was developing a desire to read and I liked the high adventure that you got in some of those comics."

Larson would purchase the comics at Cruetz' Drugstore. Because Larson missed some issues as they came out, the owner of the drugstore, Fred Cruetz, suggested that he put aside all comics that came in and have Larson pick them up periodically. As Larson recalls Fred Cruetz said, "Well, I tell you what. We'll put them away and put your name on them...and when you want to come in and get them, they'll be here." Larson accepted this arrangement. Tryg Hagen and Cecil Coop, employees at different times at the drugstore, were primarily responsible for placing Larson's name on the books which were put aside for him. It is <u>their</u> handwriting, not Larson's, that appears on the books. (This information explains the variation in the handwriting for "Larson" or "Lamont" appearing on the books, and puts to an end one of the small mysteries about the books.) This arrangement probably started some time in 1939 - Larson would have been 12 - as I am not aware of any "signed" Larsons before this date. (In fact, based on review of my "Larson" books it appears this arrangement started with books cover dated July 1939. Interestingly, his name did not appear on all titles on a consistent basis until those cover dated January 1940. This may also explain some of the gaps in the early runs. Additionally, as indicated below, it appears that certain gaps are explained by the fact that he gave some of his books away.) All comics were purchased new; no second-hand comics were purchased to fill gaps.

Mr. Larson had no explanation for the numbers written on the books, or the "P.N." or the "on" written on the books, except to state that many of the magazines sold at the drugstore, whether comics or not, would have the notation "on." To answer these questions, Larson put me in contact with Norman and Bob Cruetz, the sons of the drugstore owner. (Cruetz' Drugstore has been in continuous operation and run by the same family since 1895.) They stated that the initials identified the distributor of the books in order to make returns. "P.N." stood for "Publishers News" and "on" stood for "Omaha News". They also were able to identify <u>who</u> wrote Larson's name on the books. The flowing cursive "Larson" and "Lamont" as appears on *Funny Pages* #4/1 and *Whirlwind Comics*, respectively, was written by Tryg Hagen while the handwriting for "Larson" as it appears on *Red Raven Comics* and *Zip* #16 was written by Cecil Coop (who helped out at the drugstore after Hagen died in 1940).

As to the numbers on some of the covers, the answer is less clear. Norman Cruetz

The "Larson" name on his copy of *Marvel Mystery Comics* #3 from 1940.

believes it is a "call back" number by which the distributor identified books that were then ready to be returned. The retail outlet would then tear off the covers and return these books for credit. Cruetz believes this was the procedure for Publishers News. (Apparently after 1937 only Omaha News would be specifically indicated by a symbol on the cover.) In support of this theory it is noted that numbers do not appear on any book that has the "on" (Omaha News) symbol. This supposition of Kruetz appears to be correct in that the number for the Larson titles that do have numbers are all the same.

Larson's parents would pay for the comics. They had no problem with him reading them. Larson stated that his parents viewed it as a cheap way "to keep me out of trouble." He started reading them at the end of the Depression. As he reflected, "They were only a dime so it really wasn't a big thing, although, sometimes, that dime was kinda hard to come by." Although many of the books in the Larson collection were "reprint" books, Larson confided that he did not like these "funny books," preferring "high adventure," "far out," and "fantastic" stories. His favorite characters read like a who's who of the Golden Age: Captain America, Captain Marvel, Superman, and, his favorite, Batman (Interestingly, his "handle" for CB was "The Shadow" due to the shared name "Lamont"). He also had a tremendous interest in Dick Tracy both in comic books and Big Little Books which he adored.

Larson stated he was always careful about things he owned. Generally, he would put the comics away after he read them, although he acknowledged that some might have been thrown away. (This further explains the gaps that appear in many of the collected series.) Initially, the books were in a box in a storeroom, but when his family moved in 1940 they were stored in a barn. This outdoor storage explains the mice chews on some books and the exposure to moisture - resulting in foxing - present on many copies. (This "storage method" of subjecting books to the extremes of the Nebraskan weather while sitting of the floor of a barn in a cardboard box and yet maintaining white pages is remarkable considering the elaborate procedures advocated by "experts" on how to properly preserve one's collection.) Larson has no specific recollection of why he stopped reading comics, except to note that he had become interested in other things, such as mystery novels and anything to do with aviation. In fact, latter in life he started to collect hardback and paperback mystery novels.

Larson obtained a job as a teacher and moved away from Wausa leaving the comics in the barn. In the late 1970s, a local antique dealer, Dwaine Nelson, asked Larson's mother (for whom he did odd jobs) about the books and an arrangement was made. Larson was surprised that they had been saved. Mrs. Larson who was anxious to remove the material in the barn sold Nelson the comics and many magazines such as *The Saturday Evening Post* and *Colliers*. Nelson had the books for about 18 months before he resold them. Nelson (with whom I spoke) recollected that he sold the comics and magazines for about $50 to $100. They eventually found their way into the hands of Joe Tricarichi.

As one looks back, it was the thousands and thousands of kids who, like Lamont Larson, latching on to this new form of entertainment, catapulted the nascent comic book business into the thriving business it would be. And out of those thousands and thousands of books only a few survived through the years to be snapped up by anxious collectors today. Who would have thought that one of the most prominent collections of comic books would survive to this date, due to the idea of an owner of a drugstore in a small Nebraskan town and a boy who took good care of what he owned?

Epilogue

After my article came out in late 1994, Larson's hometown newspaper in Nebraska asked if they could reprint it. I naturally gave my permission. About two weeks after the newspaper articles appeared, I received a letter from a boyhood friend of Larson's (Larson had even been his best man.). He had read with much interest my articles. It prompted an old memory. Recently, he had cleaned out his mother's house and discovered a box of his old comics. He remembered as a boy that Larson had given him comics after he was done with them. Sure enough he found six books with "Lamont" or "Larson" on them. He "wondered" if I "might" be interested in them. MIGHT BE!

As described none of the books sounded like they were in particularly good condition. However, driven by curiosity and this incredible quirk of luck that these books even existed, I dickered over a price and purchased the books. These books are, for the record, *Smash Comics* #8 (March 1940), *Feature Comics* #34 (July 1940), *Minute Man Comics* #2 (September 5 - December 5, 1941), *Super Mystery* V2/#4 (October 1941), *Victory Comics* #3 (November 1941) and *Star Spangled Comics* #2 (November 1941). As testament to the uniqueness of the storage condition of the original collection, the "lost Larsons" are of variable condition with none grading better than VG+ and none displaying the page whiteness of the original collection.

These "lost Larsons" prompt several thoughts and observations. There are, obviously, "Larsons" that were purchased after the September 1941 cover date. However, it is clear that at this point Larson lost interest. Of the six "lost Larsons" four are from the very end of his comic reading career. The fact that he gave away the books is evidence of that. He may have been more willing to part with his comic books at this point. However, since two of the books are from 1940, the "gaps" in the Larson collection may be attributed as much to the common boyhood trait of sharing books as to the possible distribution quirks of the comic books themselves. The more intriguing question is if Larson gave away any other books. Are there more "lost Larsons" out there waiting to be found?

A version of this article originally appeared in Overstreet's Gold and Silver Quarterly #6 *(Oct.-Dec. 1994). Following that, additional information was discovered concerning this collection, most notably author Berk's acquisition of Joe Tricarichi's "Larson List." Additionally, previously unknown "Larson" copies were discovered prior to its revised publication in* Comic Book Marketplace.

AND WHEN THE VAULT WAS

It was an oddly cold day in August 1989. The mist settled in among the Manhattan skyscrapers creating a spooky EC setting as Russ Cochran and I walked over to Bill Gaines' apartment from our hotel. It still seems like only yesterday when Russ called me with the news that Bill Gaines has decided to sell his EC collection. Russ would be handling the sale and I was needed to verify the collection and to arrange the copies of each issue by grade. We both knew that he had put away twelve copies of every EC 35-40 years earlier and sealed them away in boxes. Now the time had come to open those packages.

Thoughts were rushing through our heads about the significance of the day. We had many questions to be answered. We wondered what the condition would be like, how white the pages would be, if any issues would be missing, and if something new would be discovered.

We finally arrived at the Gaines' apartment at 10:15 AM. After clearing security, we arrived at his doorstep. Bill and his wife Anne cheerfully invited us in. Their apartment was like a curio shop, filled with mementos, souvenirs, and Statues of Liberty which they had collected for many years. Over to the right were bookshelves filled with bound ECs and *MAD*s. But what really caught our eyes was a genuine shrunken head sitting on the shelf (see the *Haunt of Fear* #8 cover). After gasping and choking for a second, we settled down around a large dining room table where the work would be performed.

In the closet were six large cardboard boxes which contained the ECs. The comics were wrapped in brown paper by issue number and sealed in the boxes. Before the comic books were handled, Russ and I put on white cotton film editor's gloves.

The first box was opened and the first package of comics was set on the table. We began with *Vault of Horror* #40 and worked backwards to *War Against Crime* #10. Russ cut open each package, counted the issues and handed them to me for arrangement by grade. Anne placed the ID labels on Mylar bags while Bill supervised.

Legendary EC Publisher Bill Gaines during the evaluation of the Gaines File collection.

OPENED...

by Robert M. Overstreet
with Gary M. Carter

Haunt of Fear #17 (#3)
CGC-certified 9.6 copy
sold for $7,475 in 2005.

After each stack was graded, Russ placed them in Mylar sleeves. At this point the copies were divided into two groups, one to be sold and one to be retained by Bill. Depending on shortages, Bill wanted to keep up to four copies for his personal use.

It soon became apparent, after going through just a few packages, that we were seeing something out of the ordinary. The books were dazzling. They were essentially in brand new condition with full cover gloss and extra white pages. The cover colors were brilliant, with only a few exceptions. All of the noticeable defects either occurred during printing or trimming or the way they were wrapped. Some corners were bumped, and some issues were wrinkled.

Mad #4
CGC-certified 9.8 copy
sold for $5,750 in 2001.

We were disappointed to find no annuals or Pre-Trend comics, except for *War Against Crime* #10 and 11, and *Crime Patrol* #15 and 16. But we were surprised to find most all of the different versions of M.C. Gaines' books: *Picture Stories from the Bible*, *Science*, *American History* and *World History*. Some carried the All-American seal, some the DC seal, and others had the familiar EC seal.

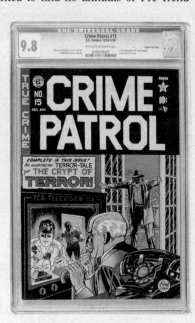

The Gaines File Pedigree is one of the most sought-after collections of comic books, with its high-grade copies selling for record prices. This **Crime Patrol** #15 CGC-graded 9.8 copy sold for $9,560 in 2008.

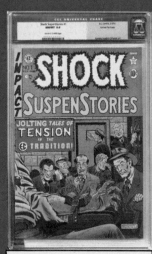

Shock SuspenStories #1
CGC-certified 9.8 copy
sold for $5,750 in 2004.

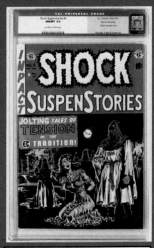

Shock SuspenStories #6
CGC-certified 9.8 copy
sold for $7,170 in 2006.

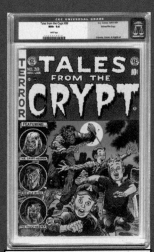

Tales From the Crypt #39
CGC-certified 9.6 copy
sold for $2,990 in 2002.

Vault of Horror #27
CGC-certified 9.8 copy
sold for $4,887 in 2005.

Robert M. Overstreet evaluates a then-freshly opened issue of **Frontline Combat** #4, documenting the now legendary Gaines File collection.

After opening a few of the packages and seeing the pristine condition of the books, we just had to check out their smell. The white pages and inks were still so fresh, that opening the books and smelling the insides swept us back to 1950. It was a smell we all remembered. Those of us who can recognize an Edgar Church Collection (Mile High) comic by its smell would have trouble distinguishing between it and the Gaines smell. It soon became obvious that we were looking at probably the best surviving sets of EC comics.

As a comparison, many of the Harvey file copies had brown edges due to the way they were stored. Some of the Dell file copies also had minor browning on the edges. Since the Gaines collection

Longtime EC enthusiast, historian and publisher Russ Cochran with **Frontline Combat** copies from the Gaines File collection.

was never read, and was wrapped air-tight, the only comparable collection would be the Church collection. In the Dell and Harvey file copies there were issues missing from the runs, and in some cases there were probably as many as 100 copies of each issue.

Bill had remembered that there were twelve copies in each package, but we found that many had been opened, probably before Gaines moved to that apartment in 1961. We found that most issues did have twelve copies, but there were many packages that contained nine, ten, or eleven copies, and a few with only seven copies, and one issue with only one copy (*Vault of Horror* #12).

The work was tedious, the days were long, but they were filled with memories that we shall never forget. As we looked at these books, we traded stories about our memories of seeing each cover for the first time, and stories of how we tracked down that particular issue for our collections. Each day we played Christmas music and sang Christmas carols as we continued processing the mountain of unopened packages. At each day's end we returned to our hotel immersed in EC dust, Christmas Spirit, and childhood memories.

After spending a few days going through these books, Russ and I agreed that it was an experience that any EC fan would have enjoyed — the historic unveiling of the Gaines File collection. It was like opening 300 little time capsules that hadn't seen the light of day for 35-40 years. Being small-town collectors we both felt privileged and honored to be present at such a historic occasion. We hope that these notes will in some way make it possible for all other collectors and fans to have been there also.

On Friday, August 11, we processed *Vault of Horror, Tales from the Crypt, Haunt of Fear, Crime SuspenStories* and *Shock SuspenStories*. On Saturday, August 12, we did *Weird Science, Weird Fantasy, Weird Science-Fantasy, Incredible Science-Fiction*, all of the New Direction titles (such as *Valor* and *Impact*), *MAD* and *Panic*. On Sunday we were joined by Russ's daughter, Sylvia, and Angie Meyer, and we did *Two-Fisted Tales, Frontline Combat*, the 3-D comics, and the various *Picture Stories* series. The actual sets of books were put together Sunday afternoon, which finished the project.

As an interesting footnote, we learned that *Impact* #1 was originally printed by Charlton Press. The printing quality was poor, so Gaines had the entire run destroyed, saving only one copy. It was then printed again and distributed to the stands.

Years later, of course, the Gaines File collection has become one of the most sought-after pedigreed collections of comic books. As has been documented in our Market Reports over the past few editions of the *Guide* and from the incredible success of Gemstone's *EC Archives* project, the interest in these classics shows no signs of waning now.

This article appeared in different form in Overstreet's Golden Age & Silver Age Quarterly *and* The Overstreet Comic Book Price Guide #38.

War Against Crime #11
CGC-certified 9.6 copy sold for
$4,600 in 2001.

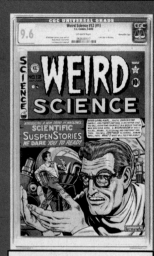

Weird Science #12 (#1)
CGC-certified 9.6 copy sold for
$8,799 in 2006.

Weird Science-Fantasy #29
CGC-certified 9.6 copy sold for
$13,255 in 2002.

THE DON AND MAGGIE THOMPSON PEDIGREE COLLECTION

By Carrie Wood

One of the more recent additions to the pedigree list is the Don and Maggie Thompson collection, which has already made serious waves at auctions since debuting in 2013. Just 86 pieces out of their immense collection were auctioned initially and they collected $748,148 by the time it was over.

When Don and Maggie first met in 1957, one of the topics of conversation that really got them going was their mutual interest in comic strips and comic books. They learned that, separately, they had been collecting their favorites and maintaining them in an age where taking care of comic books was difficult.

"My comics collecting began before I could read. I received a dime a week in allowance and spent it… on a comic book," she told Geppi's Entertainment Museum's *FAN* in August 2014. "Mom then was often condemned to read that comic book to me for the ensuing week."

When Don and Maggie were getting started on their Comic Art fanzine – perhaps the first amateur publication of its kind devoted entirely to story-telling art – they were also on the lookout for the best newsstand copy of their favorite titles. Once these stories were read, they were carefully put away and stored. And these two were meticulous about making sure they got their hands on every book as it came out, because there was no guarantee that they'd have another chance.

"If you didn't buy one month's comic book, you couldn't buy that issue a month later. That lesson learned made me pretty obsessive pretty quickly," Maggie said. "I can still tell you a couple of comic books I looked for but missed on the stands: Dell's *Easter with Mother Goose* for 1947 and – later – E.C.'s *Extra #1*. The latter never went on sale via my local newsstands."

Maggie and Don Thompson
in the early days of comic fandom

That Comic Art fanzine wasn't the duo's only foray into comic book publications; they eventually took over the editor's chair of the *Comics Buyer's Guide* until Don passed away in 1994. Maggie continued to serve in an editorial role for many years. She went on to establish two online blogs dedicated to the hobby and is still a force to be reckoned with in the comic world.

Because of how Don and Maggie were able to maintain their collection, it was established as a pedigree in 2013. A number of key titles in comic book history were included in their collection, and ended up being graded highly. Included as part of that auction was: *The Avengers* #1, CGC NM 9.4 (one of the finest copies of this book known to exist), *Journey Into Mystery* #83, CGC NM 9.2 (the first appearance of Thor), and *The Incredible Hulk* #1, CGC VF+ 8.5.

But just because the Don and Maggie Thompson Collection has hit the open market, that doesn't mean that Maggie is in any way done with the comic industry. She told *FAN* that just because some of her possessions have been sold, that shouldn't be taken as a sign that she's getting out of the business.

"I don't know who took it as that sign, but they certainly weren't paying any attention to either what I've said about it in every interview or to the work I've been doing ever since. How wrong were they? As wrong as they could be," she said. "I've lost some touch with the daily comics news, mostly because there are 24 hours in a day, I have many projects, and the incredible volume of comics output these days is stunning. But getting out? Hah!"

Even when – or if – Maggie Thompson decides to get out of the business, her impact on collecting is immense, and will live on through the Don and Maggie Thompson pedigree.

Maggie Thompson with some of her remaining collection.

COMIC BOOK
DEFINING

By Dr. Arnold T. Blumberg & J.C. Vaughn
(with additional material and
timeline graphics by Douglas Gillock)

AGES:
ERAS

In The Overstreet Comic Book Price Guide #33, *we offered the beginnings of a discussion on Comic Book Ages. This article features the results of that discussion.*

The search for agreement on comic book ages has proven to be one of those topics, the kind for which no one is without an opinion or two (or twelve). It has produced scores of animated e-mails, letters and even academic papers, all of them from collectors, dealers and historians who care deeply about where comics have been and where they're going.

As we worked to arrive at a consensus, we've heard from many different fans of the four-color medium in a wide variety of capacities. While there are still some elements to be decided, a great deal of agreement was found in some areas of understanding.

COMICS DIDN'T START IN 1933

More than 90 years before *New Fun Comics* hit the stands, *The Adventures of Obadiah Oldbuck* presented a story in sequential comic form. Someone made the decision to publish it and influenced the next generation of cartoonists. More than 50 years before *New Fun,* Palmer Cox collected his Brownies cartoons into one publication, influencing 60 years of comics publishing during which a tremendous variety of packaging and presentations were tried out.

If you still think it's the comics themselves and not the creative and business people behind them that the Ages denote, consider these questions: If Vin Sullivan and his contemporaries hadn't been looking to try something different, would *Action Comics #1* ever have happened? If Julie Schwartz hadn't been interested in reviving the superheroes, would *Showcase #4* have witnessed the reinterpretation of the Flash? If Stan Lee hadn't stepped away from the day-to-day operations at Marvel, would

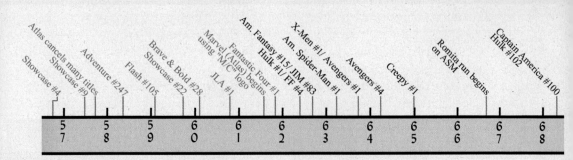

Gwen Stacy have died? If the limited series format hadn't proved successful, how would *Crisis on Infinite Earths* have been handled?

It's simple: the comics we have come to recognize as indicators of significant changes, like those noted in the previous paragraph, are the manifestations of *editorial or publishing decisions* that were made several months before. It is actually these decisions we are marking when we note the importance of the publication of *The Adventures of Obadiah Oldbuck*, the collection of Palmer Cox's Brownies into their first book, or the introduction of the Barry Allen Flash. Bill Gaines, Harvey Kurtzman and Al Feldstein wouldn't have done anything that hadn't already been done. Denny O'Neil and Neal Adams wouldn't have told their classic Green Lantern/Green Arrow tales. Gwen Stacy never would have died, the Punisher never would have appeared, and Conan would never have been a licensed comic book title.

A SEARCH FOR THE AGES

We must first acknowledge that comic book Ages really exist only to facilitate the ease of conveying information to other parties. In other words, they help create a verbal shorthand to make it easier to explain the creative, editorial or publishing work involved in a specific comic or set of comics (or the present day value we attach to a specific comic or set of comics) in comparison to other comics.

The act of splitting comics up into groups creates the illusion that these are not part of a much bigger picture, but believing that illusion would be a mistake. Comics are just one part of the much larger world of comic character collectibles, and that world itself is just a piece of the even larger entire history of popular culture.

Comic book Ages are important and they're fun, but they're truly nothing more than an intellectual exercise. If it were more serious, we'd have to take a look at why the comic book Ages run backwards (Golden, Silver, Bronze instead of Bronze, Silver, Golden as does the rest of human history). Picking the landmarks by which we navigate comics history isn't easy though, as we have often discovered.

CODIFYING THE AGES

Does one incident or single comic book issue define an Age? Surely *Action Comics* #1 begins the Golden Age just as *The Brownies* begin the Platinum Age, but some have observed that the Comics Code might be the deciding factor in dividing the various eras. That idea did in fact help to suggest an even more innovative way of looking at the whole Age issue that finally breaks away from the narrow-minded reliance on the superhero genre as the end-all be-all of Comic Book Age definition. In the final analysis, we determined that it was not the superheroes *alone* that dictated when these Ages began or ended. They were merely the superficial result of a much deeper motivating force that ultimately serves as the primary shaper of every Comic Book Age; namely, the editorial and publishing decisions that drive the industry and influence the content of the comics themselves. Seen from this perspective, the entire Age issue takes on even greater resonance and even the already established Ages fall neatly into place.

As we will see, the Comics Code can serve to illuminate this theory. Though the original incarnation of the Comics Code Authority and its system of strict self-regulation only existed for 16 years (Oct. 1954 to Jan. 1971), its influence on comic book history has been

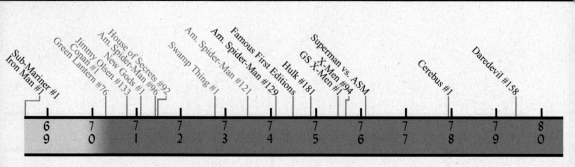

enormous. Primarily, the implementation of the CCA suggested – and perhaps necessitated – the resurrection of a stagnating superhero genre and heralded the beginnings of the Silver Age. But as this genre was given new life with the inclusion of a fresh, realism-based perspective and a growing social consciousness, creators quickly found themselves restricted by walls of content regulation that had been used in the '50s to protect an industry under public siege. It was this desire for greater content flexibility on the part of Silver Age creators that was the first sign of things to come.

Social issues had been creeping into the pages of comics for a few years, but by the end of 1970 there seems to have been a general consensus within the business that the CCA needed revision. In 1971, the Comics Magazine Association of America ratified a general overhaul of the Code, the first since its inception in 1954. Not only did this revision allow for the inclusion of content that for more than a decade had been absent from the pages of comic books, but it denoted a fundamental shift in thinking by the industry as a whole. From this point on, it was clear that the industry itself was in control of the specifics of the CCA. If they saw fit, they could change the Code to keep it current with their perception of public standards.

And change it they did. A mere three months after the original revision of the CCA, the members of the Association found themselves meeting once again to amend the specifics of the system of self-regulation. The topic at hand was the portrayal of drugs, and on April 15, 1971, an agreement was reached to allow stories depicting graphic drug use with the understanding that "narcotics addiction shall not be portrayed except as a vicious habit." This unexpected amendment was directly inspired by Stan Lee's decision at Marvel to distribute three issues of *Amazing Spider-Man* that failed to meet Code approval because of the portrayal of drug abuse. With the inconsistencies in the Code rectified, Carmine Infantino – then editor at DC – followed suit and released a Code-approved story in *Green Lantern* dealing with heroin addiction.

Just as the implementation of the Code can be seen as a defining aspect of the dawn of the Silver Age, the growing social consciousness of certain comic creators and the resulting decision to amend the CCA stands as a herald of the shift into the Bronze Age. With a revised Code, genres and topics that had been forbidden for years suddenly re-emerged in the pages of mainstream comics. The major publishers began launching a multitude of new titles and re-invigorating others that had floundered under the original content restrictions. Without a conscious decision by the industry to expand the range of allowable material, many of the characters, titles, and stories that are now considered foundational to the Bronze Age never could have been published.

In looking beyond the Bronze Age to define the Copper Age, we can see another important reconsideration of the CCA playing a role. Just as publishers had realized in the early '70s that they themselves were in control of the particulars of the Code, in the mid-'80s they decided that for certain kinds of comics the restrictions were not necessary at all. These comics were targeted at an older audience, many of whom had grown up with the socially relevant comics of the '70s. This audience realized the

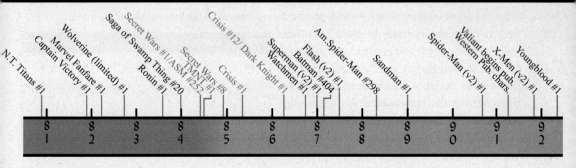

potential the medium had for a broader type of storytelling and they demanded more "mature" content. Comics like Frank Miller's *Dark Knight Returns* and Alan Moore's *Watchmen* played a major role in defining this new Copper Age and pointed the way to yet another revision of the Code in 1989.

But just as we are suggesting that no single issue can be used to wholly define an era of comic book history, it is important to point out that the CCA was not the only factor in the evolution of the industry. Many creative, social, economic, and technological factors combined to make comics what they are today. But the Code does stand out as a profound, industry-wide influence that can be very helpful in charting the progression of the medium since the mid-'50s. Only now, almost fifty years after the CCA was first imposed, are the publishers of comic books moving away from a single system of content regulation. This "deregulation" of the industry will surely be a determining factor in Ages yet to be defined.

THE SHIFTING SANDS OF TIME

Another aspect of the debate was also clarified for us during this process. For years, we have struggled to define Comic Book Ages based on a single turning point – an individual issue of one comic book from one genre and one company that straddles the line between the end of one era and the start of the next. But since these Ages are arbitrary, applied to real-world developments that never truly reach an end, the flow of history often obscures any specific turning point and instead suggests that one era might subtly segue into another over a period of time. Therefore, we establish here that the later eras on the Comic Book Age scale can be defined through gradual transitions that have start and end points. For example, while *Showcase* #4 (1956) remains an undisputed watershed moment that heralds the coming of the Silver Age (and indeed adheres strongly to our editorial and publishing theory in that it represents a decision to revive a nearly-dead genre), we propose that the transition only began with *Showcase* #4...but it ended with *Fantastic Four* #1 (1961).

This same thinking can be applied to the later Ages as well. Perhaps one of the reasons the Bronze Age has been so difficult to nail down at either its beginning or conclusion is that it represents a volatile shift in editorial and publishing philosophy on both ends. Here we propose that the Bronze Age began arriving with *Green Lantern* #76 (1970), the first of a series of books in 1970 and 1971 to break boundaries, explore new editorial and publishing opportunities in storytelling and theme, and start a march toward maturity in the medium. But where did this transformation reach its climax, signaling the death of innocence embodied by the Silver Age and opening the door to a more adult era of heightened violence and heightened consequences? *Amazing Spider-Man* #121 (1973).

Finally, we introduce a new Age: the Copper Age, spanning the years from the end of the Bronze Age in 1985 to the debut of Image Comics in 1992. As before, we propose that the transition begins with Marvel's editorial and publishing decision to embark on a twelve-issue maxi-series that ties in their entire superhero universe while introducing changes to their primary characters that would echo forward for years to come. That series was *Marvel Super-Heroes: Secret Wars* (1984-85). The Copper Age then fully arrives when DC takes the notion one step further, utilizing the same editorial and publishing concept to completely remake their fictional universe and wash away the last vestiges of the Silver and Bronze Ages with *Crisis on Infinite Earths* (1985-86).

Now, with what is hopefully a much clearer understanding of this approach to the organization of comic book history, we look forward to the future, and countless other Ages to be explored, enjoyed and defined. The adventure continues…

AGE	YEARS	CATALYSTS
Silver	1956-1970	*Showcase* #4 (1956), *FF* #1 (1961)
Bronze	1970-1984	*GL* #76 (1970), *ASM* #121 (1973)
Copper	1984-1992	*Secret Wars* (1984-85), *Crisis* (1985-86)
Modern	1992-Present	Image Comics debut

GM

(10.0) GEM MINT (GM)

GRADE DESCRIPTION:

This is an exceptional example of a given book - the best ever seen. The slightest bindery defects and/or printing flaws may be seen only upon very close inspection.

The overall look is "as if it has never been handled or released for purchase."

BINDERY/PRINTING DEFECTS - Only the slightest bindery or printing defects are allowed, and these would be imperceptible on first viewing. No bindery tears.

COVER/EXTERIOR - Flat with no surface wear. Inks are bright with high reflectivity. Well centered and firmly secured to interior pages. Corners are cut square and sharp. No creases. No dates or stamped markings allowed. No soiling, staining or other discoloration.

SPINE - Tight and flat. No spine roll or split allowed.

STAPLES - Must be original, centered and clean with no rust. No staple tears or stress lines.

PAPER/INTERIOR - Paper is white, supple and fresh. No hint of acidity in the odor of the newsprint. No interior autographs or owner signatures. Centerfold is firmly secure. No interior tears.

Collectors should thoroughly examine any book listed as 10.0. These books should also be carefully scrutinized for restoration.

BINDERY/PRINTING

only the slightest,
most imperceptible defects

COVER INKS/GLOSS

bright with high reflectivity

COVER WEAR

flat, no wear,
well centered, secure

COVER CREASES

none allowed

SOILING, STAINING

none allowed

DATES/STAMPS

none allowed

SPINE ROLL

tight and flat, no roll

SPINE SPLIT

none allowed

STAPLES

original, centered, clean

STAPLE TEARS

none allowed

RUST MIGRATION

none allowed

STRESS LINES

none allowed

CORNERS

sharp, square, no creases

CENTERFOLD

firmly secure

INTERIOR TEARS

none allowed

PAPER QUALITY/COLOR

white, supple and fresh

ACID ODOR

none allowed

MISSING PIECES

none allowed

AMATEUR REPAIRS

none allowed

COUPON CUT

none allowed

READABILITY

preserved

Green Arrow #137, October 1998. © DC Comics.
Obvious defects: None.
Hidden defects: None.
Page Quality: White.

Spine is flat
and tight

Sharp
corners

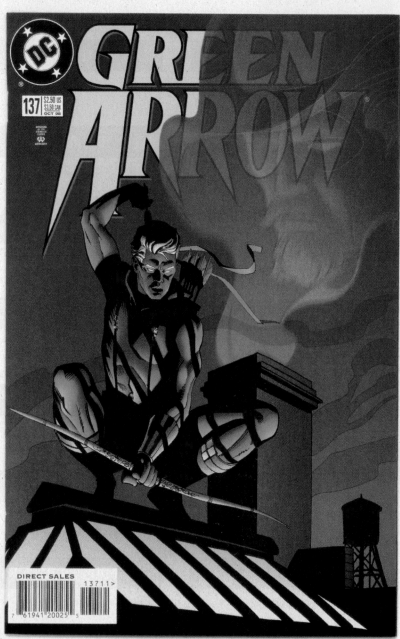

Firmly
secure
centerfold

No corner
abrasion

No edge tears or
creases

Wolverine: The Origin #1, November 2001. © Marvel Characters Inc.
Obvious defects: None.
Hidden defects: None.
Page Quality: White.

Sharp
corners

Bright reflectivity
on cover

Spine is flat
and tight

Colors are
brilliant

The Ultimates #1, March 2002. © Marvel Characters Inc.
Obvious defects: None.
Hidden defects: None.
Page Quality: White.

Sharp
corners

Spine is tight
and flat

Inks have high
reflectivity

Star Wars: Episode II –Attack of the Clones #1, April 2002. © Lucasfilm Ltd.
Obvious defects: None.
Hidden defects: None.
Page Quality: White.

Sharp
corners

No corner
abrasion

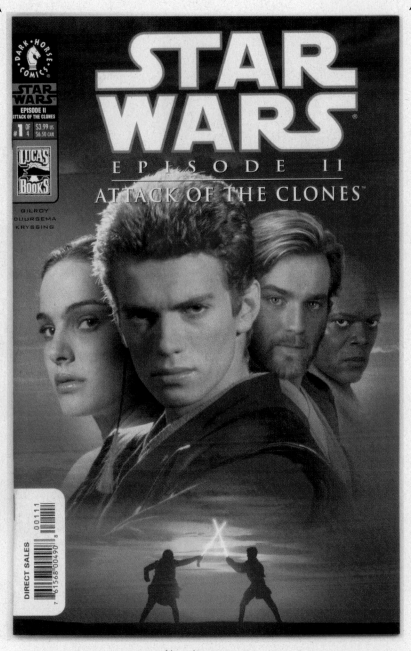

No edge tears or
creases

Transformers: Generation One #1, April 2002. © Hasbro.
Obvious defects: None.
Hidden defects: None.
Page Quality: Not applicable.

Sharp
corners

No creases or
wear on edges

Batman (2nd series) #23.1, November 2013. © DC Comics.

Obvious defects: None.

Hidden defects: None.

Page Quality: White.

3-D Lenticular front and back covers

(9.9) MINT (MT)

MT

GRADE DESCRIPTION:
Near perfect in every way.

The overall look is "as if it was just purchased."

BINDERY DEFECTS - Only subtle bindery or printing defects are allowed. No bindery tears.

COVER/EXTERIOR - Flat with no surface wear. Inks are bright with high reflectivity and minimal fading. Generally well centered and firmly secured to interior pages. Corners are cut square and sharp. No creases. Small, inconspicuous, lightly penciled, stamped or inked arrival dates are acceptable as long as they are in an unobtrusive location. No soiling, staining or other discoloration.

SPINE - Tight and flat. No spine roll or split allowed.

STAPLES - Must be original, generally centered and clean with no rust. No staple tears or stress lines.

PAPER/INTERIOR - Paper is white, supple and fresh. No hint of acidity in the odor of the newsprint. Centerfold is firmly secure. No interior tears.

Comics published before 1970 in MINT condition are extremely scarce.

BINDERY/PRINTING

only subtle defects,
no bindery tears

COVER INKS/GLOSS

bright with high reflectivity

COVER WEAR

flat, no wear,
well centered, secure

COVER CREASES

none allowed

SOILING, STAINING

none allowed

DATES/STAMPS

small, inconspicuous
dates/initials allowed

SPINE ROLL

tight and flat, no roll

SPINE SPLIT

none allowed

STAPLES

original, clean,
generally centered

STAPLE TEARS

none allowed

RUST MIGRATION

none allowed

STRESS LINES

none allowed

CORNERS

sharp, square, no creases

CENTERFOLD

firmly secure

INTERIOR TEARS

none allowed

PAPER QUALITY/COLOR

white, supple and fresh

ACID ODOR

none allowed

MISSING PIECES

none allowed

AMATEUR REPAIRS

none allowed

COUPON CUT

none allowed

READABILITY

preserved

MT

Zip Comics #7, August 1940. © MLJ Magazines.
Edgar Church (Mile High) pedigree copy.
Obvious defects: None.
Hidden defects: None.
Page Quality: White.
Note: This is the first Golden Age comic graded as a Mint 9.9 by CGC.

Slightest
bindery
defect in
corner

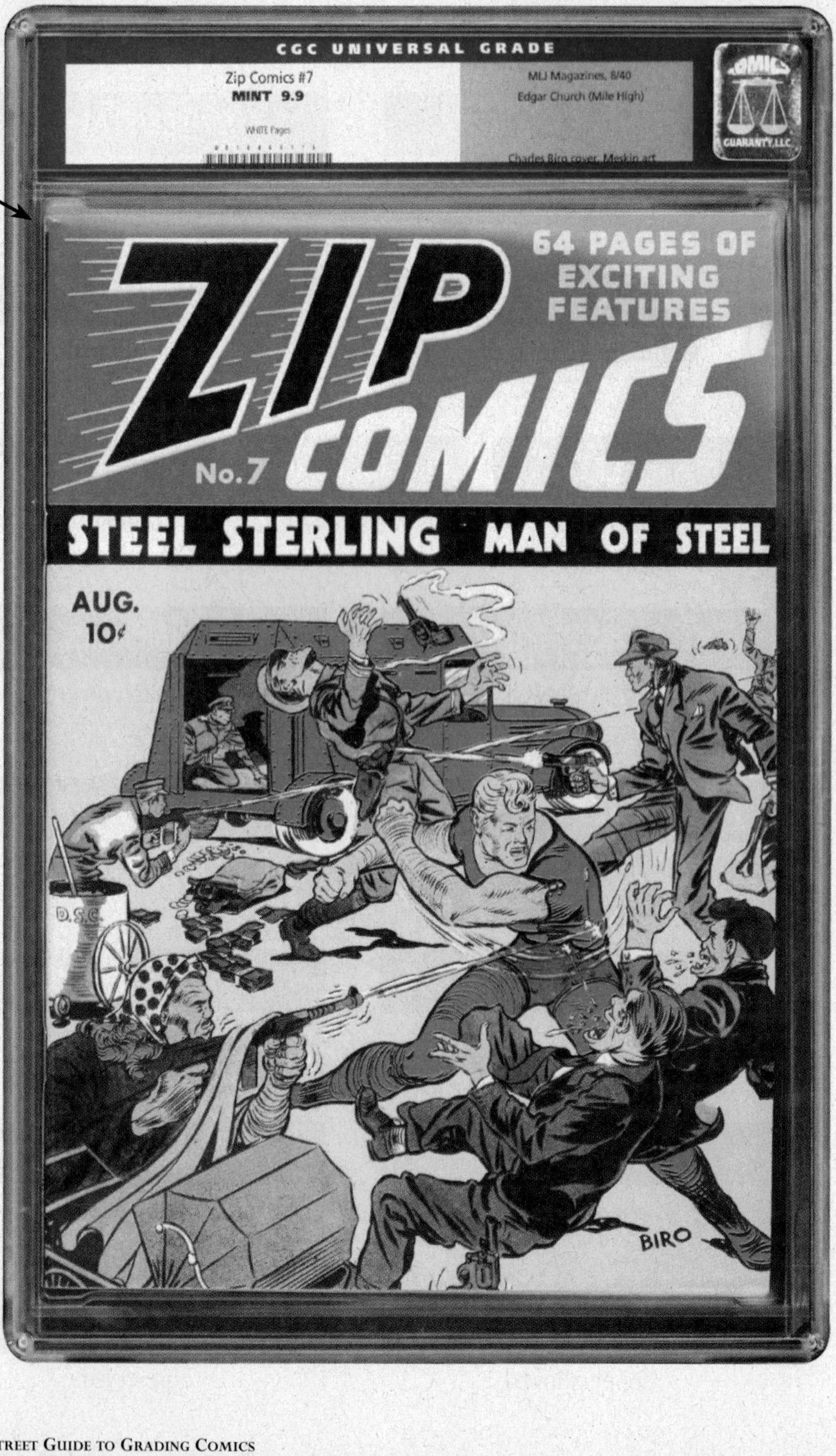

The Flash #147, September 1964. © DC Comics.
Obvious defects: Slight fading of cover inks.
Hidden defects: None.
Page Quality: White.

Spine is flat
and tight

Slight fading
on edge

Sharp
corners

No corner
abrasion

No edge tears or
creases

The Authority #14, June 2000. © WildStorm Productions.
Obvious defects: None.
Hidden defects: Small color fleck.
Page Quality: White.

Color
fleck

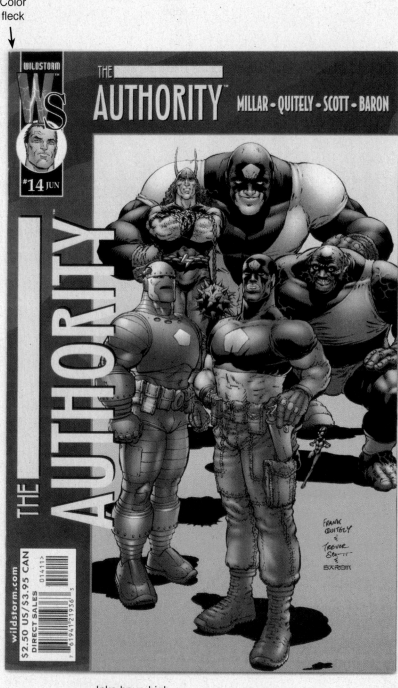

Inks have high
reflectivity

Fray #1, June 2001. © Joss Whedon.
Obvious defects: Bindery defect - slightly miswrapped cover.
Hidden defects: None.
Page Quality: White.

Cover slightly
miswrapped

MT

Batman: The 10-cent Adventure, March 2002. © DC Comics.
Obvious defects: Very subtle bend near spine.
Hidden defects: None.
Page Quality: White.

Sharp
corners

Very subtle
bend

No edge tears or
creases

The Incredible Hulk Vol. 2 #38, May 2002. © Marvel Characters Inc.
Obvious defects: Printing defect - small ink blotch.
Hidden defects: None.
Page Quality: White.

Small ink
blotch
behind
Hulk's
neck
→

(9.8) NEAR MINT / MINT (NM/MT)

GRADE DESCRIPTION:

Nearly perfect in every way with only minor imperfections that keep it from the next higher grade.

The overall look is "as if it was just purchased."

BINDERY DEFECTS - Only subtle bindery or printing defects are allowed. No bindery tears.

COVER/EXTERIOR - Flat with no surface wear. Inks are bright with high reflectivity and minimal fading. Generally well centered and firmly secured to interior pages. Corners are cut square and sharp. No creases. Small, inconspicuous, lightly penciled, stamped or inked arrival dates are acceptable as long as they are in an unobtrusive location. No soiling, staining or other discoloration.

SPINE - Tight and flat. No spine roll or split allowed.

STAPLES - Must be original, generally centered and clean with no rust. No staple tears or stress lines.

PAPER/INTERIOR - Paper is off-white to white, supple and fresh. No hint of acidity in the odor of the newsprint. Centerfold is firmly secure. Only the slightest interior tears are allowed.

NM/MT

BINDERY/PRINTING
only subtle, no bindery tears

COVER INKS/GLOSS
bright with high reflectivity

COVER WEAR
flat, no wear, well centered

COVER CREASES
none allowed

SOILING, STAINING
none allowed

DATES/STAMPS
small, inconspicuous dates/initials allowed

SPINE ROLL
tight and flat, no roll

SPINE SPLIT
none allowed

STAPLES
original, clean, generally centered

STAPLE TEARS
none allowed

RUST MIGRATION
none allowed

STRESS LINES
none allowed

CORNERS
sharp, square, no creases

CENTERFOLD
firmly secure

INTERIOR TEARS
slightest tears allowed

PAPER QUALITY/COLOR
off-white to white, supple and fresh

ACID ODOR
none allowed

MISSING PIECES
none allowed

AMATEUR REPAIRS
none allowed

COUPON CUT
none allowed

READABILITY
preserved

Crackajack Funnies #1, June, 1938. © Dell Publishing Co.
Edgar Church (Mile High) pedigree copy.
Obvious defects: None.
Hidden defects: None.
Page Quality: White.

Pencilled arrival date
does not affect grade

All corners are sharp

NM/MT

Cover
slightly mis-
wrapped

Slight
oxidatio
shadov

Grease
pencilled
number

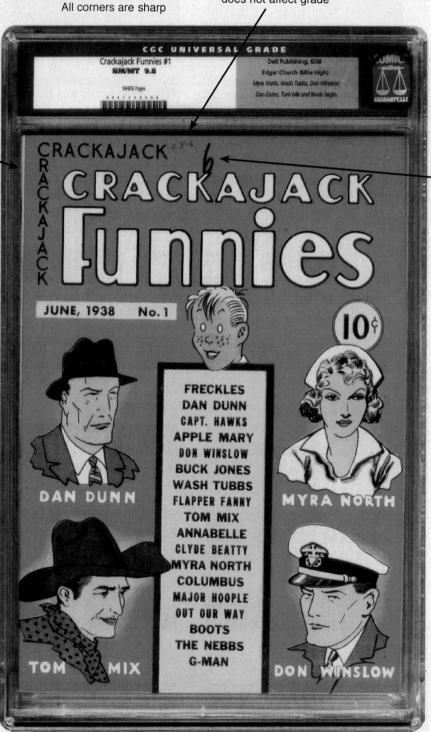

Mad #1, October-November 1956. © EC Publications.
Gaines file copy.
Obvious defects: None.
Hidden defects: None.
Page Quality: White.

Very subtle
bindery cut

All corners are sharp. This book has
one or two almost imperceptible flaws.

Witchblade #2, January, 1996. © Top Cow Productions, Inc.
Obvious defects: None.
Hidden defects: Slight fading of cover inks.
Page Quality: Not applicable.

Color
fleck

Corner
color fleck

Daredevil Volume 2 #1, November 1998. © Marvel Characters, Inc.

Obvious defects: Tiny color flecks along gatefold front cover.

Hidden defects: None.

Page Quality: Not applicable.

NM/MT

Color fleck

Color fleck

Gatefold cover

G. I. Joe #1, 2001. © Hasbro.
Obvious defects: None.
Hidden defects: Very slight interior tear. Color fleck on back cover.
Page Quality: White.

Corners are
perfect

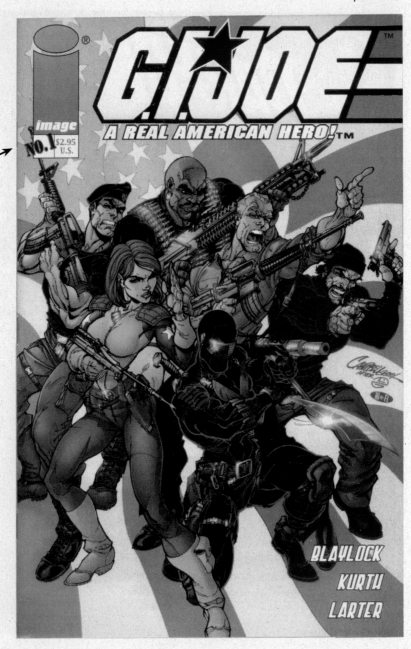

Color
fleck

Harley Quinn #7, August 2014. © DC Comics.
Obvious defects: Light spine wear which barely breaks color.
Hidden defects: None.
Page Quality: White.

Light edge wear

Very slight wear

(9.6) NEAR MINT + (NM+)

GRADE DESCRIPTION:

Nearly perfect with a minor additional virtue or virtues that raise it from Near Mint. The overall look is "as if it was just purchased and read once or twice."

BINDERY DEFECTS - Only subtle bindery or printing defects are allowed. No bindery tears are allowed, although on Golden Age books bindery tears of up to 1/8" have been noted.

COVER/EXTERIOR - Flat with no surface wear. Inks are bright with high reflectivity. Well centered and firmly secured to interior pages. One corner may be almost imperceptibly blunted, but still almost sharp and cut square. Almost imperceptible indentations are permissible, but no creases, bends, or color break. Small, inconspicuous, lightly penciled, stamped or inked arrival dates are acceptable as long as they are in an unobtrusive location. No soiling, staining or other discoloration.

SPINE - Tight and flat. No spine roll or split allowed.

STAPLES - Must be original, generally centered, with only the slightest discoloration. No staple tears, stress lines, or rust migration.

PAPER/INTERIOR - Paper is off-white, supple and fresh. No hint of acidity in the odor of the newsprint. Centerfold is firmly secure. Only the slightest interior tears are allowed.

BINDERY/PRINTING

only subtle, no tears on Silver Age
and later, 1/8" on Golden Age

COVER INKS/GLOSS

bright with high reflectivity

COVER WEAR

flat, no wear, well centered

COVER CREASES

almost imperceptible indentations
allowed

SOILING, STAINING

none allowed

DATES/STAMPS

small, inconspicuous
dates/initials allowed

SPINE ROLL

tight and flat, no roll

SPINE SPLIT

none allowed

NM+

STAPLES

original, generally cen-
tered, slight discoloration

STAPLE TEARS

none allowed

RUST MIGRATION

none allowed

STRESS LINES

none allowed

CORNERS

almost sharp, one imperceptible
blunted corner allowed

CENTERFOLD

firmly secure

INTERIOR TEARS

slightest tears allowed

PAPER QUALITY/COLOR

off-white, supple and fresh

ACID ODOR

none allowed

MISSING PIECES

none allowed

AMATEUR REPAIRS

none allowed

COUPON CUT

none allowed

READABILITY

preserved

More Fun Comics #59, September 1940. © DC Comics.
Obvious defects: Oxidation shadow. Pencil marks and color fleck.
Hidden defects: None.
Page Quality: Off-white to white.

Very light
oxidation
shadow

Pencil
marks

Very small
color fleck

Ibis The Invincible #1, January 1942. © Fawcett Publications.
Obvious defects: Light pencil marks in upper corners.
Hidden defects: None.
Page Quality: Off-white to white.

Pencil marks

Very minor blunted corner

Pencil mark

NM+

Very light stress line at spine on back cover

Crime Patrol #15, Dec. 1949-Jan 1950. © William M. Gaines.
Obvious defects: None.
Hidden defects: None.
Page Quality: Off-white.

NM+

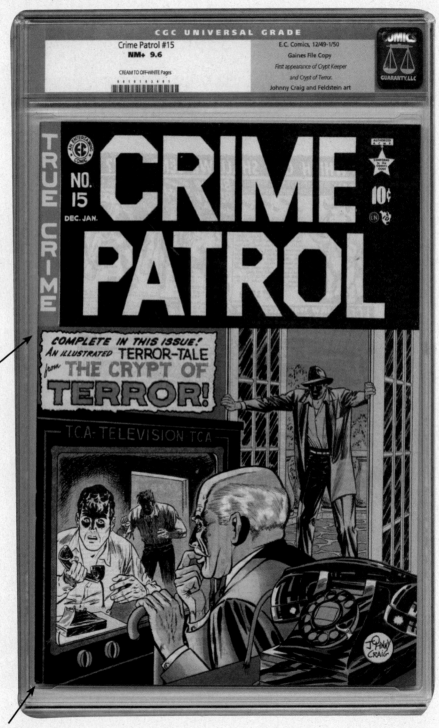

Minor
spine
stress
line

Very minor
blunted corner

The Crypt of Terror #17, April-May 1950. © William M. Gaines.
Obvious defects: None.
Hidden defects: None.
Page Quality: Off-white.

NM+

Minor
spine
stress
line

Very minor
blunted corner

Marvel Super-Heroes #18, January 1969. © Marvel Characters, Inc.
Obvious defects: Small wear on all edges of front cover.
Hidden defects: None.
Page Quality: White.

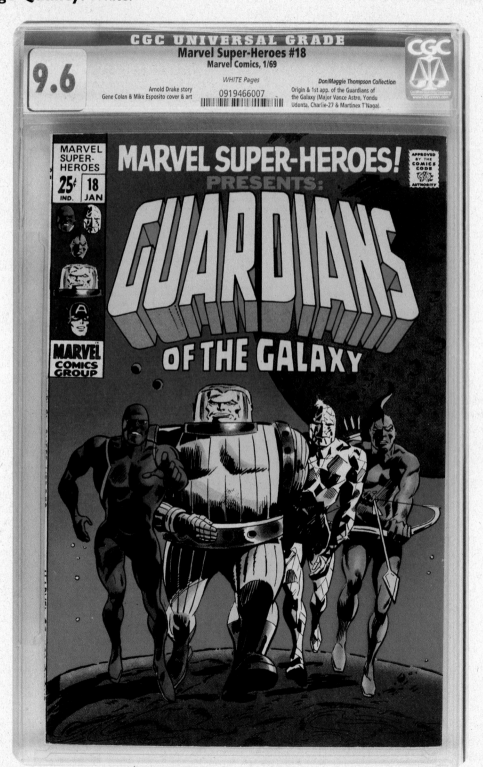

Incredible Hulk #181, November 1974. © Marvel Characters, Inc.

Obvious defects: None.
Hidden defects: Minor color flecking.
Page Quality: White.

Minor blunted
corner

Sharp
corner

NM+

Slight
indentation
on cover

Minor edge
stress

New Teen Titans #2, December 1980. © DC Comics.
Obvious defects: None.
Hidden defects: None.
Page Quality: White.

Slight corner abrasion

NM+

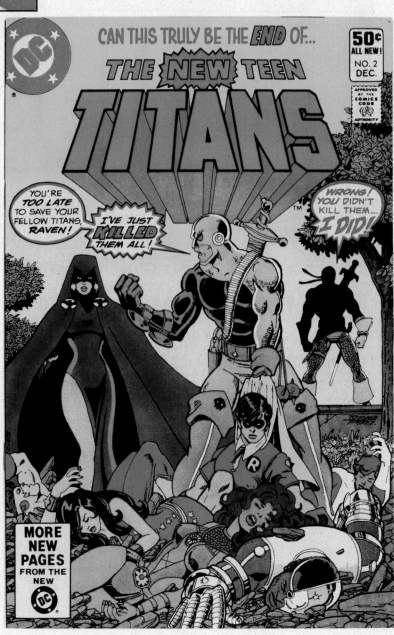

Uncanny X-Men #207, July 1986. © Marvel Characters, Inc.
Obvious defects: None.
Hidden defects: None.
Page Quality: White.

Minor corner
abrasion

Small
indentation

NM+

Walt Disney's Mickey Mouse #250, September 1989. © Walt Disney Company.
Obvious defects: Minor stress line on spine that doesn't break color.
Hidden defects: None.
Page Quality: Off-white.

Minor corner
abrasion

Small
indentation

NM+

Minor
stress
line

Strangers in Paradise Vol. 3 #1, October 1996. © Terry Moore.
Obvious defects: None.
Hidden defects: None.
Page Quality: White.

NM+

Small
indentation

No.1
OCT
$2.75
$3.95
CAN

Minor corner
abrasion

(9.4) NEAR MINT (NM)

NM

GRADE DESCRIPTION:

Nearly perfect with only minor imperfections that keep it from the next higher grade. The overall look is "as if it was just purchased and read once or twice."

BINDERY DEFECTS - Subtle defects are allowed. Bindery tears must be less than 1/16" on Silver Age and later books, although on Golden Age books bindery tears of up to 1/4" have been noted.

COVER/EXTERIOR - Flat with no surface wear. Inks are bright with high reflectivity. Generally well centered and secured to interior pages. Corners are cut square and sharp with ever-so-slight blunting permitted. A 1/16" bend is permitted with no color break. No creases. Small, inconspicuous, lightly penciled, stamped or inked arrival dates are acceptable as long as they are in an unobtrusive location. No soiling, staining or other discoloration apart from slight foxing.

SPINE - Tight and flat. No spine roll or split allowed.

STAPLES - Generally centered; may have slight discoloration. No staple tears are allowed; almost no stress lines. No rust migration. In rare cases, a comic was not stapled at the bindery and therefore has a missing staple; this is not considered a defect. Any staple can be replaced on books up to Fine, but only vintage staples can be used on books from Very Fine to Near Mint. Mint books must have original staples.

PAPER/INTERIOR - Paper is cream to off-white, supple and fresh. No hint of acidity in the odor of the newsprint. Centerfold is secure. Slight interior tears are allowed.

Comics published before 1970 in NEAR MINT condition are scarce. This grade is commonly viewed by the average collector as the best grade obtainable.

Collectors should thoroughly examine these books for restoration, particularly in the case of pre-1965 books. Expensive and key books listed as being in "high grade" frequently have some restoration. In most cases, restoration performed on otherwise NEAR MINT books will reduce the grade. A VERY FINE comic book cannot be transformed into a NEAR MINT comic book through restoration.

NM

BINDERY/PRINTING

subtle, tears up to 1/16" on Silver Age and later, 1/4" on Golden Age

COVER INKS/GLOSS

bright with high reflectivity

COVER WEAR

flat, no wear, generally centered, secure

COVER CREASES

1/16" bend with no color break allowed

SOILING, STAINING

none allowed except for slight foxing

DATES/STAMPS

small, inconspicuous dates/initials allowed

SPINE ROLL

tight and flat, no roll

SPINE SPLIT

none allowed

STAPLES

generally centered, slight discoloration

STAPLE TEARS

none allowed

RUST MIGRATION

none allowed

STRESS LINES

almost no lines

CORNERS

ever-so-slight blunting, no creases

CENTERFOLD

secure

INTERIOR TEARS

slight tears allowed

PAPER QUALITY/COLOR

cream/off-white, supple and fresh

ACID ODOR

none allowed

MISSING PIECES

none allowed

AMATEUR REPAIRS

none allowed

COUPON CUT

none allowed

READABILITY

preserved

Nickel Comics #1, May 1940. © Fawcett Publications.
Obvious defects: Lower left corner chip.
Hidden defects: Subtle color flecks.
Page Quality: Off-white.

Corner
fleck

Color
flecks

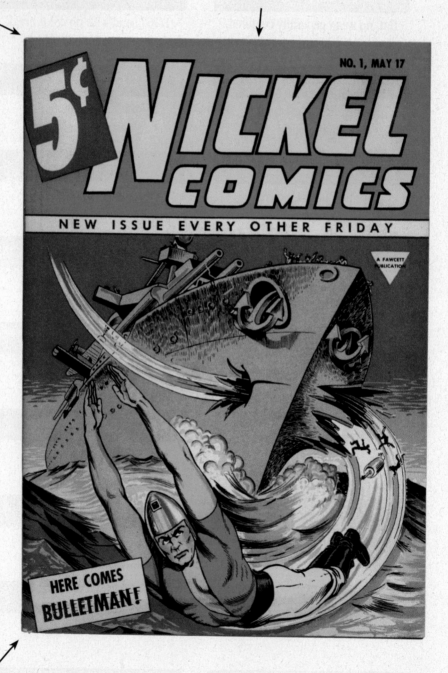

Corner
chip

All-Flash Quarterly #1, Summer 1941.© DC Comics.
Obvious defects: Slight abrasion in upper right corner.
Hidden defects: None.
Page Quality: Off-white.

Corner
chip

NM

Copy
originally
not
stapled

Spine
stress
line

A COMPLETE 64 PAGE ISSUE
CONTAINING ALL NEW, NEVER-
BEFORE-PUBLISHED EPISODES
OF *The Flash!*
—FASTEST MAN ALIVE!

Slight
foxing

Daredevil (Battles Hitler) #1, July 1941. © Lev Gleason Publications.
Obvious defects: Very minor bindery tear.
Hidden defects: None.
Page Quality: Off-white.

Very minor
bindery tear

Minor indentation

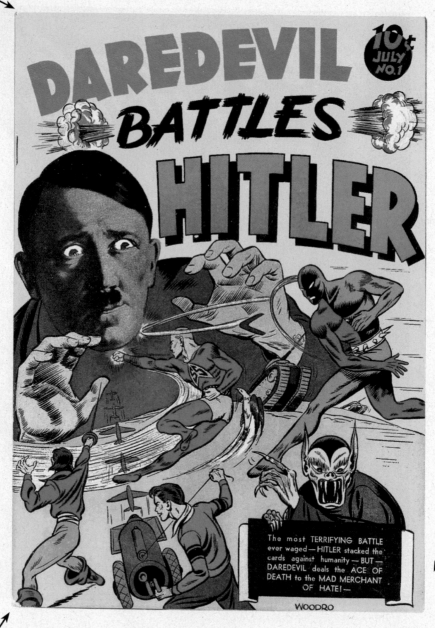

Minor corner
wear

Marvel Mystery Comics #65, July 1945. © Marvel Characters, Inc.
Obvious defects: Small tear on lower left corner.
Hidden defects: None.
Page Quality: Off-white.

Browning
on edge

Pencil
marks

Small
corner
tear

Slight edge
wear

Atomic Comics #2, March 1946. © Green Publishing Co.
Obvious defects: Cover stamp.
Hidden defects: Minor inconspicuous staining.
Page Quality: Off-white.
Note: Cover printed on non-glossy paper. Cover stamp is sufficiently inconspicuous.

Minor
corner wear

Minor
corner fleck

NM

Cover
stamp

Minor
indentation

NM

The Avengers #141, November 1975. © Marvel Characters, Inc.
Obvious defects: None.
Hidden defects: Very minor color fleck.
Page Quality: Off-white to white.

Slight
indentation

Color
fleck

Color fleck

Marvel Two-In-One #50, April 1979. © Marvel Characters, Inc.
Obvious defects: None.
Hidden defects: None.
Page Quality: Off-white.

NM

Corner not
squarely cut

Slight
staining

Abraded
corner

The Walking Dead #1, October 2003. © Robert Kirkman.
Obvious defects: Multiple bends on the spine which break color
Hidden defects: None.
Page Quality: White.

Abraded corner

NM

Multiple
spine
bends

(9.2) NEAR MINT- (NM-)

GRADE DESCRIPTION:

Nearly perfect with only a minor additional defect or defects that keep it from Near Mint. The overall look is "as if it was just purchased and read once or twice."

BINDERY DEFECTS - A limited number of minor defects are allowed.

COVER/EXTERIOR - Flat with no surface wear. Inks are bright with only the slightest dimming of reflectivity. Generally well centered and secured to interior pages. Corners are cut square and sharp with ever-so-slight blunting permitted. A 1/16-1/8" bend is permitted with no color break. No creases. Small, inconspicuous, lightly penciled, stamped or inked arrival dates are acceptable as long as they are in an unobtrusive location. No soiling, staining or other discoloration apart from slight foxing.

SPINE - Tight and flat. No spine roll or split allowed.

STAPLES - May show some discoloration. No staple tears are allowed; almost no stress lines. No rust migration. In rare cases, a comic was not stapled at the bindery and therefore has a missing staple; this is not considered a defect. Any staple can be replaced on books up to Fine, but only vintage staples can be used on books from Very Fine to Near Mint. Mint books must have original staples.

PAPER/INTERIOR - Paper is off-white to cream, supple and fresh. No hint of acidity in the odor of the newsprint. Centerfold is secure. Slight interior tears are allowed.

NM–

BINDERY/PRINTING

limited number of
minor defects

COVER INKS/GLOSS

bright with slightest
dimming of reflectivity

COVER WEAR

flat, no wear, generally centered,
secure

COVER CREASES

1/16-1/8" bend with no color
break allowed

SOILING, STAINING

none allowed except for
slight foxing

DATES/STAMPS

small, inconspicuous
dates/initials allowed

SPINE ROLL

tight and flat, no roll

SPINE SPLIT

none allowed

STAPLES

some discoloration

STAPLE TEARS

none allowed

RUST MIGRATION

none allowed

STRESS LINES

almost no lines

CORNERS

ever-so-slight blunting, no creases

CENTERFOLD

secure

INTERIOR TEARS

slight tears allowed

PAPER QUALITY/COLOR

cream to off-white,
supple and fresh

ACID ODOR

none allowed

MISSING PIECES

none allowed

AMATEUR REPAIRS

none allowed

COUPON CUT

none allowed

READABILITY

preserved

Weird Comics #1, April 1940. © Fox Features Syndicate.
Obvious defects: Minor corner abrasion and small spine tear.
Hidden defects: None.
Page Quality: Off-white.

Abraded
corner

Minor
chipping

Small spine
tear

1/8" bend
(no color
break)

Blunted
corner

Shield-Wizard Comics #1, Summer 1940. © Archie Publications.
Obvious defects: Oxidation shadow on cover's right edge.
Hidden defects: None.
Page Quality: Off-white.

Corner
chip

NM—

Oxidation
shadow

Staple
discoloration

Oxidation
shadow

Spine
stress
line

Edge
chip

Superboy #1, March-April 1949. © DC.
Obvious defects: Slightly miswrapped cover.
Hidden defects: Ink smudges.
Page Quality: Off-white.

Abraded
corner

1/8" bend
(no color break)

NM–

Slight
cover
color
dimming

Oxidation
shadow

Ink
smudges

Miswrapped
cover

Mad #1, Oct.-Nov. 1952. © EC
Obvious defects: Slightly stressed edges.
Hidden defects: Slight interior tears.
Page Quality: Cream to off-white.

Stressed
edge

NM–

Staple
stress
line

Corner
chip

Edge
stress

NM−

The Incredible Hulk #1, May 1962. © Marvel.
Obvious defects: Minor spine and corner stress.
Hidden defects: None.
Page Quality: Cream to off-white.

Corner
chip

Spine
stress

Slight
foxing

Abraded
corner

Chip

Atari Force #1, January 1984. © Atari, Inc.
Obvious defects: Blunted edges and corners.
Hidden defects: None.
Page Quality: White.

Slight
blunting

Blunted
corner

NM–

Light
rubbing

Slight blunting

Subtle
corner
wrinkles

X-Factor #1, February 1986. © Marvel Characters, Inc.
Obvious defects: Miswrapped cover.
Hidden defects: Slight interior tears.
Page Quality: Off-white to white.

Bindery defect

Slight bend

NM−

Small bumps

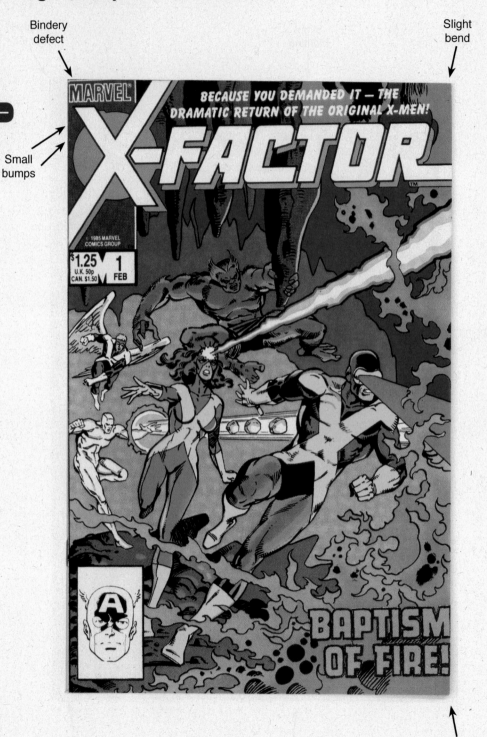

Over-cover

Walt Disney's Uncle Scrooge #235, July 1989. © Walt Disney Company.
Obvious defects: Blunted edge.
Hidden defects: None.
Page Quality: Off-white to white.

Blunted
edge

Slight staple
discoloration

Blunted
edge

NM—

Slight
bump

Slightly
impacted
corner

Gen13 #3, July 1995. © WildStorm Productions.
Obvious defects: Spine creases.
Hidden defects: None.
Page Quality: White.

Blunted
corner

Edge chip

Numerous
spine
creases

Abraded
corner

Ultimate Spider-Man #1, October 2000. © Marvel Characters, Inc.
Obvious defects: Subtle color loss near spine.
Hidden defects: Small chip in upper right corner.
Page Quality: White.

Minor
color loss

Minor corner
chip

Minor
crease
around
staple

NM—

Crescent
crease

Color
loss

(9.0) VERY FINE / NEAR MINT (VF/NM)

GRADE DESCRIPTION:

Nearly perfect with outstanding eye appeal. The overall look is "as if it was just purchased and read a few times."

BINDERY DEFECTS - A limited number of defects are allowed.

 COVER/EXTERIOR - Almost flat with almost imperceptible wear. Inks are bright with slightly diminished reflectivity. An 1/8" bend is allowed if color is not broken. Corners are cut square and sharp with ever-so-slight blunting permitted but no creases. Several lightly penciled, stamped or inked arrival dates are acceptable. No obvious soiling, staining or other discoloration, except for very minor foxing.

SPINE - Tight and flat. No spine roll or split allowed.

STAPLES - Staples may show some discoloration. Only the slightest staple tears are allowed. A very minor accumulation of stress lines may be present if they are nearly imperceptible. No rust migration. In rare cases, a comic was not stapled at the bindery and therefore has a missing staple; this is not considered a defect. Any staple can be replaced on books up to Fine, but only vintage staples can be used on books from Very Fine to Near Mint. Mint books must have original staples.

PAPER/INTERIOR - Paper is cream to off-white and supple. No hint of acidity in the odor of the newsprint. Centerfold is secure. Very minor interior tears may be present.

Collectors should thoroughly examine any such book for restoration, particularly in the case of pre-1965 books. This is a crucial grade that is often misused when a book actually falls in either Very Fine or Near Mint.

BINDERY/PRINTING

limited number of defects

COVER INKS/GLOSS

bright with slightly
diminished reflectivity

COVER WEAR

almost flat, imperceptible wear

COVER CREASES

1/8" bend with no
color break allowed

SOILING, STAINING

very minor foxing

DATES/STAMPS

several dates, stamps,
and/or initials allowed

VF/NM

SPINE ROLL

tight and flat, no roll

SPINE SPLIT

none allowed

STAPLES

some discoloration
allowed

STAPLE TEARS

only the slightest
tears allowed

RUST MIGRATION

none allowed

STRESS LINES

very minor accumulation of
nearly imperceptible lines

CORNERS

no creases

CENTERFOLD

secure

INTERIOR TEARS

very minor tears allowed

PAPER QUALITY/COLOR

cream/off-white, supple

ACID ODOR

none allowed

MISSING PIECES

none allowed

AMATEUR REPAIRS

none allowed

COUPON CUT

none allowed

READABILITY

preserved

Showcase #4, Sept.-Oct. 1956. © DC Comics.
Obvious defects: Abraded corners.
Hidden defects: None.
Page Quality: Off-white.

Abraded corner

Very slight discoloration

VF/NM

Slight staple tear

Slight spine stress lines

Abraded corner

Showcase #9, July-Aug. 1957. © DC Comics.
Obvious defects: Stressed corners.
Hidden defects: None.
Page Quality: Off-white.

Minor corner abrasion

Stressed edge

Minor discoloration

Spine stress

VF/NM

Black ink writing

Blunted corner

Blunted edge

Pep Comics #1, January 1940. © Archie Publications.
Obvious defects: Slight wear on edges and spine.
Hidden defects: None.
Page Quality: Off-white.

VF/NM

Minor edge wear

Blunted corner

Very slight spine wear and a few stress lines

Staple discoloration

Light dust shadow

Very slight rounded corner

Young Allies Comics #1, Summer 1941. © Marvel Characters, Inc.
Obvious defects: Slight corner wear.
Hidden defects: None.
Page Quality: Off-white.

Very slight
edge rub

Pencil
mark

Very slight
staple
stress

VF/NM

Staple
discoloration

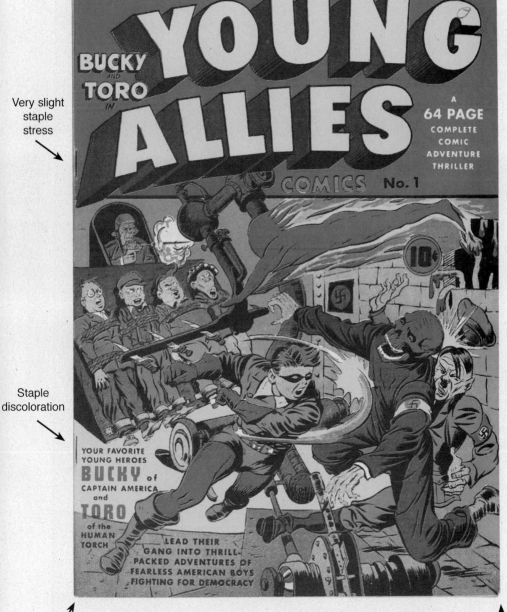

Very slight
corner rub

Blunted
corner

Amazing Spider-Man #1, March 1963. © Marvel Characters, Inc.
Obvious defects: Minor corner abrasion and small spine creases.
Hidden defects: None.
Page Quality: Off-white.

VF/NM

Minor
corner
abrasion

Minor
wear

Slight
cover
color
dimming

Staple
not
centered

Small
spine
creases

Minor
wear

Minor
wear

Teen Titans #1, Jan.-Feb. 1966. © DC Comics.
Obvious defects: "#1" written in blue ink on cover.
Hidden defects: Small edge stress marks.
Page Quality: Off-white to white.

Minor corner blunting

VF/NM

Blue ink writing

Small spine creases

Chip

Slight tear

Edge stress

Arrgh! #1, December 1974. © Marvel Characters, Inc.
Obvious defects: Over-cover.
Hidden defects: None.
Page Quality: Off-white to white.

Small tear

Minor chipping

Corner crease

VF/NM

Minor corner abrasion

Over-cover extends 1/8"

The Destructor #4, August 1975. © Seaboard Publications.
Obvious defects: None.
Hidden defects: Minor interior tears.
Page Quality: Off-white to white.

Slight blunting

Slight travelled cover

Stress line

VF/NM

Slight edge wear

3/32" spine bend

Color flecks

Marvel Team-Up #54, February 1977. © Marvel Characters, Inc.
Obvious defects: Over-cover.
Hidden defects: None.
Page Quality: Off-white.

Corner
chip out

Small stains

VF/NM

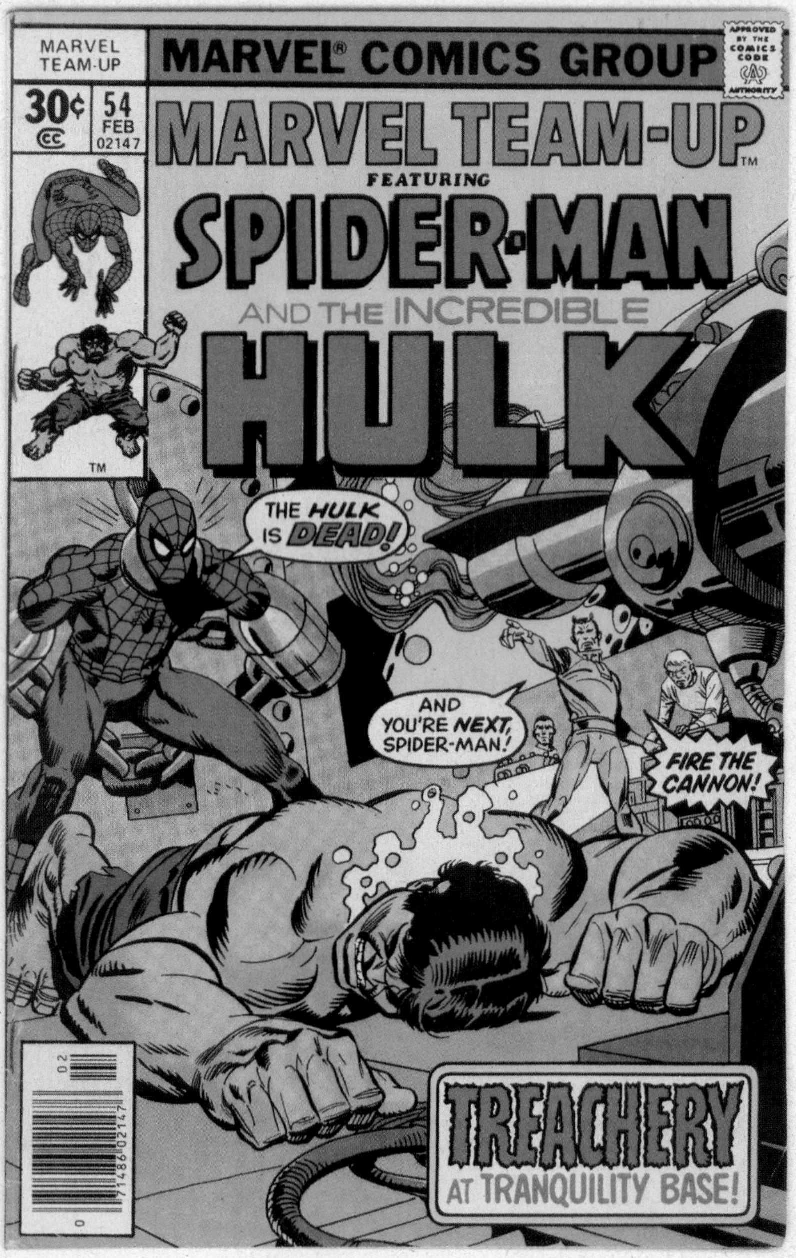

Color
fleck

Abraded
corner

Over-cover
by 1/8"

Daredevil #156, January 1979. © Marvel Characters, Inc.
Obvious defects: None.
Hidden defects: None.
Page Quality: Off-white to white.

Minor color fade

1/8" corner bend

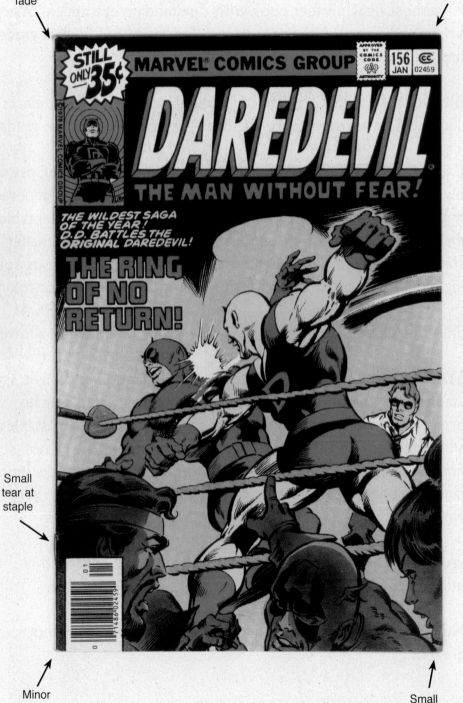

VF/NM

Small tear at staple

Minor corner abrasion

Small corner fold

(8.5) **VERY FINE +** (VF+)

GRADE DESCRIPTION:

An almost near perfect copy with outstanding eye appeal. Sharp, bright and clean with supple pages. A comic book in this grade has the appear-ance of having been carefully handled.

BINDERY DEFECTS - A limited accumulation of minor defects is allowed. One or two more than the Very Fine/Near Mint grade.

VF+

COVER/EXTERIOR - Almost flat with slight surface wear, possibly including some wear at one of the corners. Inks are generally bright with high reflectivity. A 1/8" – 1/4" bend is acceptable if color is not broken. Accumulation of several lightly penciled, stamped or inked arrival dates may be present. No obvious soiling, staining or other discoloration, except for very minor foxing.

SPINE - Almost flat with no roll. Very minor color break allowed.

STAPLES - Staples may show some discoloration. Very slight staple tears and an accumulation of very minor lines may be present. No rust migration. In rare cases, a comic is not stapled at the bindery and therefore has a missing staple; this is not considered a defect. Any staple can be replaced on books up to Fine, but only vintage staples can be used on books from Very Fine to Near Mint. Mint books must have original staples.

PAPER/INTERIOR: Paper is cream and supple. Centerfold is mostly secure. Very minor interior tears may be present.

NOTE: Certain defects are allowed if other defects are not present.

BINDERY/PRINTING

very limited accumulation of
minor defects

COVER INKS/GLOSS

generally bright with moderate to
high reflectivity

COVER WEAR

Almost flat with minimal wear

COVER CREASES

1/8" - 1/4" bend with no color
break allowed

SOILING, STAINING

very minor foxing

DATES/STAMPS

accumulation of several dates,
initials, and store stamps allowed

SPINE ROLL

almost completely flat with no roll

SPINE SPLIT

very minor color break allowed

STAPLES

some discoloration
allowed

STAPLE TEARS

only the slightest
tears allowed

RUST MIGRATION

none allowed

STRESS LINES

accumulation of very minor lines
allowed

CORNERS

no creases, very minute wear
allowed

CENTERFOLD

mostly secure

INTERIOR TEARS

very minor tears in margin allowed

PAPER QUALITY/COLOR

cream, supple

ACID ODOR

none allowed

MISSING PIECES

none allowed

AMATEUR REPAIRS

none allowed

COUPON CUT

none allowed

READABILITY

preserved

Top-Notch Comics #1, March 1939. © MLJ Magazines.
Edgar Church (Mile High) pedigree copy.
Obvious defects: Light soiling on edge. Minor spine stress.
Hidden defects: None.
Page Quality: White.

Grease
pencil
marks

VF+

Light
soiling

Minor
stress

Color
fleck

Minor
spine
stress

Minute wear
on corner

Captain Marvel Adventures #4, October 1941. © Fawcett Publications.
Obvious defects: Small chips on edge. Abraded corners.
Hidden defects: None.
Page Quality: Cream to off-white.

Corner
tear

Small
edge
chips

Slight
browning
on edge

VF+

Very
minor
chip

Abraded
corner

Small chips

The Flash #146, August 1964. © DC Comics.
Obvious defects: Light spine stress that barely breaks color.
Hidden defects: Foxing spots on back cover.
Page Quality: Off-white.

Light edge wear

Abraded corner

Astonishing Tales #25, August 1974. © Marvel Characters, Inc.
Obvious defects: Light spine stress. Creases at bottom of front cover.
Hidden defects: "Rich Buckler" written on 1st page in pen.
Page Quality: White.

Light spine stress

VF+

1/2 inch crease

Corner crease

(8.0) VERY FINE (VF)

GRADE DESCRIPTION:

An excellent copy with outstanding eye appeal. Sharp, bright and clean with supple pages. A comic book in this grade has the appearance of having been carefully handled.

BINDERY DEFECTS - A limited accumulation of minor defects is allowed.

VF

COVER/EXTERIOR - Relatively flat with minimal surface wear beginning to show, possibly including some minute wear at corners. Inks are generally bright with moderate to high reflectivity. A 1/4" crease is acceptable if color is not broken. Stamped or inked arrival dates may be present. No obvious soiling, staining or other discoloration, except for minor foxing.

SPINE - Almost flat with no roll. Possible minor color break allowed.

STAPLES - Staples may show some discoloration. Very slight staple tears and a few almost very minor to minor stress lines may be present. No rust migration. In rare cases, a comic was not stapled at the bindery and therefore has a missing staple; this is not considered a defect. Any staple can be replaced on books up to Fine, but only vintage staples can be used on books from Very Fine to Near Mint. Mint books must have original staples.

PAPER/INTERIOR - Paper is tan to cream and supple. No hint of acidity in the odor of the newsprint. Centerfold is mostly secure. Minor interior tears at the margin may be present.

NOTE: Certain defects are allowed if other defects are not present.

BINDERY/PRINTING

limited accumulation of
minor defects

COVER INKS/GLOSS

generally bright with moderate to
high reflectivity

COVER WEAR

relatively flat with minimal wear

COVER CREASES

1/4" bend with no color break
allowed

SOILING, STAINING

minor foxing

DATES/STAMPS

dates, initials, and
store stamps allowed

SPINE ROLL

almost completely flat

SPINE SPLIT

minor color break allowed

VF

STAPLES

some discoloration
allowed

STAPLE TEARS

very slight
tears allowed

RUST MIGRATION

none allowed

STRESS LINES

very minor to minor lines allowed

CORNERS

minute wear allowed

CENTERFOLD

mostly secure

INTERIOR TEARS

minor tears in margin allowed

PAPER QUALITY/COLOR

tan to cream, supple

ACID ODOR

none allowed

MISSING PIECES

none allowed

AMATEUR REPAIRS

none allowed

COUPON CUT

none allowed

READABILITY

preserved

Superman #2, Fall 1939. © DC Comics.

Obvious defects: Chipping on edges and corners. Oxidation shadow on cover bottom.

Hidden defects: None.

Page Quality: Off-white.

VF

Corner chips

Soiling line

Edge chip

Light soiling

Slight staple stress

Edge chip

Corner chip

Oxidation shadow

Blunted corner

Wonder Woman #1, Summer 1942. © DC Comics.
Obvious defects: Minor creases. Abraded corner. Small spots on title logo.
Hidden defects: None.
Page Quality: Off-white to white.

Minor
creases

Small
spots

Very
small
staple
tears

Staple
discoloration

Abraded
corner

Corner
creases

Minor
browning
on edge

Blunted
corner

VF

All Select Comics #1, Fall 1943. © Marvel Characters, Inc.
Obvious defects: Chipping on edges and corners.
Hidden defects: None.
Page Quality: Off-white.

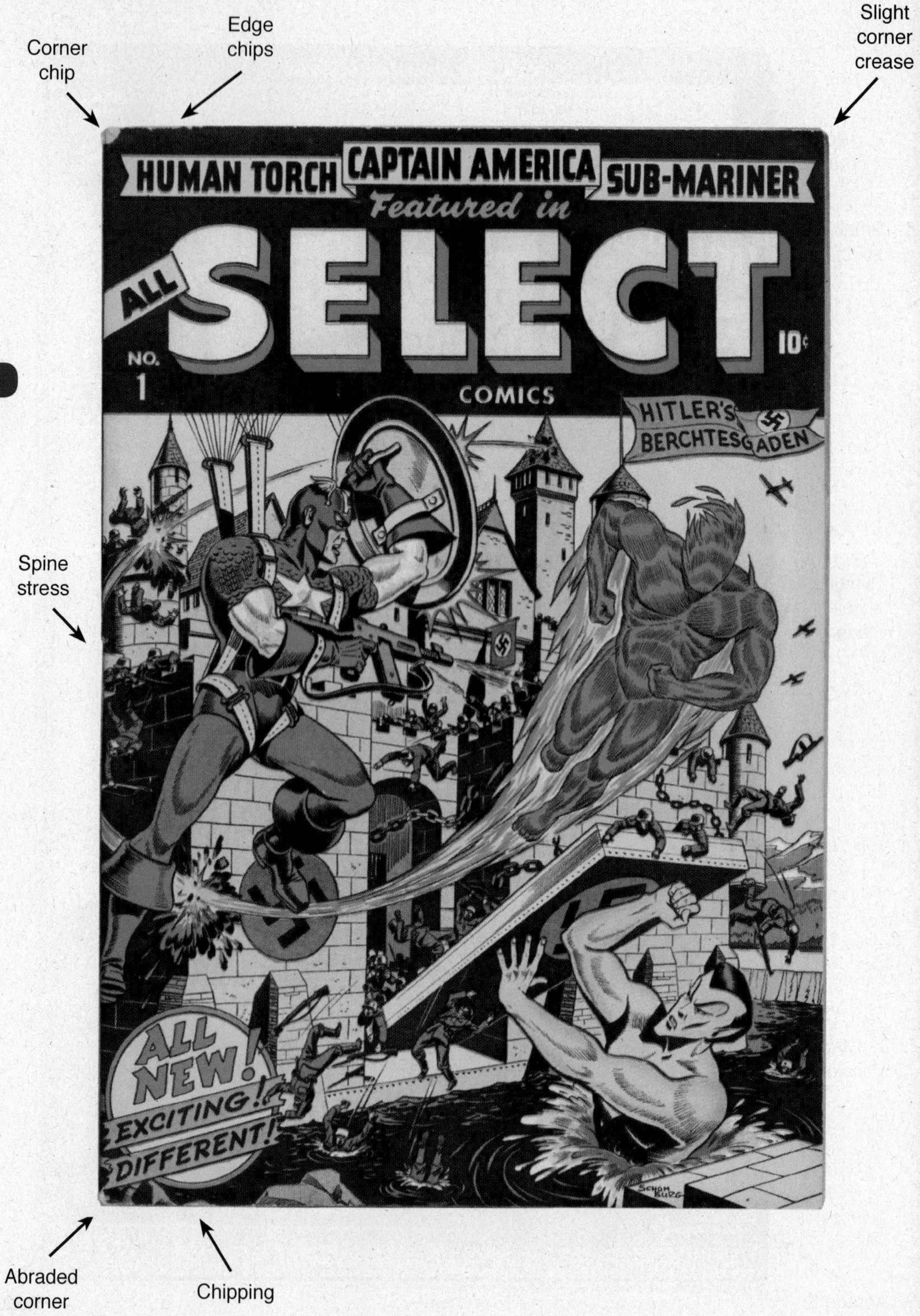

Corner
chip

Edge
chips

Slight
corner
crease

VF

Spine
stress

Abraded
corner

Chipping

Superman-Tim, May 1946. © DC Comics.
Obvious defects: Minor chipping. Color loss from handling or printer defects.
Hidden defects: None.
Page Quality: Off-white to white.

Corner chip

Stress line

Color loss

Stress line

Spine chips

VF

Color loss

Color chip

Abraded corner

Corner chip

Jughead as Captain Hero #1, October 1966. © Archie Publications.
Obvious defects: Slight browning on right edge of cover.
Hidden defects: None.
Page Quality: Off-white to white.

Slight crease

Browning along edge

VF

Rubbing

Color loss

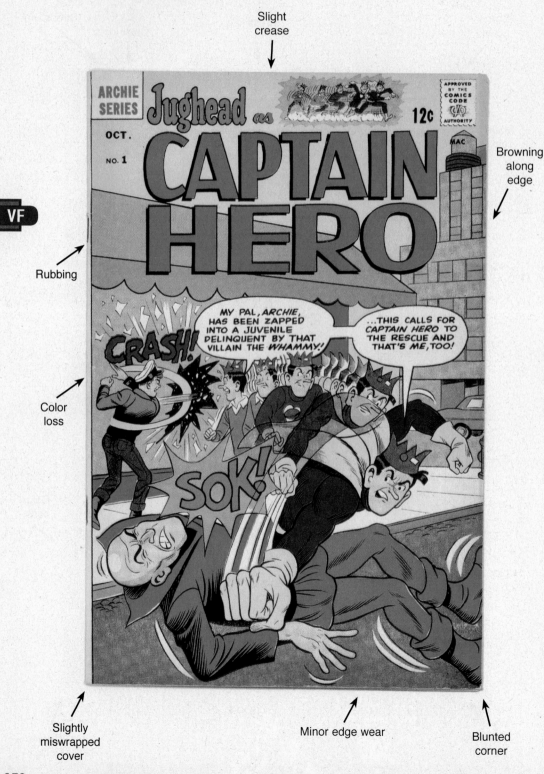

Slightly miswrapped cover

Minor edge wear

Blunted corner

Teen Titans #14, March-April 1968. © DC Comics.
Obvious defects: Small spine and corner creases.
Hidden defects: None.
Page Quality: White.

Corner
creases

Corner
creases

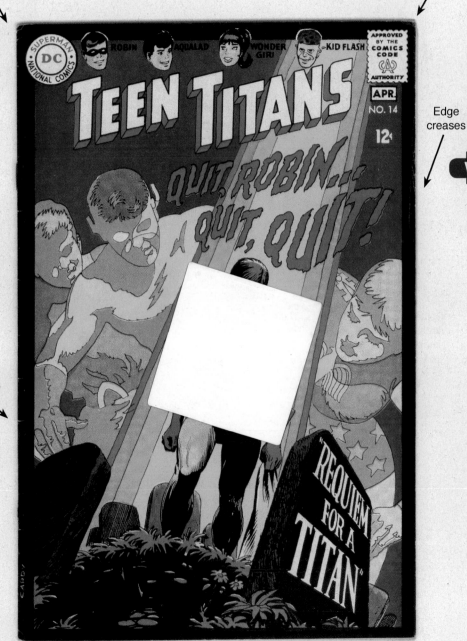

Edge
creases

VF

Spine
creases

Minor
abraded
corner

Color fleck
in corner

Silver Surfer #1, August 1968. © Marvel Characters, Inc.
Obvious defects: None.
Hidden defects: Minor soiling and fingerprints on title letters.
Page Quality: Off-white to white.

Minor corner
abrasion

Visible fingerprints and
faint ink residue on white
title letters

VF

Spine
stress
lines

Minor
pin
hole

Corner
chip

Edge stress

The Avengers #187, September 1979. © Marvel Characters, Inc.
Obvious defects: Color chips near edges.
Hidden defects: None.
Page Quality: Off-white to white.

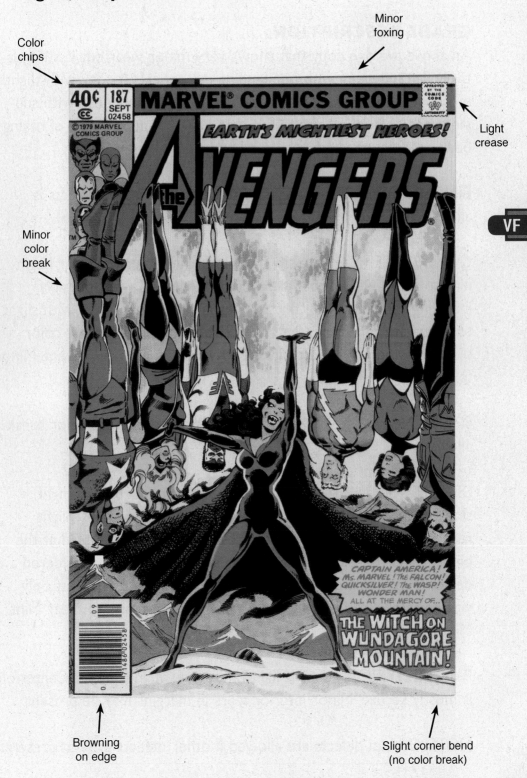

Minor
foxing

Color
chips

Light
crease

VF

Minor
color
break

Browning
on edge

Slight corner bend
(no color break)

(7.5) **VERY FINE –** (VF–)

GRADE DESCRIPTION:

An above average copy that shows very minor wear but is still relatively flat and clean with outstanding eye appeal. A copy with slightly more wear than a Very Fine copy. Sharp, bright and clean with supple pages. A comic book in this grade has the appearance of having been carefully handled.

BINDERY DEFECTS - A slight accumulation of minor defects is allowed.

COVER/EXTERIOR - Mostly flat with minimal surface wear beginning to show, with slight yellowing or tanning allowed, possibly including some wear at corners. Inks are generally bright with slight to moderate reflectivity. 1/4" to 1/2" bend with very slight color break allowed. Stamped or inked arrival dates may be present. Minor foxing may be present

SPINE - Nearly flat with a possible minor to moderate color break allowed.

STAPLES - Some discoloration allowed. Accumulation of slight staple tears and a few minor stress lines may be present. Slight rust migration allowed. In rare cases, a comic is not stapled at the bindery and therefore has a missing staple; this is not considered a defect. Any staple can be replaced on books up to Fine, but only vintage staples can be used on books from Very Fine to Near Mint. Mint books must have original staples.

PAPER/INTERIOR: Paper is light tan to cream and supple. Centerfold is mostly secure. Minor interior tears in margins may be present.

NOTE: Certain defects are allowed if other defects are not present.

BINDERY/PRINTING

limited accumulation of
minor defects

COVER INKS/GLOSS

generally bright with slight to
moderate reflectivity

COVER WEAR

mostly flat with yellowing or
tanning, minimal wear

COVER CREASES

1/4" - 1/2" bend with very slight
color break allowed

SOILING, STAINING

minor foxing

DATES/STAMPS

dates, initials, and
store stamps allowed

SPINE ROLL

nearly flat

SPINE SPLIT

minor to moderate color break
allowed

VF−

STAPLES

some discoloration
allowed

STAPLE TEARS

accumulation of
slight tears allowed

RUST MIGRATION

slight migration allowed

STRESS LINES

a few minor lines allowed

CORNERS

slight wear, blunting or abrading
allowed

CENTERFOLD

mostly secure

INTERIOR TEARS

minor tears in margin allowed

PAPER QUALITY/COLOR

tan to cream, supple

ACID ODOR

none allowed

MISSING PIECES

none allowed

AMATEUR REPAIRS

none allowed

COUPON CUT

none allowed

READABILITY

preserved

Funnies On Parade, 1933. © Eastern Color.

Obvious defects: Light soiling over most of the cover. Some corner wear visible.

Hidden defects: Light tan pages.

Page Quality: Cream.

Missing chip

Missing chip

Abraded corner

Slight discoloration

Abraded corner

Chipped edge

Corner crease

Fantastic Four #66, September 1967. © Marvel Characters, Inc.
Obvious defects: Spine stress and wear which breaks color.
Hidden defects: Light dirt on back cover.
Page Quality: Off-white to white.

Spine
stress

Minor
spine
stress

VF–

Small
corner
creases

2" crease parallel
to edge

Close up of 2" crease

Iron Man #1, May 1968. © Marvel Characters, Inc.
Obvious defects: Top of back cover not trimmed to match the rest of the comic.
Hidden defects: Some interior pages have corner tears.
Page Quality: Off-white to white.

Minor abraded corner

High cover gloss. Flat cover

Minor creases

Minor corner creases

VF–

Minor spine stress

Minor spine stress

Abraded corner

Minor color flecks

The Walking Dead #19, June 2005. © Robert Kirkman.
Obvious defects: Abrasion with multiple color chips half inch from spine.
Hidden defects: None
Page Quality: White.

Minor abraded
corner

Minor
color
flecks

Minor
color
flecks

Abrasion
with color
loss

VF–

Abraded
corner

(7.0) **FINE/VERY FINE** (F/VF)

GRADE DESCRIPTION:
An above-average copy that shows minor wear but is still relatively flat and clean with outstanding eye appeal. A comic book in this grade appears to have been read a few times and has been handled with care.

BINDERY DEFECTS - A small accumulation of minor defects is allowed.

F/VF

COVER/EXTERIOR - Minor wear beginning to show, with interior yellowing or tanning allowed, possibly including minor creases. Corners may be blunted or abraded. Inks are generally bright with a moderate reduction in reflectivity. Stamped or inked arrival dates may be present. No obvious soiling, staining or other discoloration, except for minor foxing.

SPINE - The slightest roll may be present, as well as a possible moderate color break.

STAPLES - Staples may show some discoloration. Slight staple tears and a small accumulation of light stress lines may be present. Slight rust migration. In rare cases, a comic was not stapled at the bindery and therefore has a missing staple; this is not considered a defect. Any staple can be replaced on books up to Fine, but only vintage staples can be used on books from Very Fine to Near Mint. Mint books must have original staples.

PAPER/INTERIOR - Paper is tan to cream, but not brown. No hint of acidity in the odor of the newsprint. Centerfold is mostly secure. Minor interior tears at the margin may be present.

NOTE: Certain defects are allowed if other defects are not present.

BINDERY/PRINTING

small accumulation of
minor defects

COVER INKS/GLOSS

moderate reduction in reflectivity

COVER WEAR

minimal wear, interior yellowing
or tanning allowed

COVER CREASES

minor creases allowed

SOILING, STAINING

minor foxing

DATES/STAMPS

dates, initials, and
store stamps allowed

SPINE ROLL

slightest roll allowed

SPINE SPLIT

moderate color break allowed

F/VF

STAPLES

some discoloration
allowed

STAPLE TEARS

slight tears
allowed

RUST MIGRATION

slight migration
allowed

STRESS LINES

small accumulation of
light lines

CORNERS

may be blunted or abraded

CENTERFOLD

mostly secure

INTERIOR TEARS

minor tears in margin allowed

PAPER QUALITY/COLOR

tan to cream, not brown

ACID ODOR

none allowed

MISSING PIECES

none allowed

AMATEUR REPAIRS

none allowed

COUPON CUT

none allowed

READABILITY

preserved

Billy the Kid and Oscar #1, Winter 1945. © Fawcett Publications.
Obvious defects: Out of register cover printing.
Hidden defects: Minor soiling at bottom of cover.
Page Quality: Cream to off-white.

Crumpled corner

Stamp

Library of Congress stamp

Stamp

Writing

F/VF

Slight rust migration on staple

Minor soiling

Weird Science #14, Sept.-Oct. 1950. © William M. Gaines.
Obvious defects: Missing chips. Minor spine roll.
Hidden defects: None.
Page Quality: Off-white to white.

Blunted corner

Corner chip

Slight roll

Spine creases

Slight foxing

F/VF

Slight corner stress

Minor foxing

Blunted corner

Weird Science-Fantasy Annual 1953. © William M. Gaines.
Obvious defects: Squrebound spine shows some wear.
Hidden defects: None.
Page Quality: Off-white to white.
Note: High cover gloss.

Reading
crease

High
reflectivity

Corner
creases

Abraded
corner

Spine
tear

F/VF

Tear

Corner
wear

Crease

Chip

Crease

Crease

Tales From the Crypt #41, May 1954. © William M. Gaines.

Obvious defects: Spine creases and minor browning on inside cover only.

Hidden defects: Corner chipping on numerous interior pages.

Page Quality: Off-white.

Note: High cover gloss. Copy is flat.

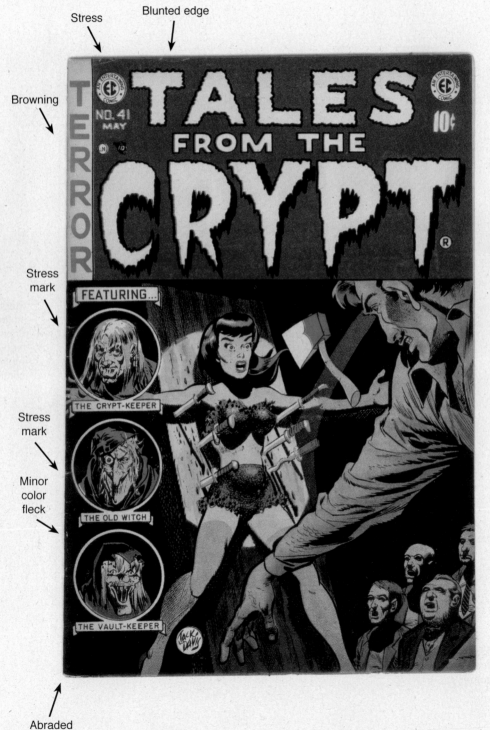

F/VF

My Little Margie #13, August 1956. © Charlton Comics Group.
Mile High pedigree copy.
Obvious defects: Bindery defect miswrapped cover.
Hidden defects: Staple holes through all interior pages.
Page Quality: Off-white.

F/VF

Miswrapped cover

Spine chip

Staple holes running through entire comic

Reading crease

Minor abraded corner

My Little Margie #13
(Back cover)

Miswrapped
cover

F/VF

Mild
soiling

Spine
creases

Ben Bowie and his Mountain Men #11, May-July 1957. © Western Publishing Co.
Pennsylvania pedigree copy shown.
Obvious defects: Arrival date written on title letters.
Hidden defects: Minor spine creases.
Page Quality: White.

Corner stress

Minor edge stress

Color flecking on edge

Writing

F/VF

Small spine creases

Two pin holes

Edge chip

Amazing Fantasy #15, August 1962. © Marvel Characters, Inc.

Obvious defects: Small creases along the entire spine.
Corner chip and abrasion.

Hidden defects: None.

Page Quality: Off-white.

Edge
crease

Corner
chip

Minor
staple
stress

Small
spine
creases

Staple
stress

Abraded
corner

Edge
wear

Minor
tears

F/VF

Justice League of America #92, September 1971. © DC Comics.
Obvious defects: Mild spine stress.
Hidden defects: Mild soiling on back cover along spine.
Page Quality: Off-white to white.

Distributor color coding

Spine
stress

F/VF

Spine
stress

Small accumulation
of light lines

Spawn #1, May 1992. © Todd McFarlane.
Obvious defects: Color scrapes near spine. Abraded corners.
Hidden defects: None.
Page Quality: White.

Abraded corner

Slight crease

Edge chip

Color scrapes

F/VF

Spine tear

Corner bend

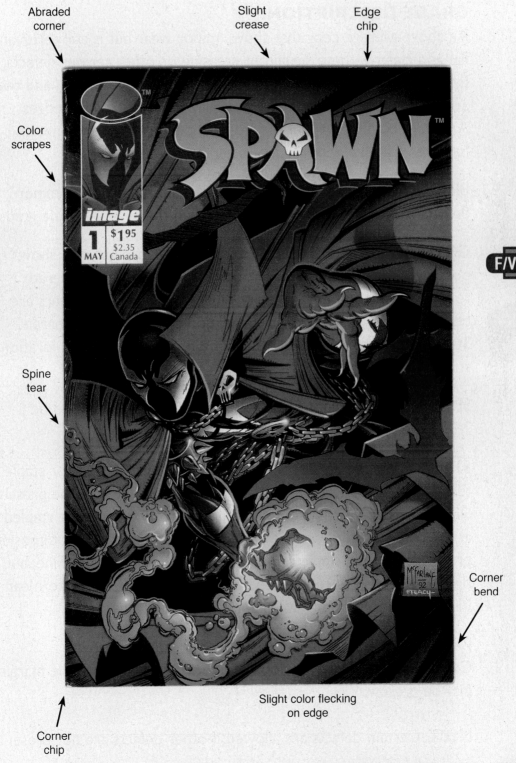

Corner chip

Slight color flecking on edge

(6.5) FINE + (FN+)

GRADE DESCRIPTION:

An above-average copy that shows minor wear but is still relatively flat and clean with no significant creasing or other serious defects. Eye appeal is slightly reduced because of light surface wear and the accumulation of small defects, especially on the spine and edges. A FINE + comic book appears to have been read a few times and has been handled with moderate care.

BINDERY DEFECTS - Small to moderate accumulation of minor defects is allowed. One or two more than the Fine/Very Fine grade.

COVER/EXTERIOR - Minimal to minor wear beginning to show, possibly including some wear at corners. Inks show a moderate to major reduction in reflectivity. Blunted or abraded corners are beginning to appear. Minor accumulation of creases are apparent. Stamped or inked arrival dates may be present. Slight discoloration, staining or foxing.

SPINE - Slight to minor spine roll is allowed. There can also be a 1/8" spine split or color break at spine.

STAPLES - Staples show some discoloration. Slight to minor staple tears and a slight accumulation of minor stress lines may be present. Slight to minor rust migration. In rare cases, a comic is not stapled at the bindery and therefore has a missing staple; this is not considered a defect. Any staple can be replaced on books up to Fine, but only vintage staples can be used on books from Very Fine to Near Mint. Mint books must have original staples.

PAPER/INTERIOR: Paper is light tan to cream, not brown. Centerfold may be slightly loose. Minor interior tears at the margin may be present.

NOTE: Certain defects are allowed if other defects are not present.

BINDERY/PRINTING

small to moderate accumulation
of minor defects

COVER INKS/GLOSS

moderate to major reduction in
reflectivity

COVER WEAR

minimal to minor wear

COVER CREASES

minor accumulation of creases

SOILING, STAINING

slight discoloration, staining,
and/or foxing

DATES/STAMPS

dates/initials/stamps allowed

SPINE ROLL

slight to minor roll allowed

SPINE SPLIT

up to 1/8" split or severe
color break allowed

STAPLES

some discoloration
allowed

STAPLE TEARS

slight to minor tears
allowed

RUST MIGRATION

slight to minor migration
allowed

FN+

STRESS LINES

accumulation of minor slight lines

CORNERS

may be blunted or abraded

CENTERFOLD

slightly loose

INTERIOR TEARS

minor tears in margin

PAPER QUALITY/COLOR

tan to cream, not brown

ACID ODOR

none allowed

MISSING PIECES

none allowed

AMATEUR REPAIRS

none allowed

COUPON CUT

none allowed

READABILITY

preserved

Captain America Comics #1, March 1941. © Marvel Characters, Inc.
Obvious defects: Spine shows some wear. Color flecks near spine.
Hidden defects: None.
Page Quality: Off-white.

Color
flecks

Missing
chip

Browning
on edge

Worn
spine

Erased
letters

FN+

Light
color
loss

Corner
chip

Edge chips

Sub-Mariner Comics #1, Spring 1941. © Marvel Characters, Inc.
Obvious defects: Slight corner wear.
Hidden defects: None.
Page Quality: Cream to off-white.

Abraded corner

Slight browning

Discolored staple

FN+

Reduction in reflectivity

Minor rubbing

Staple rust migration

Corner chip

Minor wear

Suspense Comics #3, April 1944. © Continental Magazines.
Obvious defects: Animal chews in two corners.
Hidden defects: Foxing.
Page Quality: Off-white.

FN+

Abraded corner

Foxing

Animal chew

Color flecks

Pencil marks

Animal chew

Edge chips

Suspense Comics #11, June 1946. © Continental Magazines.
Obvious defects: Spine stress.
Hidden defects: None.
Page Quality: Cream to off-white.

Bindery
tear

Slight
rolled
spine

Slight
dust
shadow

Spine
stress

Slight
edge
wear

FN+

Blunted
corner

Adventures of the Big Boy #100. © Robert C. Wian Enterprises, Inc.

Obvious defects: Rectangular tape residue on title logo. Slight water damage and slight crease on back cover.

Hidden defects: The paper cover has subtle stains, including slight soiling on back cover.

Page Quality: Off-white.

FN+

Tape residue

Minor soiling

Close-up of
tape residue

Adventures of the Big Boy #100 (back cover)

Slight
soiling

FN+

Small tear

(6.0)   **FINE**   (FN)

GRADE DESCRIPTION:

An above-average copy that shows minor wear but is still relatively flat and clean with no significant creasing or other serious defects. Eye appeal is somewhat reduced because of slight surface wear and the accumulation of small defects, especially on the spine and edges. A FINE condition comic book appears to have been read a few times and has been handled with moderate care.

BINDERY DEFECTS - Some accumulation of minor defects is allowed.

COVER/EXTERIOR - Minor wear apparent, with minor to moderate creases. Inks show a significant reduction in reflectivity. Blunted corners are more common, as is minor staining, soiling, discoloration, and/or foxing. Stamped or inked arrival dates may be present.

FN

SPINE - A minor spine roll is allowed. There can also be a 1/4" spine split or severe color break.

STAPLES - Staples may show minor discoloration. Minor staple tears and a few slight stress lines may be present, as well as minor rust migration. In rare cases, a comic was not stapled at the bindery and therefore has a missing staple; this is not considered a defect. Any staple can be replaced on books up to Fine, but only vintage staples can be used on books from Very Fine to Near Mint. Mint books must have original staples.

PAPER/INTERIOR - Paper is brown to tan and fairly supple with no signs of brittleness. No hint of acidity in the odor of the newsprint. Minor interior tears at the margin may be present. Centerfold may be loose but not detached.

FINE has historically been the most difficult grade to identify. It is the highest grade which allows a wide range of defects to occur.

NOTE: Certain defects are allowed if other defects are not present.

BINDERY/PRINTING

some accumulation of minor defects

COVER INKS/GLOSS

major reduction in reflectivity

COVER WEAR

minor wear

COVER CREASES

minor to moderate creases

SOILING, STAINING

minor discoloration, staining, and/or foxing

DATES/STAMPS

dates/initials/stamps allowed

SPINE ROLL

minor roll allowed

SPINE SPLIT

up to 1/4" split or severe color break allowed

STAPLES

minor discoloration allowed

STAPLE TEARS

minor tears allowed

RUST MIGRATION

minor migration allowed

FN

STRESS LINES

accumulation of minor lines

CORNERS

blunting or abrasion more common

CENTERFOLD

loose, not detached

INTERIOR TEARS

minor tears in margin

PAPER QUALITY/COLOR

brown to tan, supple, not brittle

ACID ODOR

none allowed

MISSING PIECES

none allowed

AMATEUR REPAIRS

none allowed

COUPON CUT

none allowed

READABILITY

preserved

Green Lantern #1, Fall 1941. © DC Comics.
Obvious defects: Chipped edge. Slightly miswrapped cover.
Hidden defects: None.
Page Quality: Off-white.

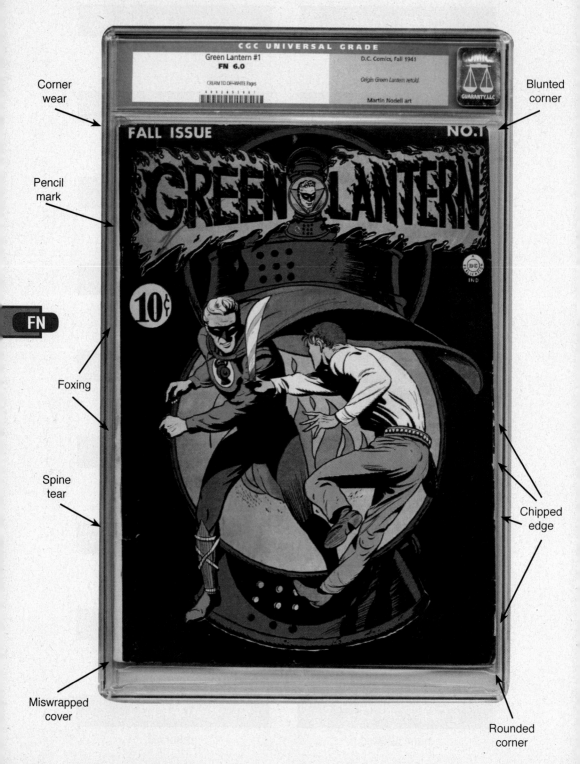

Corner wear

Pencil mark

Foxing

Spine tear

Miswrapped cover

FN

Blunted corner

Chipped edge

Rounded corner

Challengers of the Unknown #2, June-July 1958. © DC Comics.
Obvious defects: Dust shadow.
Hidden defects: Small edge chips along top.
Page Quality: Cream to off-white.

Small edge chips

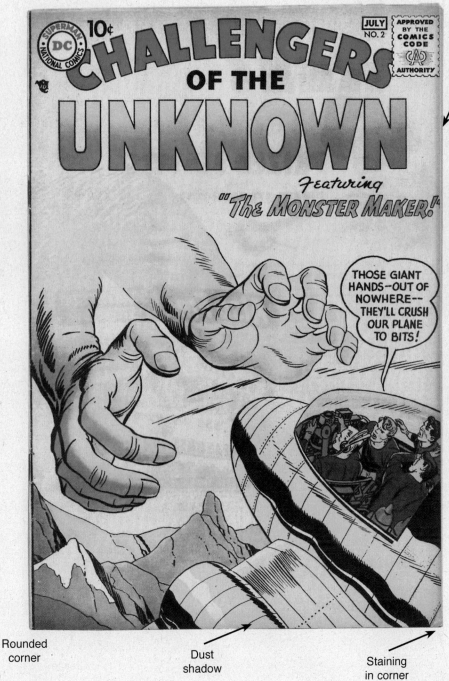

Dust
shadow

FN

Rounded
corner

Dust
shadow

Staining
in corner

Yogi Bear Visits the U.N. - Four Color #1349, 1961. © Hanna-Barbera.
Obvious defects: Cover whites have browned especially along the spine.
Hidden defects: Minor spine creases.
Page Quality: Off-white.

Corner chip out

Browning

Corner chip

FN

Browning along spine

Small spine tear

Corner chip

Crease

Underdog #1, July 1970. © Charlton Press.
Obvious defects: Oxidation shadow on top of cover.
Hidden defects: Fanned pages.
Page Quality: Off-white.

Slight
water mark

Oxidation
shadow

Oxidation
shadows

Moderate
crease

Small
cover
indentation

FN

1/4" spine
split

Minor
corner chip

Significant reduction
in reflectivity

Giant-Size Conan the Barbarian #1, September 1974. © Conan Properties.
Obvious defects: Book shape is skewed, cover is miswrapped.
Hidden defects: None.
Page Quality: White.

FN

Book trimming defect at
incorrect angle

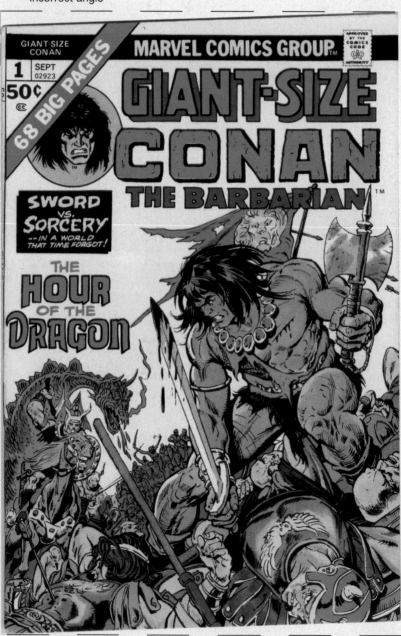

Slight
edge
stress

Blunted
corner

Corner angle is
off by this much

Amazing Spider-Man Annual #21, 1987. © Marvel Characters, Inc.
Obvious defects: Off center top staple. Water damage on bottom of cover.
Hidden defects: Light soiling.
Page Quality: Off-white.

Small corner creases

Minor crease

Off-centered

Off center staple

Small tear

Stress line

FN

Light corner crease

Minor soiling

Crease

Slight browning

Water damage

(5.5) FINE – (FN–)

GRADE DESCRIPTION:

An average to above average copy that shows moderate wear. Eye appeal is somewhat reduced because of the accumulation of defects. Still a desirable copy that has been handled with some care.

BINDERY DEFECTS - A moderate accumulation of defects allowed.

COVER/EXTERIOR - Minor surface wear showing, with heightened yellowing or tanning allowed; wear at corners more common. Inks show major reduction in reflectivity. Minor to moderate creases with slight dimpling. Stamped or inked arrival dates allowed. Minor accumulation of discoloration, staining or foxing may be present.

SPINE - A minor spine role is allowed. Spine can have a 1/4" - 1/2" split or color break at spine.

STAPLES - Staples show discoloration. Minor staple tears and an accumulation of stress lines may be present as well as minor rust migration. In rare cases, a comic is not stapled at the bindery and therefore has a missing staple; this is not considered a defect. Any staple can be replaced on books up to Fine, but only vintage staples can be used on books from Very Fine to Near Mint. Mint books must have original staples.

PAPER/INTERIOR: Paper is brown to tan and fairly supple with no signs of brittleness. Centerfold is loose, but not detatched. Minor interior tears may be present.

NOTE: Certain defects are allowed if other defects are not present.

BINDERY/PRINTING

moderate accumulation
of defects

COVER INKS/GLOSS

major reduction in reflectivity

COVER WEAR

minor wear with heightened
yellowing or tanning

COVER CREASES

minor to moderate creases with
slight dimpling

SOILING, STAINING

minor accumulation of discoloration, staining, and/or foxing

DATES/STAMPS

dates/initials/stamps allowed

SPINE ROLL

minor roll allowed

SPINE SPLIT

up to 1/4" - 1/2" split or
color break allowed

STAPLES

some discoloration
allowed

STAPLE TEARS

minor tears
allowed

RUST MIGRATION

minor migration
allowed

FN–

STRESS LINES

accumulation of minor lines

CORNERS

blunting or abrasion
more common

CENTERFOLD

loose, not detached

INTERIOR TEARS

minor tears

PAPER QUALITY/COLOR

brown to tan, supple, not brittle

ACID ODOR

none allowed

MISSING PIECES

none allowed

AMATEUR REPAIRS

none allowed

COUPON CUT

none allowed

READABILITY

preserved

The Human Torch #6, Winter 1941. © Marvel Characters, Inc.
Obvious defects: Browning on spine. Corners show wear.
Hidden defects: Slight spine roll.
Page Quality: Cream to off-white.

Corner
tear

Slight
spine roll

Corner
chip

Color
flecks

Pencil
mark

Browning

Color
flecks
down
spine

FN–

Small
stress
line

Browning

Abraded
corner

Rounded
corner

Amazing Spider-Man #109, June 1972. © Marvel Characters Inc.
Obvious defects: Several spine stress lines. Significant reduction of reflectivity on back cover.
Hidden defects: Minor stains inside back cover.
Page Quality: Off-white to white.

Creases

Moderate corner creases on back cover

Abraded corner

Several spine stress lines

Silver ink autograph

Spine crease

FN–

Moderate crease on bottom back cover

Corner crease

The Avengers #96, February 1972. © Marvel Characters, Inc.
Obvious defects: Slightly abraded corner.
Hidden defects: Subtle non-color breaking book-length crease.
Page Quality: Off-white to white.

Slightly abraded corner

Non-color breaking book-length crease

FN−

Minor stress lines

Slight edge wear

Very slight abraded corner

Minor browning

All-American Comics #16, July 1940. © DC Comics.
Obvious defects: Some chipping on edges.
Hidden defects: None.
Page Quality: Cream to off-white.

Corner chip

Pencil marks

Bundling ridge

Rounded corner

Light soiling

Crease

FN–

Foxing

Blunted corner

Abraded edge

Small crease

Small chips

(5.0) VERY GOOD/FINE (VG/FN)

GRADE DESCRIPTION:
An above-average but well-used comic book. A comic in this grade shows some moderate wear; eye appeal is somewhat reduced because of the accumulation of defects. Still a desirable copy that has been handled with some care.

BINDERY DEFECTS - An accumulation of defects is allowed.

COVER/EXTERIOR - Minor to moderate wear apparent, with minor to moderate creases and/or dimples. Inks have major to extreme reduction in reflectivity. Blunted or abraded corners are increasingly common, as is minor to moderate staining, discoloration, and/or foxing. Stamped or inked arrival dates may be present.

SPINE - A minor to moderate spine roll is allowed. A spine split of up to 1/2" may be present.

STAPLES - Staples may show minor discoloration. A slight accumulation of minor staple tears and an accumulation of minor stress lines may also be present, as well as minor rust migration. In rare cases, a comic was not stapled at the bindery and therefore has a missing staple; this is not considered a defect. Any staple can be replaced on books up to Fine, but only vintage staples can be used on books from Very Fine to Near Mint. Mint books must have original staples.

PAPER/INTERIOR - Paper is brown to tan with no signs of brittleness. May have the faintest trace of an acidic odor. Centerfold may be loose but not detached. Minor interior tears may also be present.

NOTE: Certain defects are allowed if other defects are not present.

BINDERY/PRINTING

accumulation of defects

COVER INKS/GLOSS

major to extreme reduction in
reflectivity

COVER WEAR

minor to moderate wear

COVER CREASES

minor to moderate
creases and dimples

SOILING, STAINING

minor to moderate discoloration,
staining, and/or foxing

DATES/STAMPS

dates/initials/stamps allowed

SPINE ROLL

minor to moderate roll

SPINE SPLIT

up to 1/2" split

STAPLES

minor discoloration

STAPLE TEARS

slight accumulation
of minor tears

RUST MIGRATION

minor migration

STRESS LINES

accumulation of minor lines

CORNERS

blunting or abrasion
increasingly common

CENTERFOLD

loose, not detached

INTERIOR TEARS

minor tears

PAPER QUALITY/COLOR

brown to tan, supple,
not brittle

ACID ODOR

may have the faintest odor

MISSING PIECES

none allowed

AMATEUR REPAIRS

none allowed

COUPON CUT

none allowed

READABILITY

preserved

VG/FN

Adventure Comics #40, July 1939. © DC Comics.
Obvious defects: Rat chew and light soiling.
Hidden defects: None.
Page Quality: Off-white.

Corner
chip

Light
foxing

Rat
chew

Rumpled
cover

VG/FN

Staple
stress

Abraded
corner

Star Spangled Comics #1, October 1941. © DC Comics.
Obvious defects: Browning on edges. Color chips missing from corners.
Hidden defects: None.
Page Quality: Cream.

Color chip

Color chip

Color flecks

Spine chips

Spine tear

Browning

VG/FN

Browning

1/2" spine split

Browning

Blunted corner

Green Hornet Comics #29, March 1946. © The Green Hornet Inc.
Obvious defects: Poorly trimmed interior pages.
Hidden defects: None.
Page Quality: Cream to off-white.

Torn
corner

Poorly trimmed
interior pages

Rust
migration
from
staple

Minor
tear

VG/FN

1" tear

Oxidation
shadow

Book has a
slight odor

Green Hornet Comics #29
(Interior pages)

The Lone Ranger #6, Nov.-Dec. 1948. © Lone Ranger Inc.
Obvious defects: Small creases on spine. Color flecking on edge.
Hidden defects: Some interior pages have perforations on edge from printing.
Page Quality: Off-white to white.

Worn edge

Color scrape

Chip

Numerous
small
spine
creases

VG/FN

Color
flecking

Chip out

Centerfold is
loose

Walt Disney's Comics and Stories #131, August 1951. © Walt Disney Co.

Obvious defects: Spine creases.

Hidden defects: Top of book not trimmed squarely.

Page Quality: Off-white to white.

Corner tear

Slightly worn corner

Spine wrinkling

Cover rumpled

Staple tear

Spine creases

VG/FN

Cover edge wear

Staple tear

Spine stress

Color flecks

Creases

Kid Colt Outlaw #72, May 1957. © Marvel Characters, Inc.
Circle 8 pedigree copy. Copy has high cover gloss.
Obvious defects: Frayed corners and spine.
Hidden defects: None.
Page Quality: Off-white to white.

Corner
chip out

Minor Marvel
chipping

Staple
creases

Slight tear

VG/FN

Stressed
spine

Minor
chip out

Minor
chip out

Abraded
corner

Our Army at War #138, January 1964. © DC Comics.
Obvious defects: Corner creases.
Hidden defects: Loose upper staple.
Page Quality: Off-white.

Corner
creases

Chip

Corner
chip

Loose
staple

Date
stamp

Worn
spine
(pinhole)

Edge
crease

VG/FN

Crease

Spine split

Astro Boy #1, August 1965. © NBC, Inc.

Obvious defects: Tape residue lines on lower 2" of cover. Staining on edge.

Hidden defects: None.

Page Quality: Off-white to white.

Abraded corner

Corner stains

Edge stains

VG/FN

Edge browning

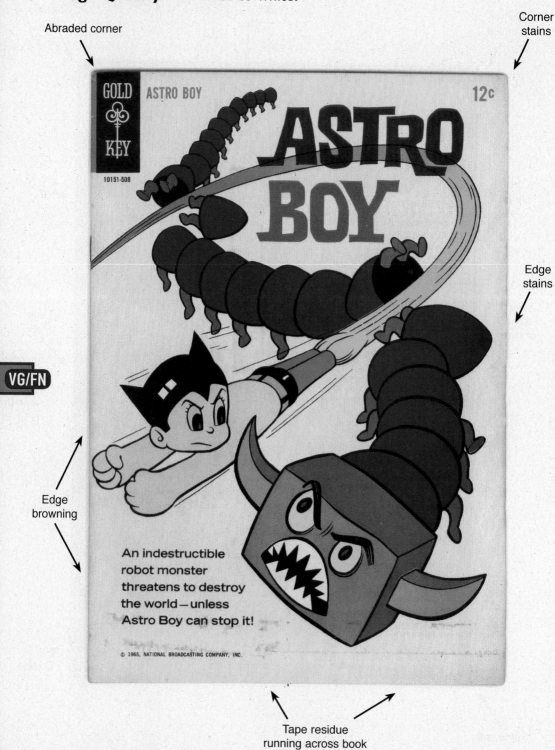

Tape residue running across book

Shazam! #1, February 1973. © DC Comics.
Obvious defects: Light soiling on front and back covers.
Hidden defects: None.
Page Quality: Off-white to white.

1/2" spine split

1/8" corner crease

Staple tear

Small spine creases

Edge tear

VG/FN

Staple stress lines

Crease

(4.5) VERY GOOD + (VG+)

GRADE DESCRIPTION:

An average comic book with less wear and defects than one in Very Good. A comic in this grade shows some moderate wear, but still has enough eye appeal to be a desirable copy.

COVER/EXTERIOR - Cover shows moderate wear, and may be loose but not completely detached. Major to extreme reduction in reflectivity. Can have moderate accumulation of creases or dimples. Corners may be blunted or abraded. Store stamps, name stamps, arrival dates, initials, etc. have no effect on this grade. Moderate discoloration, fading, and/or foxing. As much as 1/8" triangle can be missing out of the corner or edge; a missing 1/16" square is also acceptable. Only minor amateur repair allowed on otherwise high grade copies.

SPINE - Minor to moderate roll may be present and a 1/2"- 1" spine split/color break.

STAPLES - Staples discolored. Accumulation of minor staple tears and stress lines may be present, as well as rust migration.

VG+

PAPER/INTERIOR: Paper is brown to tan, supple but not brittle. A minor acidic odor can be detectable. Minor tears throughout book may be present. Centerfold may be loose or detached at one staple. Comics in this condition are still desirable and collectable. The best known copies of some pre-1965 books are in this grade range.

NOTE: Certain defects are allowed if other defects are not present.

BINDERY/PRINTING

do not affect grade

COVER INKS/GLOSS

major to extreme reduction
in reflectivity

COVER WEAR

moderate wear,
may be loose

COVER CREASES

minor to moderate accumulation
of creases or dimples

SOILING, STAINING

moderate accumulation of
discoloration, fading, foxing,
even minor soiling

DATES/STAMPS

do not affect grade

SPINE ROLL

minor to moderate roll

SPINE SPLIT

1/2" to 1" split

STAPLES

minor to major
discoloration

STAPLE TEARS

accumulation of
minor tears

RUST MIGRATION

minor to moderate
migration

STRESS LINES

minor accumulation of lines

CORNERS

blunting or abrasion
increasingly common

CENTERFOLD

loose or detached at one staple

INTERIOR TEARS

minor throughout book

VG+

PAPER QUALITY/COLOR

brown to tan, supple, not brittle

ACID ODOR

very minor odor

MISSING PIECES

1/8" triangle, 1/16" square

AMATEUR REPAIRS

very minor repairs on otherwise
high grade

COUPON CUT

none allowed

READABILITY

preserved

Marvel Mystery Comics #19, May 1941. © Marvel Characters, Inc.

Obvious defects: Spine is worn and split on ends.

Hidden defects: None.

Page Quality: Tan to cream.

Reading crease

Color flecking

Split spine

Chip out

Spine tears

Color flecking

Staple not centered

Spine stress lines

VG+

Rust migration

Split spine

Small tear

Rounded corner

Sub-Mariner Comics #4, Winter 1942. © Marvel Characters, Inc.
Obvious defects: Abraded corners. Oxidation shadows.
Hidden defects: Interior pages brown at edges.
Page Quality: Tan to cream.

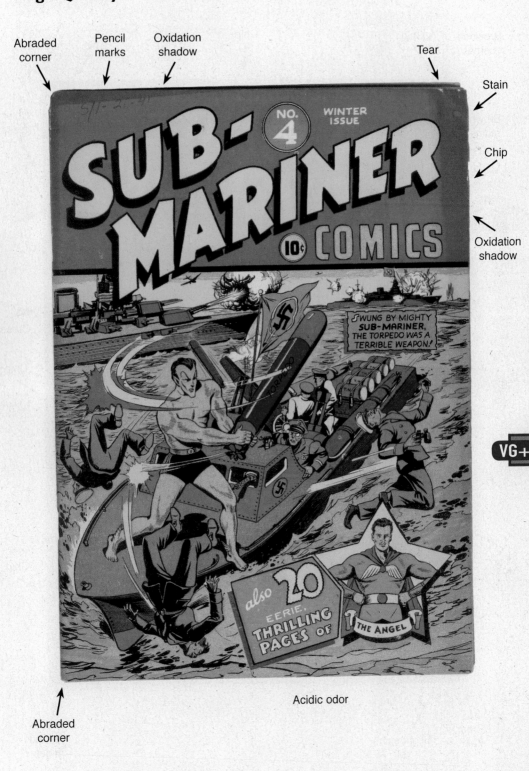

Abraded corner

Pencil marks

Oxidation shadow

Tear

Stain

Chip

Oxidation shadow

VG+

Abraded corner

Acidic odor

Strange Adventures #1, Aug.-Sept. 1950. © DC Comics.
Obvious defects: Numerous chips on cover edges.
Hidden defects: Color flecks in the cover's starry sky.
Page Quality: Cream.

Browned corner

Chip

Chip

Chip

Corner crease

Brown stains

Minor staple tears

Color flecks

Crease

Crease

Chip

VG+

Spine wear

Chip

Corner stain

Slight spine roll

Fanned pages

Roy Rogers Comics #37, January 1951. © The ROHR Co.

Obvious defects: Numerous color flecks and creases near spine. Wrinkle through the center of the cover.

Hidden defects: None.

Page Quality: Off-white.

Note: Double cover.

Pencil mark

Color flecks

Corner chip

Abraded corner

DELL COMIC

ROY ROGERS COMICS

10¢ JAN.

Spine worn around staple

Chip

Numerous spine creases

Chips

VG+

Color flecks

MERRY CHRISTMAS

Abraded corner

Crease

Action Comics #235, December 1957. © DC Comics.
Obvious defects: Color rub along spine. Pieces missing along cover bottom.
Hidden defects: None.
Page Quality: Cream to off-white.

Rounded corner

Ink stain

Rounded corner

Color rub

VG+

Staple wear

Edge piece missing

Crease

Corner piece missing

Fantastic Four #3, March 1962. © Marvel Characters, Inc.
Obvious defects: General cover wear and edge wear.
Hidden defects: Small tear on back cover.
Page Quality: Off-white to white.

Rounded corner

Pen markings

VG+

Spine stress

Corner crease

(4.0) VERY GOOD (VG)

GRADE DESCRIPTION:

The average used comic book. A comic in this grade shows some significant moderate wear, but still has not accumulated enough total defects to reduce eye appeal to the point that it is not a desirable copy.

COVER/EXTERIOR - Cover shows moderate to significant wear, and may be loose but not completely detached. Moderate to extreme reduction in reflectivity. Can have an accumulation of creases or dimples. Corners may be blunted. or abraded. Store stamps, name stamps, arrival dates, initials, etc. have no effect on this grade. Some discoloration, fading, foxing, and even minor soiling is allowed. As much as a 1/4" triangle can be missing out of the corner or edge; a missing 1/8" square is also acceptable. Only minor unobtrusive tape and other amateur repair allowed on otherwise high grade copies.

SPINE - Moderate roll may be present and/or a 1" spine split.

STAPLES - Staples discolored. Minor to moderate staple tears and stress lines may be present, as well as some rust migration.

PAPER/INTERIOR - Paper is brown but not brittle. A minor acidic odor can be detectable. Minor to moderate interior tears may be present. Centerfold may be loose or detached at one staple.

Comics in this condition are still desirable and collectable. The best known copies of some pre-1965 books are in VG condition.

There are significant differences between this grade and GOOD; over-grading sometimes occurs.

NOTE: Certain defects are allowed if other defects are not present.

BINDERY/PRINTING

do not affect grade

COVER INKS/GLOSS

major to extreme reduction in reflectivity

COVER WEAR

moderate to significant wear, may be loose

COVER CREASES

accumulation of creases or dimples

SOILING, STAINING

some discoloration, fading, foxing, even minor soiling

DATES/STAMPS

do not affect grade

SPINE ROLL

moderate roll

SPINE SPLIT

up to 1" split

STAPLES

discolored

STAPLE TEARS

minor to moderate tears

RUST MIGRATION

some migration

STRESS LINES

minor to moderate lines

CORNERS

blunted or abraded corners

CENTERFOLD

loose or detached at one staple

INTERIOR TEARS

minor to moderate tears

PAPER QUALITY/COLOR

brown, not brittle

ACID ODOR

minor odor

MISSING PIECES

1/4" triangle, 1/8" square

AMATEUR REPAIRS

minor repairs on otherwise high grade

COUPON CUT

none allowed

READABILITY

preserved

VG

Adventure Comics #59, February 1940. © DC Comics.
Obvious defects: Browning stains on cover edges.
Hidden defects: Brown interior pages.
Page Quality: Tan to cream.

Rounded corner

Loss of reflectivity

Writing on cover

Brown staining

Brown staining

Abraded spine

Edge wear

VG

Spine wear

1" spine tear

Minor fraying

Crease

Corner chip

All Star Comics #1, Summer 1940. © DC Comics.
Obvious defects: Spine is worn. Store stamp.
Hidden defects: Mold on interior pages.
Page Quality: Tan to cream.

Corner chip out

Chip missing

Rounded corner

Mold stain

Abraded spine

Store stamp

Spine tear

VG

Color chip out

Abraded corner

Impacted edge

Rounded corner

Master Comics #23, February 1942. © Fawcett Publications.
Obvious defects: Worn corners.
Hidden defects: Subtle folds and creases on cover.
Page Quality: Off-white.

Corner
chip out

Long, very
light crease

Color
flecking

Staple
tear

Numerous
spine
creases

Minor
edge fray

VG

Staple
tear

Corner
chip

Crease

Chip

Corner
chip

Leading Comics #8, Fall 1943. © DC Comics.
Obvious defects: Miswrapped cover with spine roll.
Hidden defects: Blunted corner on some interior pages.
Page Quality: Off-white to white.

Abraded corner

Color scrape

Miswrapped cover

Pencil mark

Loose centerfold

Spine roll

Color rub

VG

Abraded corner

Color scrape

Stain

Color missing abrasion

Miswrapped cover

Out of This World #1, June 1950. © Avon Publications.
Obvious defects: Large brownish transfer stain in center of cover.
Hidden defects: Loose centerfold pages.
Page Quality: Cream to off-white.

Abraded corner

Crease

Chip missing

Frayed edge

Rounded corner

Creases

Color loss

Light long crease

Edge stain

Abraded corner

Frayed edge

Abraded corner

VG

Intimate Confessions #1, July-Aug. 1951. © Realistic Comics.
Obvious defects: Stressed edges. Full length crease down the center of the cover.
Hidden defects: None.
Page Quality: Cream.

Full-length crease

Abraded corner

Edge stress

Edge stress

Abraded corner

Tear

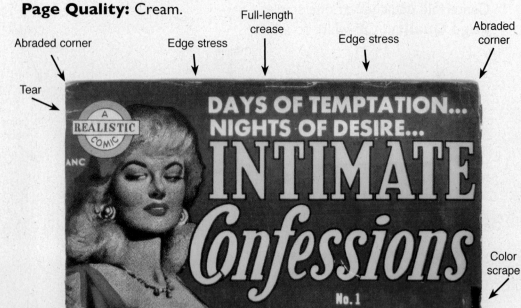

Color scrape

Staple stress

VG

Tear

Corner chips

Archie's Pal Jughead Comics #20, October 1953. © Archie Publications.
Obvious defects: Creases on the spine. Minor wrinkles near bottom of cover.
Hidden defects: Some interior pages have small holes or tears. Centerfold detached at one staple.
Page Quality: Off-white to white.

VG

Fantastic Four #13, April 1963. © Marvel Characters, Inc.
Obvious defects: Marvel chipping on cover's edge.
Hidden defects: None.
Page Quality: Off-white to white.

Abraded corner

Edge wear

Corner chip

Marvel chipping

VG

Moderate stress lines

Abraded corner

Missing chip

Edge wear

(3.5) VERY GOOD – (VG–)

GRADE DESCRIPTION:

An average comic book with more wear and defects than one in Very Good. A comic in this grade shows some significant moderate wear, but still has not accumulated enough total defects to reduce eye appeal to the point that it is not a desirable copy.

COVER/EXTERIOR - Cover shows moderate to significant wear, and may be loose and almost completely detached. Major to extreme reduction in reflectivity. Moderate accumulation of creases or dimples. Corners may be blunted or abraded. Store stamps, name stamps, arrival dates, initials, etc. have no effect on this grade. Accumulation of discoloration, fading, foxing, and even minor soiling is allowed. As much as 1/4" triangle can be missing out of the corner or edge; a missing 1/8" square is also acceptable. Only minor amateur repair allowed on otherwise high grade copies.

SPINE - Moderate roll and a 1" spine split with possible color break.

STAPLES - Staples discolored. Minor to moderate staple tears and stress lines may be present, as well as some rust migration.

PAPER/INTERIOR: Paper is brown but not brittle. A minor acidic odor can be detectable. Minor to moderate interior tears may be present. Centerfold may be loose or detached at one staple. Comics in this condition are still desirable and collectable. The best known copies of some pre-1965 books are in this grade range.

NOTE: Certain defects are allowed if other defects are not present.

BINDERY/PRINTING

do not affect grade

COVER INKS/GLOSS

major to extreme reduction
in reflectivity

COVER WEAR

significant wear,
may be loose or detached at staple

COVER CREASES

moderate accumulation of creases
or dimples

SOILING, STAINING

accumulation of discoloration,
fading, foxing, even minor soiling

DATES/STAMPS

do not affect grade

SPINE ROLL

moderate roll

SPINE SPLIT

up to 1" split with possible
color break

STAPLES

discolored; one may be
missing or replaced

STAPLE TEARS

minor to moderate
tears

RUST MIGRATION

some migration

STRESS LINES

minor to moderate lines

CORNERS

blunted or abraded corners

CENTERFOLD

loose or detached at one staple

INTERIOR TEARS

minor to moderate tears

PAPER QUALITY/COLOR

brown, not brittle

ACID ODOR

minor odor

MISSING PIECES

1/4" triangle, 1/8" square

AMATEUR REPAIRS

minor repairs on otherwise
high grade

COUPON CUT

none allowed

READABILITY

preserved

VG–

Action Comics #1, June 1938. © DC Comics.

Obvious defects: Light soiling on most of cover.

Hidden defects: Small spine split on every page. Small amount of dried glue on spine.

Page Quality: Cream to off-white.

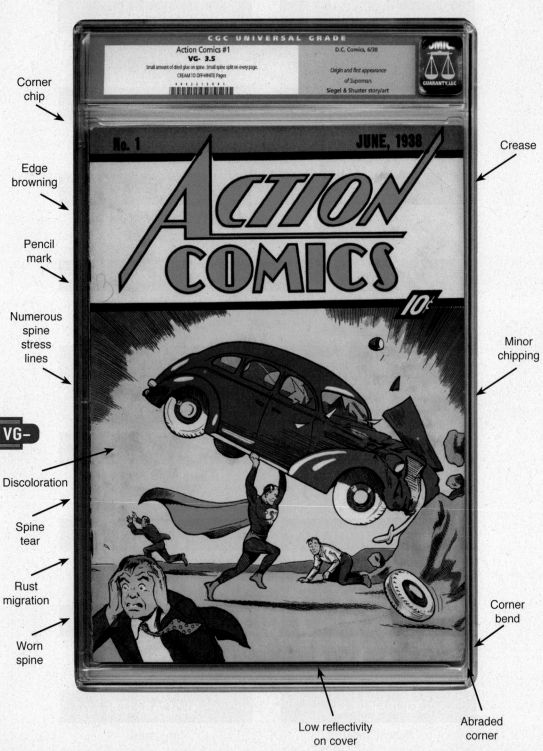

Corner chip

Edge browning

Pencil mark

Numerous spine stress lines

VG−

Discoloration

Spine tear

Rust migration

Worn spine

Crease

Minor chipping

Corner bend

Abraded corner

Low reflectivity on cover

Captain America Comics #2, April 1941. © Marvel Characters, Inc.
Obvious defects: Browning on edges. Spine crease.
Hidden defects: Mild soiling.
Page Quality: Tan to cream.

Inaccurate trimming

Corner chipping

Edge wear

Tear

Spine crease

Cover loose

Spine stress

Chip

Browning on edge

VG–

Edge chipping

Abraded corner

Mild soiling

Blunted corner

Donald Duck #147, 1947. © Walt Disney Company.
Obvious defects: Worn spine. Oxidation shadow on right edge of cover.
Hidden defects: Numerous interior pages have frayed edges.
Page Quality: Cream.

Abraded corner

Oxidation shadow

Color chip

Arrival date in pencil

Rusted staple

Staple tear

VG–

Name stamp

Corner crease

Spine creases

Corner tear

Abraded corner

Multiple dimples on cover

Initials written in black ink

Corner tear

Fantastic Four #48, March 1966. © Marvel Characters, Inc.

Obvious defects: Bindery defect of front cover wrapped 1/4" onto back.

Hidden defects: Frayed edges on some interior pages.

Page Quality: Off-white to white.

Abraded corner

Creases

Loose chip

Corner chip and creases

Front cover image wraps onto back by 1/4"

Numerous spine creases

VG–

Chip

Reading crease

Crease with color loss

Crease

(3.0) GOOD / VERY GOOD (GD/VG)

GRADE DESCRIPTION:
A used comic book showing some substantial wear. A copy in this grade has all pages and covers, although there may be small pieces missing. Still a reasonably desirable copy and completely readable.

COVER/EXTERIOR - Cover shows significant wear, and may be loose or even detached at one staple. Cover reflectivity is very low. Can have a book-length crease and/or minor dimples. Corners may be blunted, abraded or even rounded. Store stamps, name stamps, arrival dates, initials, etc. have no effect on this grade. An accumulation of discoloration, fading, foxing, and even minor to moderate soiling is allowed. A triangle from 1/4" to 1/2" can be missing out of the corner or edge; a missing 1/8" to 1/4" square is also acceptable. Tape and other amateur repair may be present.

SPINE - Moderate roll likely. May have a spine split of anywhere from 1" to 1-1/2".

STAPLES - Staples may be rusted or replaced. Minor to moderate staple tears and moderate stress lines may be present, as well as some rust migration.

PAPER/INTERIOR - Paper is brown but not brittle. A minor to moderate acidic odor can be detectable. Centerfold may be loose or detached at one staple. Minor to moderate interior tears may be present.

NOTE: Certain defects are allowed if other defects are not present.

BINDERY/PRINTING

do not affect grade

COVER INKS/GLOSS

very low reflectivity

COVER WEAR

significant wear, loose,
may be detached at one staple

COVER CREASES

book-length creases,
minor dimples

SOILING, STAINING

accumulation of discoloration,
fading, foxing,
minor to moderate soiling

DATES/STAMPS

do not affect grade

SPINE ROLL

moderate roll likely

SPINE SPLIT

up to 1-1/2" split

STAPLES

rusted or replaced

STAPLE TEARS

minor to moderate
tears

RUST MIGRATION

some migration

STRESS LINES

moderate lines

CORNERS

blunted or abraded,
may be slightly rounded

CENTERFOLD

loose or detached at one staple

INTERIOR TEARS

minor to moderate tears

GD/VG

PAPER QUALITY/COLOR

brown, not brittle

ACID ODOR

minor to moderate odor

MISSING PIECES

1/4" to 1/2" triangle,
1/8" to 1/4" square

AMATEUR REPAIRS

may be present

COUPON CUT

none allowed

READABILITY

preserved

Nickel Comics #1, May 1940. © Fawcett Publications.
Obvious defects: Abraded spine with foxing.
Hidden defects: Foxing on interior pages.
Page Quality: Cream.

Corner tear

Chip

Chip

Chip

Corner chip

Cover hole

Foxing

Chips

Color faded area

Abraded spine

GD/VG

Loose piece

Abraded corner

Foxing

Foxing

Bulletman #1, Summer 1941. © Fawcett Publications.
Obvious defects: Numerous spine chips and abrasions. Browning on edges.
Hidden defects: Loose interior pages.
Page Quality: Tan to cream.

Back cover spine

Abraded corner

Minor soiling

Chip

Loose and missing pieces

Spine chips

Browning on edge

Spine chips

Color flecks

GD/VG

Abraded spine

Mis-trimmed cover

Browning on edge

More Fun Comics #103, May-June 1945. © DC Comics.
Obvious defects: Excessive spine wear. Rusted staples.
Hidden defects: None.
Page Quality: Off-white.

Corner tear

Stains in title logo

Soilng

Crease

Rust migration

Rusted staple

Worn spine

Pencil mark

Rusted staple

GD/VG

Tear

Abraded corner

Creases

Rounded corner

Peter Porkchops #2, Jan-Feb. 1950. © DC Comics.

Obvious defects: Spine is damaged, especially at the bottom.
Numerous small tears on the right edge of the cover.

Hidden defects: Stains on the inside front cover show through to the front.

Page Quality: Off-white.

Reading crease

Numerous tears

Corner fold

Corner chip

Staple tears

Spine tear

Split spine

52 BIG PAGES

PETER PORKCHOPS

10¢

NO.2
JAN.FEB.

PETER PORKCHOPS'
DANCING SCHOOL

IMMEDIATE RESULTS
GUARANTEED!

Tear

Tear

Tear

Tear

GD/VG

Tear

Foxing

Foxing

Funny Folks #2, June-July 1946. © DC Comics.

Obvious defects: Numerous chips missing from cover's top edge. Cover is mis-wrapped, leaving unprinted area on right edge. Staples are rusty, with rust migration on back cover staples.

Hidden defects: None.

Page Quality: Cream to off-white.

Abraded corner

Creases

Numerous chips missing

Missing chip

Black ink writing

Color scrape

Color scrapes

Small chips off cover

Color scrape

GD/VG

Abraded corner

Frayed edge

Mis-wrapped cover

Funny Folks #2
(Back cover)

Rusted
staple

Rusted
staple
with rust
migration

GD/VG

Amazing Adventures #1, November 1950. © Ziff-Davis Publishing Co.
Obvious defects: Numerous chips and tears near spine.
Hidden defects: None.
Page Quality: Off-white.

Rounded corner

Corner chip

Crease

Chip

Worn spine

GD/VG

Chips

Spine piece missing

Chipping all along edge

Corner chip

Eddie Stanky, Baseball Hero #1, 1951. © Fawcett Publications.
Obvious defects: Center crease on cover.
Hidden defects: Center crease on interior pages.
Page Quality: Off-white to white.

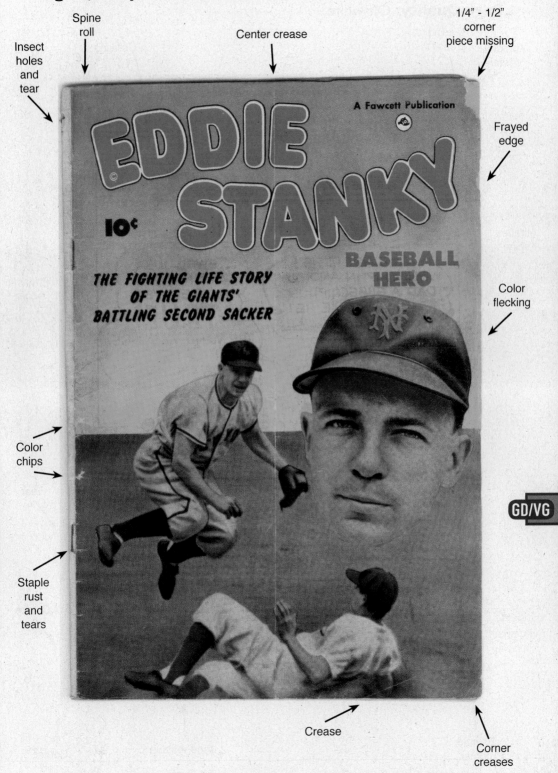

Spine roll

Center crease

1/4" - 1/2" corner piece missing

Insect holes and tear

Frayed edge

Color flecking

Color chips

Staple rust and tears

Crease

Corner creases

GD/VG

Archie's Pals 'n' Gals #1, 1952-53. © Archie Publications.
Obvious defects: Squarebound spine missing bottom half inch.
Reading creases.
Hidden defects: None.
Page Quality: Off-white.

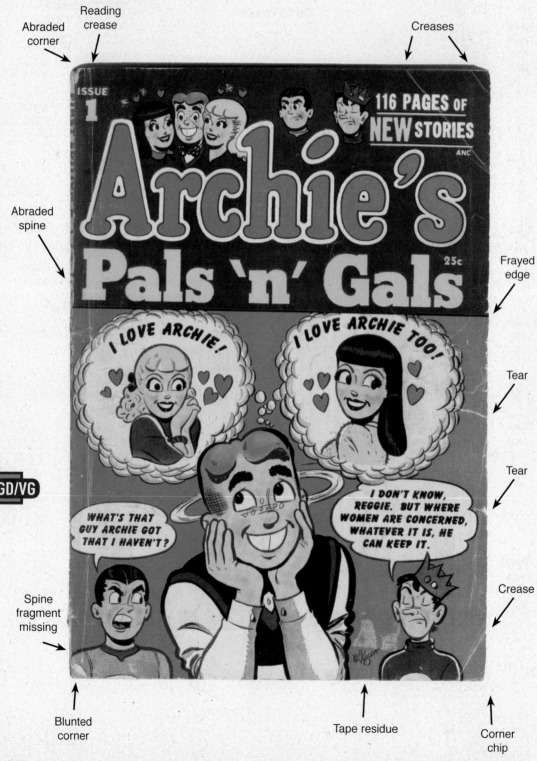

Abraded corner

Reading crease

Creases

Abraded spine

Frayed edge

Tear

Tear

GD/VG

Crease

Spine fragment missing

Blunted corner

Tape residue

Corner chip

Detective Comics #283, September 1960. © DC Comics.
Obvious defects: Frayed right edge on cover.
Hidden defects: Pencil marks on interior pages.
Page Quality: Off-white.

Corner
chip out

Comic has moderate
acidic odor

Loose
piece
still
attached

Chip
out

Frayed
edge

Numerous
spine
creases

GD/VG

Staple
tears

Abraded
corner

Edge wear

Corner
creases

Showcase #14, May-June 1958. © DC Comics.
Obvious defects: Numerous creases on spine and edges.
Hidden defects: Back cover poorly trimmed.
Page Quality: Off-white to white.

Abraded corner

Numerous stress lines

Corner creases

Abraded spine

Staple tears

Numerous spine stress lines

GD

Corner chip out

Significant wear on cover. Very low reflectivity

Edge creases

Corner creases

Showcase #14
(Back cover)

Poorly trimmed
back cover

Amateur
repairs
evident

GD

(2.5) GOOD + (GD+)

GRADE DESCRIPTION:

This grade shows substantial wear but less than a good copy. Comics in this grade have all pages and covers, although there may be small pieces missing. Books in this grade are commonly creased, scuffed, abraded, soiled, but still completely readable.

COVER/EXTERIOR - Cover shows significant wear and may even be loose or partially detached. Nearly none to no reflectivity. Store stamp, name stamp, arrival date and initials are permitted. Near book-length creases and dimples may be present. Blunted, abraded or slightly rounded corners are common. Moderate soiling, staining, discoloration and foxing may be present. The largest piece allowed missing from the front or back cover is usually 1/2" triangle or a 1/4" square. Tape and other forms of amateur repair are common in Silver Age and older books.

SPINE - Moderate roll is likely. May have up to an 1-1/2" split with accumulation of color breaks.

STAPLES - Staples may be rusted or replaced. Moderated staple tears and stress lines may be present, as well as some rust migration.

GD+

PAPER/INTERIOR: Paper brown but not brittle. A minor to moderate acidic odor may be present. Centerfold may be loose or detached. Moderate interior tears may be present.

A comic book in Good+ condition can have a moderate to large accumulation of defects but still preserves readability with all coupons still intact.

NOTE: Certain defects are allowed if other defects are not present.

BINDERY/PRINTING

do not affect grade

COVER INKS/GLOSS

nearly no reflectivity
to no reflectivity

COVER WEAR

significant wear,
loose or detached at staples

COVER CREASES

book-length creases
with minor dimples

SOILING, STAINING

accumulation of discoloration,
fading, foxing,
or moderate soiling

DATES/STAMPS

do not affect grade

SPINE ROLL

moderate roll likely

SPINE SPLIT

up to 1-1/2" split with
accumulation of color breaks

STAPLES

rusted or replaced

STAPLE TEARS

moderate tears

RUST MIGRATION

some migration

STRESS LINES

moderate lines

CORNERS

bluunted, abraded or slightly
rounded corners

CENTERFOLD

loose or detached

INTERIOR TEARS

moderate tears

PAPER QUALITY/COLOR

brown, not brittle

ACID ODOR

minor to moderate odor

GD+

MISSING PIECES

1/4" - 1/2" triangle,
1/8" - 1/4" square

AMATEUR REPAIRS

may be present

COUPON CUT

none allowed

READABILITY

preserved

Boy Commandos #1, Winter 1942-43. © DC Comics.
Obvious defects: Spine roll. Rusted staples. Mold on back cover.
Hidden defects: Brittle pages.
Page Quality: Brown, brittle.

Spine roll

Edge tears

Foxing

Rusted staple

Rusted staple

Edge tear

GD+

Boy Commandos #1
(Back cover)

Mold

Close-up of mold

Whiz Comics #9, October 1940. © Fawcett Publications.
Obvious defects: Cover corner piece missing.
Hidden defects: Blunted edges on some interior pages.
Page Quality: Tan to cream.

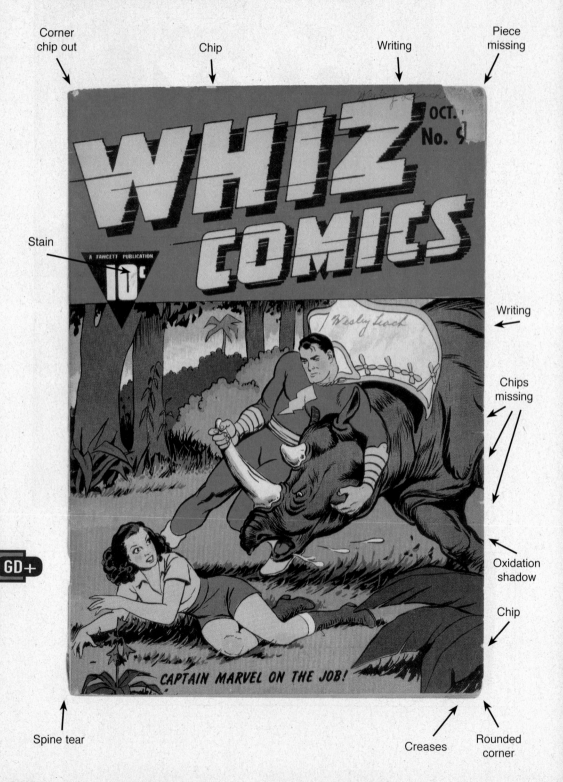

Corner chip out

Chip

Writing

Piece missing

Stain

Writing

Chips missing

Oxidation shadow

Chip

GD+

Spine tear

Creases

Rounded corner

Looney Tunes and Merrie Melodies Comics #3, January 1942. © Warner Bros.
Obvious defects: Water stain with paper residue attached.
Hidden defects: None.
Page Quality: Cream to off-white.

Abraded corner

Reading crease

Crease

Rounded corner

Loose piece

Numerous spine tears and creases

Tear with missing chip

Water stain from glass

GD+

Spine creases

Creases

Corner chip

Air Ace Vol. 2 #1, January 1944. © Street and Smith Publications.
Obvious defects: Corner piece missing. Ink smudges and pencil marks.
Hidden defects: Some interior pages have brittle edges.
Page Quality: Tan to cream.

Edge tear   Edge tear   Ink smudges   Pencil mark   Corner chip

Ink smudges

Pencil marks

GD+

Corner chip   Frayed edge   1/2" corner piece missing

The Flash #129, June 1962. © DC Comics.
Obvious defects: Large diagonal cover crease. Large piece missing from lower left cover
Hidden defects: Spine roll.
Page Quality: Off-white.

Rounded corner

Long diagonal crease

Edge tear

Abraded spine

Tear

Chip

Split spine

Missing corner piece

Loose piece

Wrinkled area

Corner creases

GD+

Tales To Astonish #13, November 1960. © Marvel Characters, Inc.
Obvious defects: Multiple creases which break color.
Hidden defects: Interior foxing.
Page Quality: Off-white.

Abraded corner

Edge tears

Corner creases

Light red ink

Spine creases

Spine creases

Abrasion

Abrasion

GD+

Small spine tears

Multiple creases

Tales To Astonish #13
(Back cover)

Torn corner

Foxing

Foxing

Spine tear

GD+

(2.0) GOOD (GD)

GRADE DESCRIPTION:

This grade shows substantial wear; often considered a "reading copy." Comics in this grade have all pages and covers, although there may be small pieces missing. Books in this grade are commonly creased, scuffed, abraded, soiled, but still completely readable.

COVER/EXTERIOR - Cover shows significant wear and may even be detached. Nearly no reflectivity to no reflectivity. Store stamp, name stamp, arrival date and initials are permitted. Book-length creases and dimples may be present. Rounded corners are more common. Moderate soiling, staining, discoloration and foxing may be present. The largest piece allowed missing from the front or back cover is usually a 1/2" triangle or a 1/4" square, although some Silver Age books such as 1960s Marvels have had the price corner box clipped from the top left front cover and may be considered Good if they would otherwise have graded higher. Tape and other forms of amateur repair are common in Silver Age and older books.

SPINE - Definite roll likely. May have up to a 2" spine split.

STAPLES - Staples may be degraded, replaced or missing. Moderate staple tears and stress lines are common, as well as rust migration.

PAPER/INTERIOR - Paper is brown but not brittle. A moderate acidic odor may be present. Centerfold may be loose or detached. Moderate interior tears may be present.

GD

Some of the most collectable comic books are rarely found in better than GOOD condition. Most collectors consider this the lowest collectable grade because comic books in lesser condition are often incomplete and/or brittle. Traditionally, collectors have sometimes found it difficult to differentiate this grade from the next lower grade, FAIR. This task can be simplified if one remembers that a comic book in GOOD condition can have a moderate to large accumulation of defects but still preserves readability.

NOTE: Certain defects are allowed if other defects are not present.

BINDERY/PRINTING

do not affect grade

COVER INKS/GLOSS

nearly no reflectivity to
no reflectivity

COVER WEAR

significant wear,
may be detached

COVER CREASES

book-length creases with minor to
moderate creases, dimples

SOILING, STAINING

discoloration, fading, foxing,
or moderate soiling

DATES/STAMPS

do not affect grade

SPINE ROLL

roll likely

SPINE SPLIT

up to 2" split

STAPLES

degraded, replaced
or missing

STAPLE TEARS

moderate tears

RUST MIGRATION

may have migration

STRESS LINES

lines are common

CORNERS

rounded corners more common

CENTERFOLD

loose or detached

INTERIOR TEARS

moderate tears

PAPER QUALITY/COLOR

brown, not brittle

ACID ODOR

moderate odor

MISSING PIECES

1/2" triangle, 1/4" square

AMATEUR REPAIRS

common in Silver Age and older

COUPON CUT

none allowed

READABILITY

preserved

GD

Superman #2, Fall 1939. © DC Comics.
Obvious defects: Tape on spine. Browning near edges.
Hidden defects: Brittle interior pages.
Page Quality: Tan to cream.

Amateur glue repair

Crease

Rounded corner

Tape on spine

Browning

Chip missing

Stains

Browning

Low reflectivity

GD

Spine split

Tear

Color flecks and chips

Rounded corner

Captain Marvel Adventures #5, December 1941. © Fawcett Publications.
Obvious defects: Two pieces missing from cover.
Hidden defects: None.
Page Quality: Cream.

Corner
chip out

Piece missing

Color
scrape

Spine
loose at
staple

Animal
chew
extends
through
3/4 of all
pages

GD

Piece missing

Corner
crease

Comics on Parade #35, January 1942. © United Features Syndicate.
Obvious defects: Out of register printing.
Hidden defects: Color flecking near spine. Rounded corners on interior pages.
Page Quality: Tan to cream.

Abraded corner

Pencil writing

Foxing

Browning

Out of register

Color chip

Staple wear

Edge wrinkle

Loose chips

Spine tear

Color flecking

GD

Abraded area

Rounded corner

Little Al of the F.B.I. #10, 1950. © Ziff-Davis.
Obvious defects: Rolled spine, worn edges and numerous creasings.
Hidden defects: Cover is wrinkled with brittle pages inside.
Page Quality: Cream.

Abraded corner

Dirt smudge and ink on title letters

Ink writing on cover

Heavy edge wear

Corner chip

Edge tear

Spine tear

Long 4" crease

Spine tears

Color flecks

Tears around a rusted staple

Spine roll

Long center crease

Walt Disney's Comics & Stories #146, November 1952. © Walt Disney Co.
Obvious defects: Numerous cover creases with color loss.
Hidden defects: Minor spine roll.
Page Quality: Off-white to white.

Cover creasing heaviest along spine

Pen writing

Pencil writing

Stress marks

Blunted edge

Pencil writing and ink marks

Rubbing and stress marks

Significant cover wear

Slightly miswrapped cover

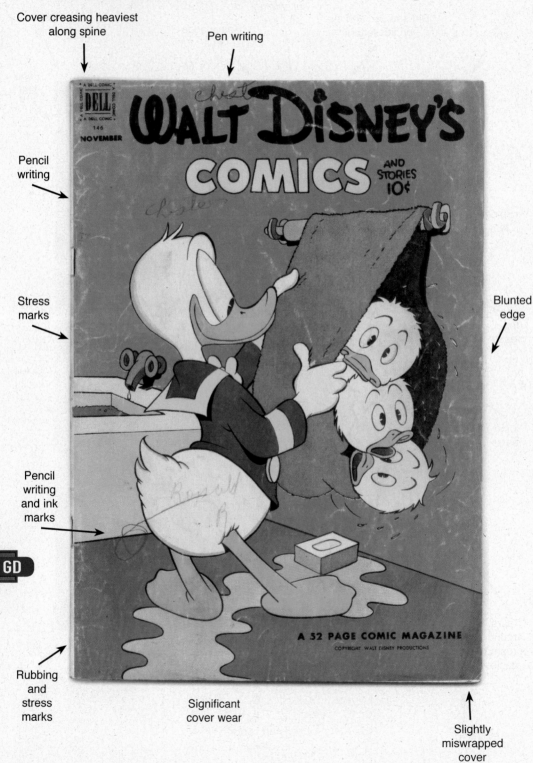

GD

Showcase #17, Nov.-Dec. 1958. © DC Comics.
Obvious defects: Spine is abraded and wrinkled. Numerous creases.
Color loss in bottom left corner.
Hidden defects: Interior pages wrinkled.
Page Quality: Off-white.

Rounded
corner

Numerous edge
tears and creases

Long crease

Corner
creases

Worn
spine

Numerous
stress
lines

Staple
tears

GD

Loose
piece

Spine
tear

Reading
creases

Color missing

Corner
creases

Mystery in Space #71, November 1961. © DC Comics.
Obvious defects: Numerous creases and wrinkles.
Hidden defects: Light soiling. Pen indentations.
Page Quality: Off-white to white.

Abraded corner

Wrinkled edge

Center crease

Crease

Abraded spine

Spine tear

Small tears along edge

Corner crease

Corner chip with color flecking

Crease

Color flecking

Poorly trimmed edge

Rounded corner

GD

Life With Archie #50, June 1966. © Archie Publications.
Obvious defects: Cover is detached. Cover has light soiling and stress lines.
Hidden defects: None.
Page Quality: Cream to off-white.

Rounded corner

Color flecking

Crease with color loss

Corner chip

Abraded staple holes

Numerous spine tears

Creases

Color scrape

Stains

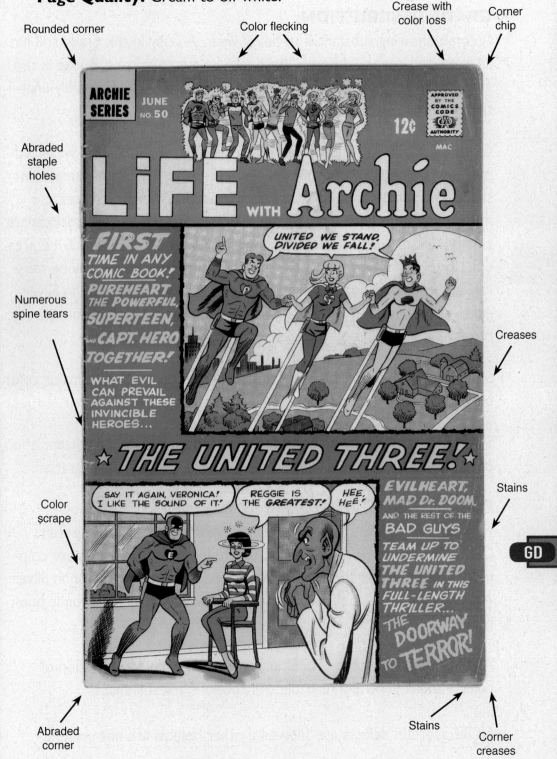

Abraded corner

Stains

Corner creases

GD

(1.8) GOOD – (GD-)

GRADE DESCRIPTION:

A comic showing substantial to heavy wear. A copy in this grade still has all pages and covers, although there may be pieces missing. Books in this grade are commonly creased, scuffed, abraded, soiled, and possibly unattractive, but still readable.

COVER/EXTERIOR - Cover shows significant to considerable wear and may even be detached. Nearly none to no reflectivity. Store stamp, name stamp, arrival date and initials are permitted. Book-length creases and major dimpling may be present. Blunted, abraded or rounded corners are common. Significant discoloration, staining, foxing and soiling may be present. Up to 1/2" triangle or a 1/4" square of the back cover may be missing. Tape and other forms of amateur repair are very common in Silver Age and older books, although tape should never be used in comic book repair.

SPINE - Roll is more likely. May have spine split up to 2" with major color breaks.

STAPLES - Staples may be degraded, replaced or missing. An accumulation of staple tears and stress lines are common, as well as rust migration.

PAPER/INTERIOR: Paper is brown and may be beginning to show very slight brittleness around the edges. Acidic odor may be present.

GD-

Centerfold may be loose or detached. Moderate interior tears are common. Tape and other forms of amateur repair are very common in Silver Age and older books, although tape should never be used in comic book repair.

A comic book in Good– condition can have a large accumulation of defects and is generally readable. All coupons are still intact.

NOTE: Certain defects are allowed if other defects are not present.

BINDERY/PRINTING

do not affect grade

COVER INKS/GLOSS

nearly no reflectivity
to no reflectivity

COVER WEAR

signifcant considerable wear,
may be detached

COVER CREASES

creases, tears, and folds;
major dimpling

SOILING, STAINING

significant discoloration, fading,
foxing and soiling

DATES/STAMPS

do not affect grade

SPINE ROLL

roll more likely

SPINE SPLIT

up to 2" split with
major color breaks

STAPLES

degraded, replaced,
one missing

STAPLE TEARS

accumulation of
moderate tears

RUST MIGRATION

may have migration

STRESS LINES

lines are common

CORNERS

rounded corners
common

CENTERFOLD

loose or detached

INTERIOR TEARS

moderate tears

PAPER QUALITY/COLOR

brown, very slight brittleness

ACID ODOR

moderate odor

GD–

MISSING PIECES

up to 1/2" triangle,
1/4" square

AMATEUR REPAIRS

very common in
Silver Age and older

COUPON CUT

none allowed

READABILITY

generally preserved

Modern Love #2, Aug.-Sept. 1949. © William M. Gaines.
Obvious defects: Severely rusted staples. Water damage on spine.
Abundant soiling.
Hidden defects: Loose centerfold and interior pages.
Page Quality: Tan to cream.

Abraded corner

Spine roll

Crease

Rounded corners

Rusted staple with rust migration

Chip

Foxing

Worn edge

Rusted staple

GD–

Blunted corner

Modern Love #2
(Back cover)

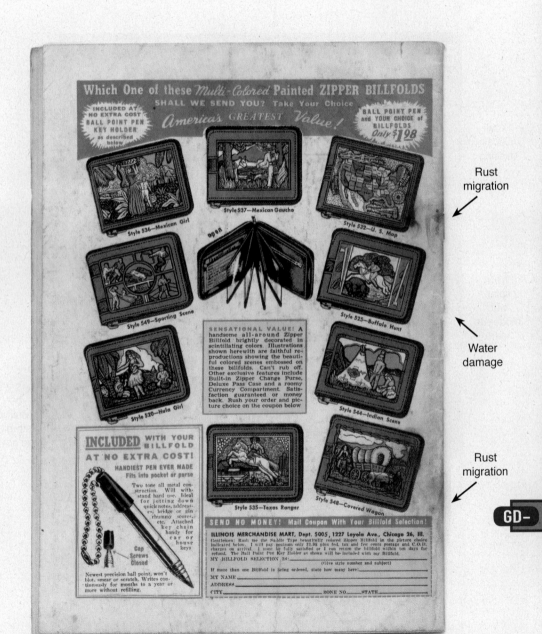

Rust
migration

Water
damage

Rust
migration

Walt Disney's Comics and Stories #153, June 1953. © Walt Disney Company.
Obvious defects: Worn spine and abundant creases.
Hidden defects: Cover detached at upper staple.
Note: Subscription label does not affect grade.
Page Quality: Cream to off-white.

Abraded corner

Length-wide crease

Small pieces missing

Worn spine with moderate tears

GD−

Multiple dimples on cover

Corner chips missing

Heavy cover wear

Corner chips missing

Peanuts #9, May-July 1961. © United Features Syndicate.
Obvious defects: Substantial writing on cover. Piece missing
Hidden defects: Slightly rusted staple.
Page Quality: Off-white.

Slightly
miswrapped
cover

Slightly
rusted
staple

Numerous
stress
lines

Rust
migration

Piece
missing

GD–

Moderate
soiling

Light
crease

(1.5) **FAIR / GOOD** (FR/GD)

GRADE DESCRIPTION:

A comic showing substantial to heavy wear. A copy in this grade still has all pages and covers, although there may be pieces missing. Books in this grade are commonly creased, scuffed, abraded, soiled, and possibly unattractive, but still generally readable.

COVER/EXTERIOR - Cover shows considerable wear and may be detached. Nearly no reflectivity to no reflectivity remaining. Store stamp, name stamp, arrival date and initials are permitted. Book-length creases, tears and folds may be present. Rounded corners are increasingly common. Soiling, staining, discoloration and foxing is generally present. Up to 1/10 of the back cover may be missing. Tape and other forms of amateur repair are increasingly common in Silver Age and older books.

SPINE - Roll is common. May have a spine split between 2" and 2/3 the length of the book.

STAPLES - Staples may be degraded, replaced or missing. Staple tears and stress lines are common, as well as rust migration.

PAPER/INTERIOR - Paper is brown and may show brittleness around the edges. Acidic odor may be present. Centerfold may be loose or detached. Interior tears are common.

NOTE: Certain defects are allowed if other defects are not present.

BINDERY/PRINTING

do not affect grade

COVER INKS/GLOSS

nearly no reflectivity
to no reflectivity

COVER WEAR

considerable wear,
may be detached

COVER CREASES

creases, tears, and folds

SOILING, STAINING

generally present

DATES/STAMPS

do not affect grade

SPINE ROLL

roll common

SPINE SPLIT

between 2" and 2/3 length

STAPLES

degraded, replaced,
one missing

STAPLE TEARS

tears are common

RUST MIGRATION

may have migration

STRESS LINES

lines are common

CORNERS

rounded corners
very common

CENTERFOLD

loose or detached

INTERIOR TEARS

tears are common

PAPER QUALITY/COLOR

brown, edges show brittleness

ACID ODOR

odor present

FR/GD

MISSING PIECES

up to 1/10 of the
back cover missing

AMATEUR REPAIRS

increasingly common in
Silver Age and older

COUPON CUT

none allowed

READABILITY

generally preserved

Action Comics #17, October 1939. © DC Comics.
Obvious defects: 3 inch tear out from spine. Browning on cover edges.
Hidden defects: Spine split from bottom to lower staple.
Page Quality: Brown to tan.

Corner chip out

Corner creases

Rounded corner

Browning

Corner crease

Browning

Writing

Frayed spine

Frayed edge

Color chip out

3 inch tear

Edge wear

FR/GD

2" spine split

Rounded corner

Special Edition Comics #1, August 1940. © Fawcett Publications.
Obvious defects: Cover pieces missing and cover soiling.
Hidden defects: Mold spots and staining.
Page Quality: Cream.

Chip

Corner creases

Mold and stains

Piece missing

Rusty staples

Worn spine

Holes and tears

Mold spots

Piece out

Browning

Crease

FR/GD

Corner piece missing

Tear

Pieces out

New York World's Fair Comics, 1940. © DC Comics.
Obvious defects: Squarebound spine is heavily worn.
Hidden defects: Brittle pages.
Page Quality: Brown to tan.

Chip missing

Numerous creases

Chip missing

Abraded corner

Tape residue

Pencil marks

Cover soiling

Pencil marks

Color flecks

FR/GD

Abraded corner

Missing pieces

Numerous tears

Corner creases and abrasion

New York World's Fair Comics 1940
(Back cover)

Abraded
corner

Numerous
creases

Tape
residue

Numerous
chips
missing

Tear

Corner creases
and abrasion

Abraded
corner

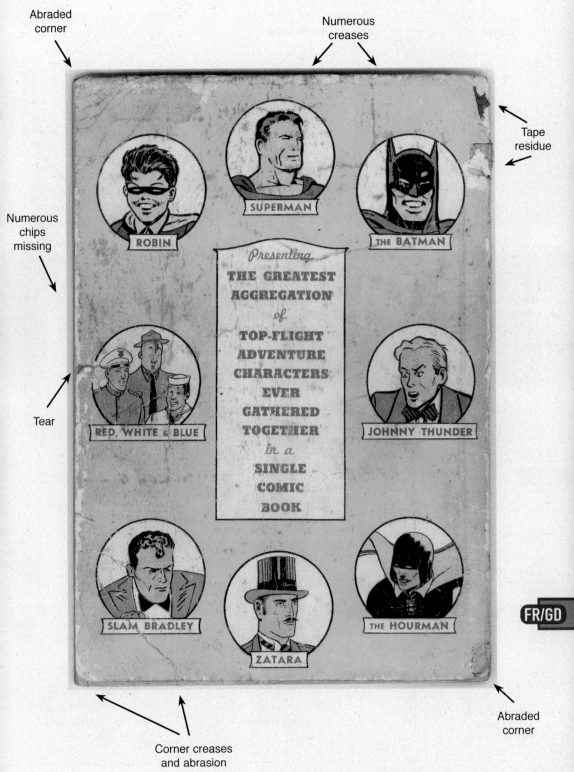

FR/GD

Air Fighters Comics Volume 2 #10, Fall 1945. © Hillman Periodicals.
Obvious defects: Worn spine and corners. Water stains on cover.
Hidden defects: Loose centerfold.
Page Quality: Cream to off-white.

Abraded corner

Frayed edge

Rounded corner

Pencil marks

Worn spine

Water stains

Tape on spine

FR/GD

Rounded corner

Long crease

Corner is worn and stained

Shock SuspenStories #17, Oct.-Nov. 1954. © William M. Gaines.

Obvious defects: Excessive cover creases and spine wear. Writing on cover.

Hidden defects: Loose interior pages.

Page Quality: Brown to tan.

Abraded corner

Writing in title logo

Corner creases

Spine tear

Heavily worn spine

Writing in center

FR/GD

Corner tear

Center crease

Piece missing

Corner creases

Poppo of the Popcorn Theatre #1, 1955. © George Gale.
Obvious defects: Large piece missing from cover.
Hidden defects: None.
Page Quality: Off-white.

Abraded corner

Large crease

Acidic odor present

Rounded corner

Staple not centered

Worn spine

Staple wear

1" piece missing

FR/GD

Rounded corner

Heavy surface wear

Corner creases

Showcase #3, July-August 1956. © DC Comics.
Obvious defects: Heavy color loss and spine damage.
Hidden defects: Wrinkled interior pages.
Page Quality: Cream to off-white.
Note: Mildew smell is obvious.

Abraded corner

Heavy color loss

Numerous stress lines

Corner creases

Staple tears

Abraded spine

Staple tears

Rounded corner

Color loss

Large crease

Corner creases

FR/GD

Super Duck #21, August 1958. © Archie Publications.
Obvious defects: Excessive staining and bundling creases
Hidden defects: Loose inner pages.
Page Quality: Tan to cream.

Corner chip out

Foxing

Bundling crease

Staining

Rat chew

Color flecks

Mold and stains

Bundling crease

Edge crease

Edge tear

Hole in cover

Abraded corner

Abraded edge

Bundling crease

Poorly trimmed interior pages

Corner crease

FR/GD

The Avengers #9, October 1964. © Marvel Characters, Inc.

Obvious defects: Stress lines at top of cover. Abraded corners. Spine split. 1/10th of the back cover missing.

Hidden defects: Brittle pages.

Page Quality: Brown to tan.

Abraded corner

Numerous stress lines

Corner creases

1 1/2" spine split

Spine creases

Foxing

Rusty staple

FR/GD

Abraded corner

Edge tears

Multiple dimples and stress lines on cover

Corner creases

The Incredible Hulk #103, May, 1968. © Marvel Characters, Inc.
Obvious defects: Worn spine and ragged edges.
Hidden defects: Loose interior pages.
Page Quality: Cream to off-white.

Abraded corner

Reading creases

Numerous stress lines

Soiling on white title letters

Loose interior pages

Foxing

Issue no. digit cut from cover

Large dimple at center of cover

Numerous stress lines

Numerous stress lines

Tears around staple

FR/GD

2 1/2" long crease

Abraded corner

Chipping

Abraded corner

Issue no. digit cut from cover

The Incredible Hulk #103 (Back cover)

2" tear

Abraded corner

Abraded corner

FR/GD

(1.0)   **FAIR**   (FR)

GRADE DESCRIPTION:

A copy in this grade shows heavy wear. Some collectors consider this the lowest collectible grade because comic books in lesser condition are usually incomplete and/or brittle. Comics in this grade are usually soiled, faded, ragged and possibly unattractive. This is the last grade in which a comic remains generally readable.

COVER/EXTERIOR - Cover may be detached, and inks have lost all reflectivity. Creases, tears and/or folds are prevalent. Corners are commonly rounded or absent. Soiling and staining is present. Books in this condition generally have all pages and most of the covers, although there may be up to 1/4 of the front cover missing or no back cover, but not both. Tape and other forms of amateur repair are more common.

SPINE - Spine roll is more common; spine split can extend up to 2/3 the length of the book.

STAPLES - Staples may be missing or show rust and discoloration. An accumulation of staple tears and stress lines may be present, as well as rust migration.

PAPER/INTERIOR - Paper is brown and may show brittleness around the edges but not in the central portion of the pages. Acidic odor may be present. Accumulation of interior tears. Chunks may be missing. The centerfold may be missing if readability is generally preserved (although there may be difficulty). Coupons may be cut.

Demand for comics in this grade from the 1930s through the 1960s is high, but FR books should be examined for brittleness. Some POOR condition books have missing pages replaced with pages from a different issue or title to give the appearance of a FAIR book.

BINDERY/PRINTING
do not affect grade

COVER INKS/GLOSS
no reflectivity

COVER WEAR
may be detached

COVER CREASES
creases, tears and folds

SOILING, STAINING
present

DATES/STAMPS
do not affect grade

SPINE ROLL
roll more common

SPINE SPLIT
up to 2/3 length

STAPLES
may be missing

STAPLE TEARS
accumulation
of tears

RUST MIGRATION
may have migration

STRESS LINES
accumulation of lines

CORNERS
rounded or absent

CENTERFOLD
may be missing

INTERIOR TEARS
accumulation of tears

PAPER QUALITY/COLOR
brown, edges show brittleness

ACID ODOR
odor present

MISSING PIECES
up to 1/4 front cover or
entire back cover, and/or chunks

AMATEUR REPAIRS
more common

COUPON CUT
coupon may be cut

READABILITY
generally preserved to difficulty

FR

More Fun Comics #15, November 1936. © DC Comics.

Obvious defects: Poorly trimmed right edge. Staples replaced, center-fold detached. Coupon cut inside. No reflectivity on cover.

Hidden defects: Color touch.

Page Quality: Tan to cream.

Frayed edge

Poorly retrimmed edge

3" spine split

Untrimmed interior page

Soiling

Ink stains

Soiling

Staples replaced

FR

Frayed edge

Crease

Corner creases

Abraded corner

Color
touch

Color touch

More Fun Comics #15
(Back cover)

FR

Walt Disney's Comics and Stories #1, October 1940. © Walt Disney Company.
Obvious defects: Cover chunk missing. Rusted staples. Coupon cut on back cover.
Hidden defects: Torn interior pages. Water damage on back cover.
Page Quality: Tan to cream.

Chunk missing

Back cover spine

Multiple spine stress lines

Rusted staple

Spine chips

Rusted staple

Large stain

FR

True Comics #2, June 1941. © The Parents' Institute.
Obvious defects: Taped spine. Edge chips and tears. Center crease.
Hidden defects: None.
Page Quality: Brown to tan.

Tape along
spine

Chips

Worn
spine

Tears

Chips

Tape along
spine

Some brittleness
along edge

6" crease

Rounded
corner

FR

Tom & Jerry Comics #76, November 1940. © Loew's Inc.
Obvious defects: Heavy creasing.
Hidden defects: Vertical tears on top of interior pages
Page Quality: Cream to off-white.

Abraded corner

Worn spine

Staple is rusty and not centered

Heavy creases

Heavy creases and crumpling

Heavy creases and crumpling

FR

Heavy creases

Heavily blunted edge

Heavy creases

Classics Illustrated #52, October 1948. © Gilberton.
Obvious defects: Water stains. Cover piece missing.
Mold on back cover.
Hidden defects: None.
Page Quality: Brown to tan.

Water
stains

Piece
issing

Mold

Back
cover

FR

Popeye #8, August-September 1949. © King Features Syndicate.
Obvious defects: Cover staining with pieces missing. Foxing on cover.
Hidden defects: Foxing on interior pages.
Page Quality: Brown.

Staining

Missing pieces

Foxing

Spine
wear

Foxing

Missing
edge

FR

Wedding Bells #1. February 1954. © Comic Magazines.
Obvious defects: 7" spine split. Water stains on outer and inner covers.
Hidden defects: Small tears on some interior pages.
Page Quality: Off-white.

Edge tears

Browning on edges

Water spots

7" spine split

Water stain

Edge tear

1" spine split

Chips missing

FR

Corner chip

Shows slight brittleness

Stalker #1, June-July 1975. © DC Comics.
Obvious defects: Substantial cat chew damage on front and back covers.
Hidden defects: Small tears and holes on interior pages.
Page Quality: Off-white.

Crease

Corner creases

Staple tear

Numerous creases and stress lines

FR

Cat chew

Crease

Crease

Cat chew

Buffy the Vampire Slayer #9, May 1999. © 20th Century Fox.

Obvious defects: Massive cover abrasion/tear with underlying damage extending through 10 interior pages. Spine creases

Hidden defects: None.

Page Quality: Not applicable.

Massive
cover trauma

Close-up on
first interior
page

Spine
creases

Spine
creases

FR

Numerous
diagonal folds

(0.5) POOR (PR)

GRADE DESCRIPTION:

Most comic books in this grade have been sufficiently degraded to the point where there is little or no collector value; they are easily identified by a complete absence of eye appeal. Comics in this grade are brittle almost to the point of turning to dust with a touch, and are usually incomplete.

COVER/EXTERIOR - Extreme fading may render the cover almost indiscernible. May have extremely severe stains, mildew or heavy cover abrasion to the point that some cover inks are indistinct/absent. Covers may be detached with large chunks missing. Can have extremely ragged edges and extensive creasing. Corners are rounded or virtually absent. Covers may have been defaced with paints, varnishes, glues, oil, indelible markers or dyes, and may have suffered heavy water damage. Can also have extensive amateur repairs such as laminated covers.

SPINE - Extreme roll present; can have extremely ragged spines or a complete, book-length split.

STAPLES - Staples can be missing or show extreme rust and discoloration. Extensive staple tears and stress lines may be present, as well as extreme rust migration.

PAPER/INTERIOR - Paper exhibits moderate to severe brittleness (where the comic book literally falls apart when examined). Extreme acidic odor may be present. Extensive interior tears. Multiple pages, including the centerfold, may be missing that affect readability. Coupons may be cut.

PR

BINDERY/PRINTING

do not affect grade

COVER INKS/GLOSS

extreme fading

COVER WEAR

detached with chunks missing

COVER CREASES

extreme creases, ragged edges

SOILING, STAINING

extreme soiling, staining and discoloration

DATES/STAMPS

do not affect grade

SPINE ROLL

extreme roll

SPINE SPLIT

extremely ragged or completely split

STAPLES

missing or extremely rusted, discolored

STAPLE TEARS

extensive tears

RUST MIGRATION

extreme migration

STRESS LINES

many lines

CORNERS

rounded or absent

CENTERFOLD

may be missing

INTERIOR TEARS

extensive tears

PAPER QUALITY/COLOR

moderate to severe brittleness

ACID ODOR

extreme odor

MISSING PIECES

large chunks of front cover and back cover, and/or interior

AMATEUR REPAIRS

extensive repairs

COUPON CUT

coupon(s) may be cut

READABILITY

multiple pages missing

PR

Wonder Comics Vol. 2 #2, July 1945. © Great Publications.
Obvious defects: Substantial water damage and discoloration. Text from other publication transfered onto cover. Cover surface is wrinkled.
Hidden defects: Water damage and discoloration on inside pages.
Page Quality: Brown to tan.

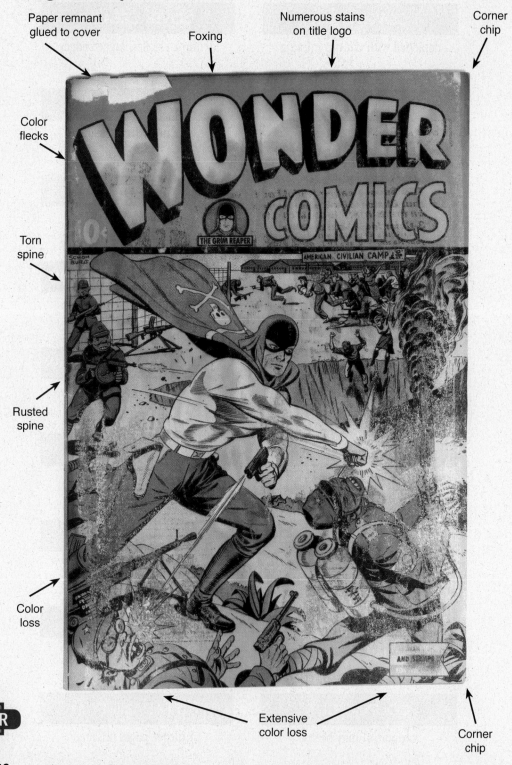

Paper remnant glued to cover

Foxing

Numerous stains on title logo

Corner chip

Color flecks

Torn spine

Rusted spine

Color loss

Extensive color loss

Corner chip

Wonder Comics Vol. 2 #2
(Back cover)

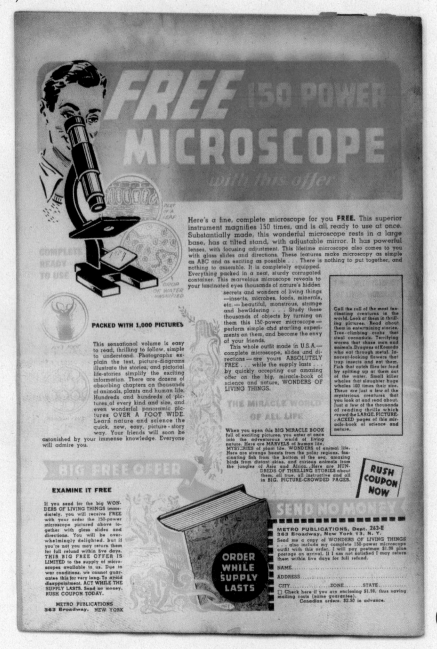

Pogo Possum #8, January-March 1952. © Walt Kelly.

Obvious defects: Substantial water damage and discoloration. Staples are rusted and rust migration is evident. Paper is wrinkled.

Hidden defects: Water damage and discoloration on inside pages.

Page Quality: Off-white.

Severely rusted staple

Severely rusted staple

Incomplete cover from water damage

Discoloration

Pogo Possum #8
(Back cover)

Discoloration

Discoloration

Incomplete cover
from water damage

(0.3) INCOMPLETE (INC)

GRADE DESCRIPTION:

These designations are only used for the purpose of authentication. Numerous collectors and comic fans will purchase coverless comics to either read or to obtain a filler copy of a book for their collection.

Books that are coverless, but are otherwise complete, will receive a grade of 0.3, as will covers missing their interiors.

Copies in this designation typically will in most cases be beyond collectability to the majority of the hobby.

Detective Comics #27, May 1939.
© DC Comics.
Coverless.

Batman #1, Spring 1940. © DC Comics.
Obvious defects: Coverless.
Hidden defects: Spines of inner wraps are split and detached.
Page Quality: Brittle.

(0.1) INCOMPLETE (INC)

GRADE DESCRIPTION:
These designations are only used for the purpose of authentication. Numerous collectors and comic fans will purchase coverless comics to either read or to obtain a filler copy of a book for their collection.

Coverless copies that have incomplete interiors, wraps or single pages will receive a grade of 0.1, as will just front covers or just back covers.

Copies in this designation typically will in most cases be beyond collectability to the majority of the hobby.

Rare key comics and incomplete pages i.e. centerfolds are considered to be valuable by the collecting community for either restoration purposes or for individuals who just wish to own a piece of comic history.

Action Comics #1, June 1938.
© DC Comics.
Partial front cover only.

Incredible Hulk #2, July 1962. © Marvel Characters, Inc.
Obvious defects: Coverless.
Hidden defects: Most of 12th page missing.
Page Quality: Off-white to white.

THE SHRINKING SCALE - THE ATOM #25

Although this book contains a plethora of examples of most grades in the 10 Point Scale, it's difficult to visualize the degradation that takes place as you move from the best example of a given comic to the worst copy. To demonstrate this progression, we've taken one specific comic book - DC Comics' *The Atom #25* - and presented it here in conditions ranging from 9.6 to 1.0, to further illustrate how a comic might degrade as it moves down the major steps of the 10 Point Scale. Who better than the Atom to aid us with this quick visual guide to the amazing shrinking scale?

9.6 Near Mint +

The overall look is "as if it was just purchased and read once or twice."

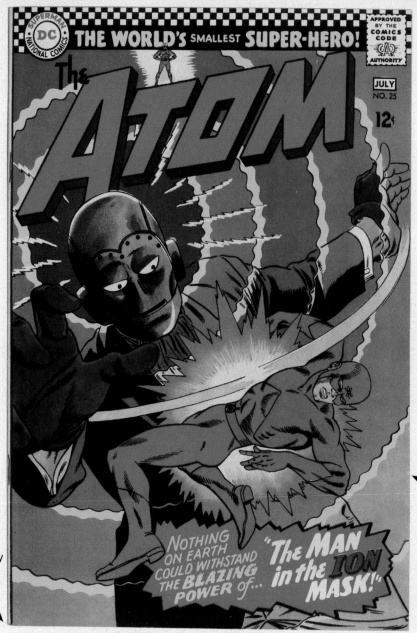

Color fleck

Almost imperceptibly blunted corner

©DC Comics

Slight staple stress lines

Slight staple stress lines

High cover reflectivity

©DC Comics

Slight edge wear

8.0 Very Fine

A comic book in this grade has the appearance of having been carefully handled.

Minor spine wear

Slight staple stress lines

Slight staple stress lines

©DC Comics

Minor spine wear

Cornerwear

1/8" light crease

Light spine wear

Staple stress lines

©DC Comics

Light spine wear along spine

1/8" light crease

Cover travelled

Corner wear

Staples not centered

Stress lines

Cover indentations

©DC Comics

Minor corner tear

Blunted corner

5.0 Very Good/Fine

An above-average but well-used comic book.

1/8" minor corner crease

Minor edge wear

Cover indentations

Staple stress lines

Spine stress

Staple stress

Spine stress

Moderate wear

Cover indentations

©DC Comics

Cover travelled

Cover inks have low reflectivity

Rounded corner

Staples not centered

Numerous spine stress lines

Edge wear

©DC Comics

Rounded corner

Surface has multiple dimples and general wear

1/4" moderate crease

Rounded corner

Cover shows
substantial wear

Rusted
staple

Edge
wear

Spine
stress
and
tears

Browning

Corner
wear

Edge wear

©DC Comics

Corner
creases

Cover has low reflectivity and
numerous dimples and overall
cover wear

Corner wear

Significant wear on cover

Rounded corner

Color fleck

Edge wear

Moderate spine wear

Pencil marks

Staple tears

Creases

1/8" color scrape

Corner wear

Cover has low reflectivity and numerous dimples

©DC Comics

Spine roll

Center crease

Cover shows heavy wear

Color fleck

Corner wear

Heavy spine wear

2" spine split

Staple tears

Edge wear

Long crease

Corner crease

©DC Comics

1 1/2" piece missing

Color scraped

Corner crease

To again demonstrate the progression of the best example of a given comic to the worst copy, we've taken Marvel Comics' *The Amazing Spider-Man* #50 - and presented it here in conditions ranging from 9.8 to 1.0, to further illustrate how a comic might degrade as it moves down the major steps of the 10 Point Scale.

9.8 Near Mint/Mint   The overall look is "as if it was just purchased."

© Marvel Characters, Inc.

Color fleck

Slightly stressed edge

Corner chip

Slight staple stress lines

Corner crease

High cover reflectivity

© Marvel Characters, Inc.

Slightly stressed edge

Slight staple stress lines

Missing staple

Corner crease

Corner chip

Crease

©Marvel Characters, Inc.

7.0 Fine/Very Fine

An above-average copy that shows minor wear ...with outstanding eye appeal.

Small edge tear

Blunted edge

Slight browning

© Marvel Characters, Inc.

Color chip

Staple stress lines

Corner chip

Minor color fleck

6.0 Fine

An above-average copy that shows minor wear but is still relatively flat and clean with no significant creasing or other serious defects.

Stains

Edge chip

Stressed edge

Spine creases

Staple not centered

Minor spine creases

Staple not centered

the AMAZING SPIDER-MAN

APPROVED BY THE COMICS CODE AUTHORITY

MARVEL COMICS GROUP

12¢ IND. 50 JULY

"SPIDER-MAN NO MORE!"

© Marvel Characters, Inc.

Full length reading crease

Color flecks

Corner chip

Corner chip

Minor edge wear

Spine crease

Cover crease

Color crease

Edge chip

Spine stress

Corner creases

© Marvel Characters, Inc.

Minor edge chips

4.0 Very Good

Significant moderate wear, not accumulated enough total defects to reduce eye appeal to the point that it is not a desirable copy.

Abraded corner

Foxing on title logo

Stressed edge

Date stamp

Color chips

Numerous spine stress lines

Color chip

Edge wear

Rounded corner

Surface has numerous color chips

© Marvel Characters, Inc.

1/4" moderate crease

Abraded corner

Center crease

Stressed edge

Staple is rusted and not centered

Edge tear

Browning

Color chip

Spine stress and tears

Staple not centered

Edge chips

Spine tear

Cover has low reflectivity

© Marvel Characters, Inc.

Corner creases

Rounded corner

Edge tear

Corner piece missing

Miswrapped cover

Moderate spine wear

Ink spots

Severe staple tear

Edge chip

Corner wear

Numerous edge chips

© Marvel Characters, Inc.

Corner wear

Cover shows heavy wear with widespread color loss

Corner wear

Corner wear

Staple tears

Heavy spine wear

Edge wear

Edge tear

Staple tears

Corner crease

Abraded corner

Edge wear

© Marvel Characters, Inc.

Abraded corner

COMIC BOOK COVER INDEX

GLOSSARY

ABRADED CORNER - Grinding of corner area caused by improper handling or storage.

ABRADED STAPLE HOLE - See Staple Hole.

AD - Abbreviation for Arrival Date.

ALLENTOWN COLLECTION - A collection discovered in 1987-88 just outside Allentown, Pennsylvania. The Allentown collection consisted of 135 Golden Age comics, characterized by high grade and superior paper quality.

ANILINE - A poisonous oily liquid, colorless when pure, obtained from coal tar and especially from nitro benzene, used in making inks, dyes and perfumes; also found in certain medicines, plastics, resins, etc. The oxidation of aniline produces quinone, which can cause transfer stains and paper discoloration. See Quinone.

APO - Abbreviation for Ad Page Out.

ARRIVAL DATE - The date written (often in pencil) or stamped on the cover of comics by either the local wholesaler, newsstand owner, or distributor. The date precedes the cover date by approximately 15 to 75 days, and may vary considerably from one locale to another or from one year to another.

Arrival Date

ASHCAN - A publisher's in-house facsimile of a proposed new title. Most ashcans have black and white covers stapled to an existing coverless comic on the inside; other ashcans are totally black and white. In modern parlance, it can also refer to promotional or sold comics, often smaller than standard comic size and usually in black and white, released by publishers to advertise the forthcoming arrival of a new title or story.

AT - Abbreviation for Archival safe Tape.

ATOM AGE - Comics published from approximately 1946-1956.

BACK-UP FEATURE - A story or character that usually appears after the main feature in a comic book; often not featured on the cover.

BAD GIRL ART - A term popularized in the early '90s to describe an attitude as well as a style of art that portrays women in a sexual and often action-oriented way.

BAXTER PAPER - A high quality, heavy, white paper used in the printing of some comics.

BBC - Abbreviation for Bottom of Back Cover.

BC - Abbreviation for Back Cover.

BI-MONTHLY - Published every two months.

BI-WEEKLY - Published every two weeks.

BINDER - The person that oversees the bindery process.

BINDER HOLES - Either two or three holes punched into the spine of comics in order to fit them into a two or three ring binder.

BINDER PERFS - See Perforations.

BINDERY - The location where comic books are assembled, trimmed, and stapled and/or glued.

BINDERY CORNER - Small, triangular spine corner tears that occur during binding.

BINDERY DEFECT - Defects associated with the binding process, including mistrimming, miswrapping, inaccurate stapling, etc.

BINDERY TRIMMING DEFECT TAXONOMY - Comic is not cut/trimmed correctly at the bindery.

Type 1 - Cover cut squarely:

1a - Cover square; rectangular part of back cover shows along spine or right edge of front or back cover.

1b - Cover square; triangular part of back cover shows along spine or right edge of front or back cover.

1c - Cover square; white unprinted rectangular strip shows along top or bottom of front or back cover, indicating that cover travelled before trimming.

1d - Cover square; white unprinted triangular strip shows along top or bottom of front or back cover, indicating that cover travelled before trimming.

Type 2 - Cover not cut squarely:

2a, 2b, 2c, 2d - Cover not square; otherwise same as above.

2e - Cover not square; no other defects.

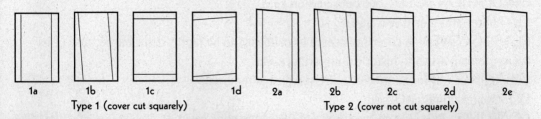

1a   1b   1c   1d   2a   2b   2c   2d   2e

Type 1 (cover cut squarely)   Type 2 (cover not cut squarely)

BLACK COVER - A comic cover where black is the predominant color. These covers more readily show wear. Because they rarely occur in high grade, black covers are in great demand by collectors.

BLUNTED CORNER - See **Corner Blunting**.

BONDAGE COVER - Usually denotes a female in bondage.

BOUND COPY - A comic that has been bound into a book. The process requires that the spine be trimmed and sometimes sewn into a book-like binding.

BOUND SHORT - See **Siamese Pages**.

BRITTLENESS - A severe condition of paper deterioration where paper loses its flexibility and thus chips and/or flakes easily.

BRN - Abbreviation for Brown.

BRONZE AGE - Comics published from approximately 1970 through 1985.

BROWNING - (1) The aging of paper characterized by the ever-increasing level of oxidation characterized by darkening; (2) The level of paper deterioration one step more severe than tanning and one step before brittleness.

BRT - Abbreviation for Brittle.

BUG - Abbreviation for Bug Chew.

CAMEO - The brief appearance of one character in the strip of another.

CBCS - Abbreviation for the certified comic book grading company, Comic Book Certification Service.

CC - Abbreviation for **Coupon Cut**.

CCA - Abbreviation for **Comics Code Authority**.

CE - Abbreviation for Canadian Edition.

CENTER CREASE - See **Subscription Copy**.

CENTERFOLD or CENTER SPREAD - The two folded pages in the center of a comic book at the terminal end of the staples.

CENTIMETER - For handy reference -

CERTIFIED GRADING - A process provided by a professional grading service that certifies a given grade for a comic and seals the book in a protective enclosure. See **Slab**.

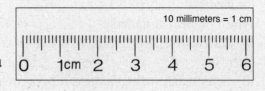

CF - Abbreviation for **Centerfold**.

CFL - Abbreviation for Centerfold Loose.

CFO - Abbreviation for Centerfold Out.

CGC - Abbreviation for the certified comic book grading company, Comics Guaranty, LLC.

CHIP CUT - Missing piece smaller than 1 square millimeter.

CHP - Abbreviation for edge Chipping.

CIRCULATION COPY - See **Subscription Copy**.

CIRCULATION FOLD - See **Subscription Fold**.

CL - Abbreviation for **Cover Loose**.

CLASSIC COVER - A cover considered by collectors to be highly desirable because of its subject matter, artwork, historical importance, etc.

CLEANING - A process in which dirt and dust is removed.

CO - Abbreviation for Cut Out.

COCKLING - Bubbling on the surface of the comic book cover.

Color touch

COLOR FLAKE - The color layer has been lost, making the white paper substrata visible. Color flakes are larger than 1 square millimeter and smaller than 2 square millimeters.

COLOR FLECK - The color layer has been lost, making the white paper substrata visible. Color flecks are no larger than 1 square millimeter.

COLOR TOUCH - A restoration process by which colored ink is used to hide color flecks, color flakes, and larger areas of missing color. Short for Color Touch-Up.

COMIC BOOK DEALER - (1) A seller of comic books; (2) One who makes a living buying and selling comic books.

COMIC BOOK REPAIR - When a tear, loose staple or centerfold has been mended without changing or adding to the original finish of the book. Repair may involve tape, glue or nylon gossamer, and is easily detected; it is considered a defect.

COMPLETE RUN - All issues of a given title.

CON - A convention or public gathering of fans.

CONDITION - The state of preservation of a comic book, often inaccurately used interchangeably with **Grade**.

CONSERVATION - The European Confederation of Conservator-Restorers' Organizations (ECCO) in its professional guidelines, defines conservation as follows: "Conservation consists mainly of direct action carried out on cultural heritage with the aim of stabilizing condition and retarding further deterioration."

CORNER BLUNTING - Compression folds at approximately

Corner blunting

45 degrees to the ends and sides of the comic, as if the corner of the comic were dropped against a hard surface.

CORNER CREASE - Permanent crease located within 1" of a corner, usually the upper right hand or lower right hand corner.

CORNER FOLD - A linear dent indicating folding within 1" of the corner, usually the upper right hand or lower right hand corner.

COSMIC AEROPLANE COLLECTION - A collection from Salt Lake City, Utah discovered by Cosmic Aeroplane Books, characterized by the moderate to high grade copies of 1930s-40s comics with pencil check marks in the margins of inside pages. It is thought that these comics were kept by a commercial illustration school and the check marks were placed beside panels that instructors wanted students to draw.

COUPON CUT or COUPON MISSING - A coupon has been neatly removed with scissors or razor blade from the interior or exterior of the comic as opposed to having been ripped out.

COVER GLOSS - The reflective quality of the cover inks.

COVERLESS - A comic with no cover attached. There is a niche demand for coverless comics, particularly in the case of hard-to-find key books otherwise impossible to locate intact. See **Remainders**.

COVER LOOSE - (1) Cover has become completely detached from the staples; (2) Cover moves around on the staples but is not completely detached.

COVER MISSING - See **Coverless**.

COVER OFF - Cover is completely detached from the staples.

COVER REATTACHED - Cover has been repaired/restored to hold staples and reattached to comic interior.

COVER TRIMMED - Cover has been reduced in size by neatly cutting away rough or damaged edges.

C/P - Abbreviation for Cleaned and Pressed.

CREASE - A fold which causes ink removal, usually resulting in a white line. See **Corner Crease** and **Reading Crease**.

CRN - Abbreviation for Corner.

CRS - Abbreviation for **Crease**.

CT - Abbreviation for **Color Touch**.

CVLS - Abbreviation for **Coverless**.

CVR - Abbreviation for Cover.

DATE STAMP - Arrival or other date printed in ink somewhere in or on the comic by use of a stamp and stamp pad. Also see **Arrival Stamp**.

DBL - Abbreviation for **Double**.

DEALER - See **Comic Book Dealer**.

DEACIDIFICATION - Several different processes that reduce acidity in paper.

DEBUT - The first time that a character appears anywhere.

DEFECT - Any fault or flaw that detracts from perfection.

DEFECTIVES - Comics which, through flaws, are imperfect.

DEFORMED STAPLE - A staple that has not penetrated all the pages properly or is bent and/or misshapen. See **Shallow Staple**.

DENT - An indentation, usually on the cover, that does not penetrate the paper nor remove any material or gloss.

DENVER COLLECTION - A collection consisting primarily of early 1940s high grade number one issues bought at auction in Pennsylvania by a Denver, Colorado dealer.

DIE-CUT COVER - A comic book cover with areas or edges pre-cut by a printer to a special shape or to create a desired effect.

DIMPLE - A surface indentation on the cover, usually caused by excessive thumb/finger pressure at the edge of the cover.

Dimples

DIRT - Inorganic and organic substances that can be removed from paper by cleaning.

DISTRIBUTOR STRIPES - Color brushed or sprayed on the edges of comic book stacks by the distributor/wholesaler to code them for expedient exchange at the sales racks. Typical colors are red, orange, yellow, green, blue, and purple. Distributor stripes are not a defect.

Distributor stripes

DMP - Abbreviation for **Dimple**.

DOG - Abbreviation for Dog-eared.

DOUBLE - A duplicate copy of the same comic book.

DOUBLE COVER - When two covers are stapled to the comic interior instead of the usual one; the exterior cover often protects the interior cover from wear and damage. This is considered a desirable situation by some collectors and may increase collector value; this is not considered a defect.

DRY PRESS - Machine used to flatten comics with rolled spines and/or folds.

DS - Abbreviation for **Dust Shadow**.

DUOTONE - Printed with black and one other color of ink. This process was common in comics printed in the 1930s.

DUST SHADOW - Darker, usually linear area at the edge of some comics stored in stacks. Some portion of the cover was not covered by the comic immediately above it and it was exposed to settling dust particles. Also see **Oxidation Shadow** and **Sun Shadow**.

EDGAR CHURCH COLLECTION - See **Mile High Collection**.

EMBOSSED COVER - A comic book cover with a pattern, shape or image pressed into the cover from the inside, creating a raised area.

ENCAPSULATION - Refers to the process of sealing certified comics in a protective plastic enclosure. Also see **Slabbing**.

ENTROPY - An inescapable fact of the physical universe, and the primary enemy of comic book collectors; basically, all ordered systems, including living things, have a tendency to break down and deteriorate over time. Fight it all you like with Mylar and backing boards, but entropy claims all things in the end.

ERASER MARK - Damage left when pencil marks are removed from the cover or inside of a comic; most identifiable when cover gloss is dulled.

EXT - Abbreviation for Extensive.

EXTENDERS - See **Staple Extenders**.

EYE APPEAL - A term which refers to the overall look of a comic book when held at approximately arm's length. A comic may have nice eye appeal yet still possess defects which reduce grade.

FADING - Loss of color due to exposure to sunlight or certain fluorescent lights which give off a moderate to high percentage of ultraviolet light.

FANNED PAGES - A condition caused by a rolled spine which progressively pulls interior pages away from the edge, creating a fanned appearance.

FANZINE - An amateur fan publication.

FC - Abbreviation for Front Cover.

FIBER FURNISH - The fibrous composition of the paper pulp.

FILE COPY - A high grade comic originating from the publisher's file; contrary to what some might believe, not all file copies are in Gem Mint condition. An arrival date on the cover of a comic does not indicate that it is a file copy, though a copyright date may.

FINGER OILS - Natural oils from the skin left when handling comics with bare hands; oil accelerates the collection of dust and dirt.

FIRST APPEARANCE - See Debut.

FLE - Abbreviation for color Flecking.

FLECK - See Color Fleck.

FOIL COVER - A comic book cover that has had a thin metallic foil hot stamped on it. Many of these "gimmick" covers date from the early '90s, and might include chromium, prism and hologram covers as well.

FOLDING ERROR - A bindery defect in which the comic is folded off-center, resulting in part of the front cover appearing on the back cover, or more seriously, part of the back cover appearing on the front cover.

FOLDED OFF-CENTER - See Folding Error.

FOLDS - Linear dents in paper that do not result in the loss of ink; not a crease.

FOLIO - A sheet of paper, folded once in the middle, making 2 leaves or 4 pages; 32 interior pages are made up of 8 folios. The centerfold, cover, and first wraparound are examples of folios.

FOUR COLOR - Series of comics produced by Dell, characterized by hundreds of different features; named after the four color process of printing. See One Shot.

FOUR COLOR PROCESS - The process of printing with the three primary colors: red (magenta), yellow, and blue (cyan) plus black.

FOX - Abbreviation for Foxing.

FOXING - Defect caused by mold growth which results in a spotting effect usually at the edges of comic books.

Foxing

FREEZE DRY - Process used to preserve wet paper before mildew damage can occur.

GATEFOLD COVER - A double-width fold-out cover.

GENRE - Categories of comic book subject matter; e.g. Science Fiction, Super-Hero, Romance, Funny Animal, Teenage Humor, Crime, War, Western, Mystery, Horror, etc.

GIVEAWAY - Type of comic book intended to be given away as a premium or promotional device instead of being sold.

GLASSES ATTACHED - In 3-D comics, the special blue and red cellophane and cardboard glasses are still attached to the comic.

GLASSES DETACHED - In 3-D comics, the special blue and red cellophane and cardboard glasses are not still attached to the comic; obviously less desirable than **Glasses Attached**.

GLUE or GLUED - Restoration and/or conservation method in which some form of glue is used to repair or reinforce a comic book defect.

GOLDEN AGE - Comics published from approximately 1938 (*Action Comics* #1) to 1945.

GRADE or GRADING - That's what this whole book is about!

GREASE PENCIL - A wax-based marker commonly used to write on cardboard.

GREASE PENCIL ON COVER - Indicates that someone marked the cover of a comic with a grease pencil, usually with a resale price or an arrival date.

GREY-TONE COVER - A cover art style in which pencil or charcoal underlies the normal line drawing, used to enhance the effects of light and shadow, thus producing a richer quality. These covers, prized by most collectors, are sometimes referred to as **Painted Covers** but are not actually painted.

HC - Abbreviation for Hardcover.

HEAVY CREASING - A crease that is longer than 2 inches.

HLP - Abbreviation for Hole Punched.

HOT STAMPING - The process of pressing foil, prism paper and/or inks on cover stock.

HRN - Abbreviation for Highest Reorder Number. This refers to a method used by collectors of Gilberton's *Classic Comics* and *Classics Illustrated* series to distinguish first editions from later printings.

IBC - Abbreviation for Inside Back Cover.

IFC - Abbreviation for Inside Front Cover.

ILLO - Abbreviation for Illustration.

IMPAINT - Another term for **Color Touch**.

INDICIA - Publishing and title information usually located at the bottom of the first page or the bottom of the inside front cover. In some pre-1938 comics and some modern comics, it is located on internal pages.

INFINITY COVER - Shows a scene that repeats itself to infinity.

INITIALS ON COVER - Someone's initials in pencil, pen, or grease pencil written on the cover.

INIT. ON CVR - Short for **Initials on Cover**.

INK SKIP - Printing defect in which the printing roller momentarily receives no ink, causing a streak or blank spot.

INK SMUDGE - Printing defect in which ink is smeared, usually by handling, before the ink is completely dry; these defects commonly look like fingerprints.

INTRO - Same as **Debut**.

INVESTMENT GRADE COPY - (1) Comic of sufficiently high grade and demand to be viewed by collectors as instantly liquid should the need arise to sell; (2) A comic in VF or better condition; (3) A comic purchased primarily to realize a profit.

ISSUE NUMBER - The actual edition number of a given title.

ISH - Short for Issue.

JOINED PAGES - (1) Bindery defect in which pages are "trimmed long" and are not separated at right hand corner(s) or along right edge. See **Siamese Pages**; (2) A rare printing defect where a new roll of paper is glued to the spent roll while still on the press. This glued intersection appears as a vertical stripe of double thick newsprint on one of the interior pages.

KEY, KEY BOOK or KEY ISSUE - An issue that contains a first appearance, origin, or other historically or artistically important feature considered especially desirable by collectors.

LAMINATED - Clear plastic with adhesive used by early collectors to protect comics; an outdated and destructive technique which virtually eliminates collector value.

LAMONT LARSON - Pedigreed collection of high grade 1940s comics with the initials or name of its original owner, Lamont Larson.

LATERAL BAR - See **Staple Lateral Bar**.

LBC - Abbreviation for Left [Side or Edge of] Back Cover.

LENTICULAR COVERS or "FLICKER" COVERS - A comic book cover overlayed with a ridged plastic sheet such that the special artwork underneath appears to move when the cover is tilted at different angles perpendicular to the ridges.

LETTER COL or LETTER COLUMN - A feature in a comic book that prints and sometimes responds to letters written by its readers.

LFC - Abbreviation for Left [Side or Edge of] Front Cover.

LFT - Abbreviation for Left. Not much of an abbreviation, is it?

LGC - Abbreviation for **Logo Cut**.

LIGHT CREASING - A crease 2" long or less.

LINE DRAWN COVER - A cover published in the traditional way where pencil sketches are overdrawn with india ink and then colored. See also **Grey-Tone Cover**, **Photo Cover**, and **Painted Cover**.

LLBC - Abbreviation for Lower Left [Corner of] Back Cover.

LLFC - Abbreviation for Lower Left [Corner of] Front Cover.

LOGO - The title of a strip or comic book as it appears on the cover or title page.

LOGO CUT - See **Remainders**.

LOOSE STAPLE - Staple that can be easily moved and no longer holds comic pages tightly. See **Popped Staple**.

LRBC - Abbreviation for Lower Right [Corner of] Back Cover.

LRFC - Abbreviation for Lower Right [Corner of] Front Cover.

LS - Abbreviation for **Loose Staple**.

LSH - Abbreviation for Legion of Super-Heroes.

LT - Abbreviation for Light.

MAGIC LIGHTNING COLLECTION - A collection of high grade 1950s comics from the San Francisco area.

MANUFACTURING FOLD - A defect in which some page(s) of the comic (usually the cover) is folded during the printing and/or the paper manufacturing process.

MARRIED - A married comic book is one in which the issue includes wrap(s), page(s) or cover replaced from another copy of the same issue. This is generally done to replace missing or damaged portions of an issue. When graded by CGC, if restoration (such as reinforcement) is detected, that comic book will be given the "Restored" purple label; otherwise it is certified with the green "Qualified" label.

MARVEL CHIPPING - A bindery (trimming/cutting) defect that results in a series of chips and tears at the top, bottom, and right edges of the cover, caused when the cutting blade of an

Marvel chipping

industrial paper trimmer becomes dull. It was dubbed Marvel Chipping because it can be found quite often on Marvel comics from the late '50s and early '60s but can also occur with any company's comic books from the late 1940s through the middle 1960s.

MAVERICK PAGES or MAVERICK SIGNATURE - Interior pages that are not the same size or shape as the rest of the interior; most commonly a bindery defect.

MAVERICK STAPLE - See Deformed Staple.

MID-SPINE - Between the staples.

MILE HIGH COLLECTION - High grade collection of over 22,000 comics discovered in Denver, Colorado in 1977, originally owned by Mr. Edgar Church. Comics from this collection are now famous for extremely white pages, fresh smell, and beautiful cover ink reflectivity.

Miswrapped cover

MIN - Abbreviation for Minor.

MISCUT or MISTRIMMED - Bindery defect where cover and/or pages are not cut square or are cut to wrong size.

MISWRAPPED - Bindery defect where staple and fold do not intersect the center of the cover, causing some of the back cover to appear on the front of the comic or some of the front cover to ride around to the back.

MOD - Abbreviation for Moderate.

MODERN AGE - A catch-all term usually applied to comics published from 1992 to the present.

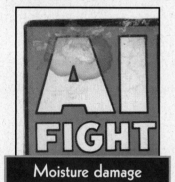
Moisture damage

MOISTURE DAMAGE - Wrinkling and/or stains caused by absorption of a liquid.

MOISTURE DAMAGE or MOISTURE RING - Wrinkling and/or stains, often circular, caused by absorption of moisture, often from the bottom of a cup or glass.

MOTH BALL SMELL - The aroma that infuses some comic books because of their storage with moth balls. Some comics from specific collections can be identified by this characteristic odor.

MS - Abbreviation for Missing Staple.

MULTIPLE BINDERY STAPLES - Bindery defect in which the comic book is stapled additional times unnecessarily.

MYLAR[TM] - An inert, very hard, space-age plastic used to make high quality protective bags and sleeves for comic book storage. "Mylar" is a trademark of the DuPont Co.

NAME STAMP - Indicates that an ink stamp with someone's name (and sometimes address) has been stamped in or on the comic book.

NBC - Abbreviation for No Back Cover.

NC - Abbreviation for No Cover.

ND - Abbreviation for No Date.

NFC - Abbreviation for No Front Cover.

NGL - Abbreviation for No (3-D) Glasses.

NN - Abbreviation for No Number.

NO COVER - Come on, do you really need a definition for this one? See Coverless...if you have to.

NO DATE - When there is no date given on the cover or indicia page.

NO NUMBER - No issue number is given on the cover or indicia page; these are usually first issues or one-shots.

NOC - Abbreviation for Name on Cover.

OFF-CENTER FOLDING - See Folding Error.

OFF-SET COVER - See Folding Error.

OIL DAMAGE or OIL STAIN - A defect in which oil has penetrated the cover and /or interior pages, causing them to become translucent in the area of the stain.

ONE-SHOT - When only one issue is published of a title, or when a series is published where each issue is a different title (e.g. Dell's *Four Color Comics*).

ORIGIN - When the story of a character's creation is given.

OS - Abbreviation for Oxidation Shadow.

OVER-COVER - A condition common in 1950s comic books where the cover extends approximately 1/16 of an inch beyond the interior pages. Because this margin is unsupported by the interior pages, it is more susceptible to damage.

O/W - Abbreviation for Otherwise.

OWL - Overstreet Whiteness Level, a scale for evaluating paper color established in the original *The Official Overstreet Comic Book Grading Guide.*

Oxidation shadow

OXIDATION SHADOW - Darker, usually linear area at the edge of some comics stored in stacks. Some portion of the cover was not covered by the comic immediately above it, and it was exposed to the air. Also see Dust Shadow and Sun Shadow.

PAGES MISSING - One or more pages have been removed from the comic.

PAGES OUT OF ORDER - A rare bindery defect in which the pages of a comic book are bound together in the wrong order.

PAGES TRIMMED - The top, bottom and right-hand edges of the comic (or possibly interior pages) have been trimmed with a paper cutter, hand blade, or pneumatic cutter to hide edge defects.

PAGES UPSIDE DOWN - A rare bindery defect in which the cover orientation is reversed relative to the orientation of the interior pages.

PAINTED COVER - (1) Cover taken from an actual painting instead of a line drawing; (2) Inaccurate name for a grey-toned cover.

PANELOLOGIST - One who researches comic books and/or comic strips.

PANNAPICTAGRAPHIST - One possible term for someone who collects comic books; can you figure out why it hasn't exactly taken off in common parlance?

PAPER ABRASION - Rough patch or area where the paper has been abraded on a rough surface, leaving a rough texture that is often faded.

PAPER COVER - Comic book cover made from the same newsprint as the interior pages. These books are extremely rare in high grade.

PARADE OF PLEASURE - A book about the censorship of comics.

PB - Abbreviation for Paperback.

PC - Abbreviation for Piece.

PEDIGREE - A book from a famous and usually high grade collection - e.g. Allentown,

Lamont Larson, Edgar Church/Mile High, Denver, San Francisco, Cosmic Aeroplane, etc. Beware of non-pedigree collections being promoted as pedigree books; only outstanding high grade collections similar to those listed qualify.

PERFECT BINDING - Pages are glued to the cover as opposed to being stapled to the cover, resulting in a flat binded side. Also known as **Square Back or Square Bound**.

PERFORATIONS - Small holes at the page margins which sometimes occur as part of the manufacturing process; not considered a defect. Perforations are sometimes used to tell if a comic is an unread copy. In such a copy, tell-tale clicks are heard when the book is opened for the first time as the perforations separate.

PG - Abbreviation for Page.

PHOTO COVER - Comic book cover featuring a photographic image instead of a line drawing or painting.

PHOTO-REACTIVE COLORS or INKS - Certain inks used in the printing of comics that contain a higher proportion of metals, thus decreasing their stability and resistance to fading; comics with these inks/colors commonly have faded covers. Examples are: "DC dark green" (e.g. *Showcase* #8, *Superman* #100), blue (*Showcase* #13), purple (*Showcase* #14), and orange-red (*Showcase* #4).

PICKLE SMELL - A colloquial description of the odor of acetic acid, often associated with browning and/or brittle paper. See **Vinegar Smell**.

PICTORIAL COVER - Another term for **Photo Cover**.

PIN HOLES - Tiny holes often passing through the covers and multiple pages of a comic where a pin was used to tack the comic to a board. In some cases, the paper displaced by the pin may still be present but frayed; in other cases, removal of the pin may have torn away miniscule pieces of paper around the hole.

PLATINUM AGE - Comics published from approximately 1883-1938.

PNEUMATIC CUTTER - An industrial tool used to shear large amounts of paper.

PNL - Abbreviation for Panel.

POC - Abbreviation for Pencil On Cover.

POLYPROPALENE - A type of plastic used in the manufacture of comic book bags; now considered harmful to paper and not recommended for long term storage of comics.

POOO - Abbreviation for **Pages Out Of Order**.

POPPED STAPLE - A term used to describe a condition where the cover has split at the staple and has become detached or popped loose. See **Loose Staple**.

POST-CODE - Describes comics published after February 1955 and usually displaying the CCA stamp in the upper right-hand corner.

POUGHKEEPSIE - Refers to a large collection of Dell Comics file copies believed to have originated from the warehouse of Western Publishing in Poughkeepsie, NY.

PP - Abbreviation for Pages.

PRESSING - A term used to describe a variety of processes or procedures, professional and amateur, under which an issue is pressed to eliminate wrinkles, bends, dimples and/or other perceived defects and thus improve its appearance. Some types of pressing involve disassembling the book and performing other work on it prior to its pressing and reassembly. Some methods are generally easily discerned by professionals and amateurs. Other types of pressing, however, can pose difficulty for even experienced professionals to detect. In all cases, readers are cautioned that unintended damage can occur in some instances. Related defects will diminish an issue's grade correspondingly rather than improve it.

PRICE STICKERS - Adhesive stickers applied to comic covers to alter the cover price; often considered a defect.

PRINTERS' SMUDGE - See Ink Smudge.

PRINTING DEFECT - A defect caused by the printing process. Examples would include paper wrinkling, miscut edges, misfolded spine, untrimmed pages, off-registered color, off-centered trimming, misfolded and unbound pages. It should be noted that these are all defects that lower the grade of the book.

PRINT-THROUGH - The printing on the inside of the front cover is visible (to varying degrees) from the front cover as if one were looking through the front cover. This is not always considered a defect. See Transparent Cover.

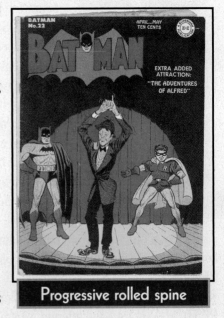

Progressive rolled spine

PROGRESSIVE ROLLED SPINE - A spine roll that is more pronounced on one end than the other.

PROVENANCE - When the owner of a book is known and is stated for the purpose of authenticating and documenting the history of the book. Example: A book from the Stan Lee or Forrest Ackerman collection would be an example of a value-adding provenance.

PULP - Cheaply produced magazine made from low grade newsprint. The term comes from the wood pulp that was used in the paper manufacturing process.

PUZZLE FILLED IN - Game or puzzle inside a comic book that has been written on, thus reducing the value of the comic.

QUARTERLY - Published every three months (four times a year).

QUINONE - (1) The substance in ink that promotes oxidation and discoloration and is associated with transfer stains; (2) A yellowish, crystalline compound with an irritating odor, obtained by the oxidation of aniline, and regarded as a benzene with two hydrogen atoms replaced by two oxygen atoms. It is used in tanning and making dyes. Quinone will oxidize another material and itself reduce to hydroquinone. Bet you wished you paid attention in chemistry class now. See Aniline.

R - Abbreviation for Reprint.

RARE - 10-20 copies estimated to exist.

RAT CHEW - Damage caused by the gnawing of rats and mice.

RBC - Abbreviation for Right [Side or Edge of] Back Cover.

RBCC - Abbreviation for Rockets Blast Comic Collector, one of the first and most prominent adzines instrumental in developing the early comic book market.

Rat chew

READING COPY - A comic that is in FAIR to GOOD condition and is often used for research; the condition has been sufficiently reduced to the point where general handling will not degrade it further.

READING CREASE - Book-length, vertical front cover crease at staples, caused by bending the cover over the staples. Square-bounds receive these creases just by opening the cover too far to the left.

Reading crease

RECESSED STAPLES - When the staple lateral bar penetrates below the plane of the cover without breaking through.

REGLOSSING - A repair technique where silicone or other clear sprays are applied to comic book covers in an attempt to restore cover ink reflectivity. This is not generally viewed as an ethical practice and therefore reduces the value of the comic.

REMAINDERS - Comic books that remain unsold at the newsstand. In the past, the top 1/4 to 1/3 of the cover (or in some cases the entire cover) was removed and returned to the publisher for credit; this is the reason many comics from 1936-1965 are sometimes found as **Coverless**, **Three-Fourths**, or **Two-Thirds** cover copies.

REPRINT COMICS - In earlier decades, comic books that contained newspaper strip reprints; modern reprint comics usually contain stories originally featured in older comic books.

RES - Abbreviation for Restored.

RESEARCH COPY - See **Reading Copy**.

RESTORATION - Any attempt, whether professional or amateur, to enhance the appearance of an aging or damaged comic book using additive procedures. These procedures may include any or all of the following techniques: recoloring, adding missing paper, trimming, re-glossing, reinforcement, glue, etc. Amateur work can lower the value of a book, and even professional restoration has now gained a negative aura in the modern marketplace from some quarters. In all cases a restored book can never be worth the same as an unrestored book in the same condition. There is no consensus on the inclusion of pressing, non-aqueous cleaning, tape removal and in some cases staple replacement in this definition. Until such time as there is consensus, we encourage continued debate and interaction among all interested parties and reflection upon the standards in other hobbies and art forms.

RESTORED COPY - A comic book that has had restoration work.

RETURN or RETURN COPY - See **Remainders**.

RFC - Abbreviation for Right [Side or Edge of] Front Cover.

RICE PAPER - A thin, transparent paper commonly used by restorers to repair tears and replace small pieces on covers and pages of comic books.

RIP - An uneven rough tear; different from a split or cut.

RLS - Abbreviation for **Rolled Spine**.

ROLLED SPINE - A condition where the left edge of a comic book curves toward the front or back; a defect caused by folding back each page as the comic was read. See **Progressive Rolled Spine**.

Rolled spine

ROUGH SPINE - See **Abraded Spine**.

ROUND BOUND - Standard saddle stitch binding typical of most comics.

ROUNDED CORNER - See **Abraded Corner**.

RT - Abbreviation for Right.

RUN - A group of comics of one title where most or all of the issues are present. See **Complete Run**.

RUST MIGRATION - Rust stains that have moved from the staples to the adjacent paper.

RUST STAIN - (1) A red-brown stain caused by proximity to a rusty object; (2) A stain associated with rusty staples. This is considered a defect.

RUSTY STAPLES - Staples that have oxidized through exposure to moisture in the air.

Rusty staple

SADDLE STITCH - The staple binding of magazines and comic books.

SC - Abbreviation for **Subscription Crease**.

SCARCE - 20-100 copies estimated to exist.

SCRAPED STAPLE - A staple which has had rust or other discoloration removed by scraping the surface. This condition is readily identifiable under a hand lens or magnifying glass.

SCUFF or PAPER SCUFF - A light paper abrasion.

SEDUCTION OF THE INNOCENT - An inflammatory book written by Dr. Frederic Wertham and published in 1953; Wertham asserted that comics were responsible for rampant juvenile deliquency in American youth.

SET - (1) A complete run of a given title; (2) A grouping of comics for sale.

SEMI-MONTHLY - Published twice a month, but not necessarily **Bi-Weekly**.

SEWN SPINE - A comic with many spine perforations where binders' thread held it into a bound volume. This is considered a defect.

SF - Abbreviation for Science Fiction (the other commonly used term, "sci-fi," is often considered derogatory or indicative of more "low-brow" rather than "literary" science fiction, i.e. "sci-fi television."

SHALLOW STAPLE - A staple that has not penetrated all of the pages and is not visible at the centerfold. See **Deformed Staple**.

SIAMESE PAGES - A bindery defect in which pages are "trimmed long" and are not separated at right-hand corner(s) or along right edge. See **Joined Pages**.

SIGNATURE or SIG - A large sheet of paper printed with four, or a multiple of four, pages. When folded, it becomes a section of one comic book.

SIGNATURE DUPLICATED - A rare bindery defect in which a signature is inadvertently duplicated. This may also displace and/or replace an adjacent signature.

SIGNATURE OUT OF ORDER - A rare bindery defect in which signatures are bound in the wrong sequence. For example, a 32-page comic book with this defect usually has pages in the following order: 9-16, 1-8, 25-32, 17-24.

SIGNATURE REVERSED - A rare bindery defect in which the orientation of one of the signatures is reversed and appears upside down and backwards.

SILVER AGE - Comics published from approximately 1956 (*Showcase* #4) to 1970.

SILVER PROOF - A black and white actual size print on thick glossy paper hand-painted by an artist to indicate colors to the engraver.

SIZING - The glaze applied to newsprint at the end of the manufacturing process.

SLAB - Colloquial term for the plastic enclosure used by grading certification companies to seal in certified comics.

SLABBING - Colloquial term for the process of encapsulating certified comics in a plastic enclosure.

SLICK COVER - Any cover that is made from clay-coated paper stock.

SLT - Abbreviation for Slight.

SM - Abbreviation for Small.

SMOKE DAMAGE - Grey or black discoloration caused by smoke. This is considered a defect.

SOILING - Organic and inorganic substances and residues on the surface of the paper; different from stains, smudges, and mildew.

SOTI - Abbreviation for **Seduction of the Innocent**.

SPINE - The left-hand edge of the comic that has been folded and stapled.

SPINE CHIP - A small piece missing from the area of the spine.

SPINE ROLL - See **Rolled Spine** and **Progressive Rolled Spine**.

SPINE SPLIT - An even separation at the spine fold, commonly above or below the staple.

SPINE STRESS - A small fold, usually less than 1/4 inch long, perpendicular to the spine.

SPL - Abbreviation for **Spine Split**.

SPLASH PAGE - A **Splash Panel** that takes up the entire page.

SPLASH PANEL - (1) The first panel of a comic book story, usually larger than other panels and usually containing the title and credits of the story; (2) An oversized interior panel.

Stains

SPLIT SPINE - See **Spine Split**.

SPN - Abbreviation for **Spine**.

SQUARE BACK or SQUARE BOUND - See **Perfect Binding**.

SS - Abbreviation for **Store Stamp**.

STAINS - Discoloration caused by a foreign substance.

STAMP PAGE - Page devoted to the sale and discussion of stamp collecting; common in comics of the 1930s.

STAPLE EXTENDERS - The portion of the staple that actually penetrates the paper and can be seen at the centerfold; the portion of the staple that is bent either upwards or downwards toward the center of the staple.

STAPLE HOLE - A punched-out area in cover and interior pages caused by staple extender. This hole becomes enlarged (abraded) when staples are removed and replaced several times.

STAPLE LATERAL BAR - The portion of the staple that does not penetrate the paper and lies on top of the cover parallel to the spine; the part of the staple visible on the outside of the comic.

STAPLE PAGE - Term used by early collectors to describe the **Centerfold**.

STAPLE REINFORCED - (1) To strengthen with additional materials the cover paper at the site of staple contact; (2) To strengthen with additional materials the centerfold and/or other pages at the points of staple contact.

STAPLE RUST MIGRATION - Rust stains have moved from the staple to the paper.

STAPLE TEAR - Most often indicates paper separation at the staple.

STAPLE POPPED - Staple tear; staple has "popped" loose from the cover.

STICKER ON COVER - Price, name, or other sticker adhered to cover.

STN - Abbreviation for Staining.

Store stamp

STORE STAMP - Store name (and sometimes address and telephone number) stamped in ink via rubber stamp and stamp pad.

STP - Abbreviation for Staples.

STRESS LINES - Light, tiny wrinkles occuring along the spine, projecting from the staples or appearing anywhere on the covers of a comic book.

STRESS SPLIT - Any clean paper separation caused by pressure; most common at the spine.

SUBSCRIPTION COPY - A comic sent through the mail directly from the publisher or publisher's agent. Most are folded in half, causing a subscription crease or fold running down the center of the comic from top to bottom; this is considered a defect.

SUBSCRIPTION CREASE - See **Subscription Copy**.

SUBSCRIPTION FOLD - See **Subscription Copy**. Differs from a **Subscription Crease** in that no ink is missing as a result of the fold.

SUN - Abbreviation for **Sun Shadow**.

SUN SHADOW - Darker, usually linear area at the edge of some comics stored in stacks. Some portion of the cover was not covered by the comic immediately above it, and it suffered prolonged exposure to light. A serious defect, unlike a **Dust Shadow**, which can sometimes be removed. Also see **Oxidation Shadow**.

SUPPLE - The condition of paper with little or no deterioration. This kind of paper is bendable, pliant, and limber; the other end of the spectrum from **Brittleness**.

SWIPE - A panel, sequence, or story obviously borrowed from previously published material.

TANNIN LINE - A brownish stain line of tannin that occurs when wet comic book paper dries.

TAPE PULL - Loss of artwork or color when a piece of tape stuck to the cover has been improperly removed from the paper surface.

Tape residue

TAPE RESIDUE - Adhesive substance from tape which has penetrated paper fibers.

TAPE STAIN - See **Tape Residue**.

TEAR - An irregular separation of the paper; different from a split or cut.

TEAR SEALED - A tear that has been glued together.

TEXT ILLO. - A drawing or small panel in a text story that almost never has a dialogue balloon.

TEXT PAGE - A page with no panels or drawings.

TEXT STORY - A story with few if any illustrations commonly used as filler material during the first three decades of comics.

3-D COMIC - Comic art that is drawn and printed in two color layers, producing a 3-D effect when viewed through special glasses.

3-D EFFECT COMIC - Comic art that is drawn to appear as if in 3-D but isn't.

THREE-FOURTHS COVER - See **Remainders**.

TITLE - The name of the comic book.

TITLE PAGE - First page of a story showing the title of the story and possibly the creative credits and indicia.

TOBC - Abbreviation for Top Of Back Cover.

TOFC - Abbreviation for Top Of Front Cover.

TOS - (1) Abbreviation for Tape On Spine; (2) Abbreviation for *Tales of Suspense*.

TP - Abbreviation for **Tape Pull**.

TR - Abbreviation for **Tear**.

TRANSFER STAIN - Ink from the first page rubs off onto the inside front cover, causing certain portions to appear yellowed; often mistaken for paper deterioration. Can also occur on inside back cover.

TRANSPARENT COVER - The printing on the inside front cover is visible (to varying degrees) from the outside front cover. This is not always considered a defect. See **Print-Through**.

TRIMMED - (1) A bindery process which separates top, right, and bottom of pages and cuts comic books to the proper size; (2) A repair process in which defects along the edges of a comic book are removed with the use of scissors, razor blades, and/or paper cutters. Comic books which have been repaired in this fashion are considered defectives.

TTA - Abbreviation for *Tales to Astonish*.

TWO-THIRDS COVER - See **Remainders**.

UK - Abbreviation for British edition (United Kingdom).

ULBC - Abbreviation for Upper Left Corner Of Back Cover.

ULFC - Abbreviation for Upper Left Corner Of Front Cover.

UPGRADE - To obtain another copy of the same comic book in a higher grade.

URBC - Abbreviation for Upper Right Corner Of Back Cover.

URFC - Abbreviation for Upper Right Corner Of Front Cover.

VARIANT COVER - A different cover image used on the same issue.

VERY RARE - 1 to 10 copies estimated to exist.

VICTORIAN AGE - Comics published from approximately 1828-1883.

VINEGAR SMELL - The smell of acetic acid in newsprint that is deteriorating.

WAREHOUSE COPY - Originating from a publisher's warehouse; similar to file copy.

WATER DAMAGE - See **Moisture Damage**.

WC - Abbreviation for **White Cover**.

WD - Abbreviation for **Water Damage**.

WHITE COVER - A comic cover where white is the predominant color. These covers are easily stained and/or damaged and readily show wear. Because they rarely occur in high grade, white covers are in great demand by collectors.

WHITE MOUNTAIN COLLECTION - A collection of high grade 1950s and 1960s comics which originated in New England.

WHITE PAGES - A term used to describe interior pages in the best state of preservation; the preferred state of interior pages.

WHITENESS LEVEL - The whiteness of interior pages compared against a whiteness standard like the OWL scale.

WOC - Abbreviation for Writing On Cover.

WORM HOLE - Small holes eaten into paper caused by a variety of insects and boring worms.

WP - Abbreviation for **White Pages**.

WR - Abbreviation for Writing.

WRAP - A single sheet of paper folded to form four pages of story (counting both sides) and bound into a comic; the center-fold is a wrap, as is the cover and all successive pages. The "first" or "outer" wrap is the first interior page after the cover.

WRP - Abbreviation for **Wrap**.

WRONG COVER - A rare bindery defect in which the cover from one comic is stapled to the interior pages of another comic.

WS - Abbreviation for Water Stain.

YEL - Abbreviation for Yellowing.

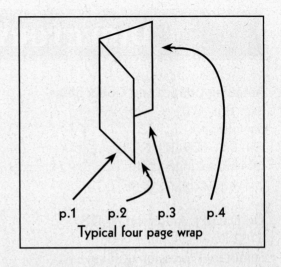

p.1   p.2   p.3   p.4
Typical four page wrap

ADVERTISER INDEX

DIRECTORY LISTINGS

Amazing Comics and Collectibles
P.O. Box 470
Sayville, NY 11782
PH: 631-605-0143
info@amazingco.com
www.amazingco.com

Dr. David J. Anderson, D.D.S.
5192 Dawes Avenue
Seminary Professional Village
Alexandria, VA 22311
PH/FAX: 703-578-1222
DJA2@cox.net

ArchAngels
4629 Cass Street #9
Pacific Beach, CA 92109
PH: 310-480-8105
rhughes@archangels.com
www.archangels.com

Bill Cole Enterprises
P.O. Box 60
Randolph, MA 02368-0060
PH/FAX: 781-986-2653
sales@bcemylar.com
www.bcemylar.com

Certified Guaranty Company (CGC)
P.O. Box 4738
Sarasota, FL 34230
PH: (877) NM-COMIC
FAX: (941) 360-2558
www.CGCcomics.com

Comic Book Certification Service (CBCS)
P.O. Box 33048
St. Petersburg, FL 33733-8048
PH: 727-803-6822
PH: 844-870-CBCS (2227)
www.CBCScomics.com

ComicConnect.com
873 Broadway, Suite 201
New York, NY 10003
PH: 888-779-7377
PH: 212-895-3999
FAX: 212-260-4304
support@comicconnect.com
www.comicconnect.com

Comic Investors LLC
PH: 844-MYCOMIC
joe@comicinvestors.com
www.comicinvestors.com

ComicLink Auctions & Exchange
PH: 617-517-0062
buysell@ComicLink.com
www.ComicLink.com

Diamond Comic Distributors
10150 York Rd.
Suite 300
Hunt Valley, MD 21030
PH: 443-318-8001

Diamond International Galleries
1940 Greenspring Drive
Suite I
Timonium, MD 21093
GalleryQuestions@DiamondGalleries.com
www.DiamondGalleries.com

Stephen A. Geppi
10150 York Rd.
Suite 300
Hunt Valley, MD 21030
PH: 443-318-8203
gsteve@diamondcomics.com

Geppi's Entertainment Museum
301 West Camden Street
Baltimore, MD 21201
PH: 410-625-7089
FAX: 410-625-7090
www.geppismuseum.com

E. Gerber Products
1720 Belmont Ave.; Suite C
Baltimore, MD 21244
PH: 888-79-MYLAR

Hake's Americana
P.O. Box 12001
York, PA 17402
PH: 866-404-9800
www.hakes.com

Heritage Auctions
3500 Maple Avenue; 17th Floor
Dallas, TX 75219-3941
PH: 800-872-6467
www.HA.com

Metropolis Collectibles
873 Broadway, Suite 201
New York, NY 10003
PH: 800-229-6387
FAX: 212-260-4304
E-Mail: buying@metropoliscomics.com
www.metropoliscomics.com

MyComicShop.com
PH: 817-860-7827
buytrade@mycomicshop.com
www.mycomicshop.com/sell
PH: 682-232-4855
consignment@mycomicshop.com
www.mycomicshop.com/consign

Pedigree Comics
12541 Equine Lane
Wellington, FL 33414
PH: 561-422-1120
PH: 561-596-9111
DougSchmell@pedigreecomics.com
www.PedigreeComics.com

That's Entertainment
56 John Fitch Highway
Fitchburg, MA 01420
PH: 978-342-8607
fitch@thatse.com
www.thatse.com

That's Entertainment
244 Park Ave.
Worcester, MA 01609
PH: 508-755-4207
ken@thatse.com
www.thatse.com

OVERSTREET ADVISORS

DARREN ADAMS
Pristine Comics
Seattle, WA

WELDON ADAMS
Comics Historian
Fort Worth, TX

GRANT ADEY
Halo Certification
Brisbane, QLD,
Australia

BILL ALEXANDER
Collector
Sacramento, CA

DAVID T. ALEXANDER
David Alexander
Comics
Tampa, FL

TYLER ALEXANDER
David Alexander
Comics
Tampa, FL

LON ALLEN
Heritage Comics
Auctions
Dallas, TX

DAVE ANDERSON
Want List Comics
Tulsa, OK

STEPHEN BARRINGTON
Flea Market Comics
Chickasaw, AL

LAUREN BECKER
Warp 9 Comics
Clawson, MI

ROBERT BEERBOHM
Robert Beerbohm
Comic Art
Fremont, NE

JON BERK
Collector
Hartford, CT

JIM BERRY
Collector
Portland, OR

JON BEVANS
Collector
Baltimore, MD

**PETER BILELIS,
ESQ.**
Collector
South Windsor, CT

**DR. ARNOLD T.
BLUMBERG**
Collector
Baltimore, MD

STEVE BOROCK
Comic Book
Certification Service
St Petersburg, FL

KEVIN BOYD
Collector
Toronto, ONT
Canada

SCOTT BRADEN
Comics Historian
Hanover, PA

RICHARD BROWN
Collector
Detroit, MI

MICHAEL BROWNING
Collector
Danville, WV

SHAWN CAFFREY
Finalizer/Modern Age
Specialist
CGC

MICHAEL CARBONARO
Bestincomics.com
New York

BRETT CARRERAS
Brett's Comic Pile
Richmond, VA

GARY CARTER
Collector
Coronado, CA

CHARLES CERRITO
Hotflips
Farmingdale, NY

JEFF CERRITO
Hotflips
Farmingdale, NY

JOHN CHRUSCINSKI
Tropic Comics
Lyndora, PA

PAUL CLAIRMONT
PNJ Comics
Winnipeg, MB
Canada

ART CLOOS
Collector/Historian
Flushing, NY

GARY COLABUONO
Dealer/Collector
Arlington Heights, IL

BILL COLE
Bill Cole Enterprises,
Inc.
Randolph, MA

TIM COLLINS
RTS Unlimited, Inc.
Lakewood, CO

ANDREW COOKE
Writer/Director
New York City, NY

JON B. COOKE
Editor - Comic Book
Artist Magazine
West Kingston, RI

JACK COPLEY
Coliseum of Comics
Florida

JESSE JAMES CRISCIONE
Jesse James Comics
Glendale, AZ

FRANK CWIKLIK
Metropolis Comics
New York, NY

BROCK DICKINSON
Collector
St. Catharines, ONT
Canada

PETER DIXON
Paradise Comics
Toronto, ONT Canada

GARY DOLGOFF
Gary Dolgoff Comics
Easthampton, MA

JOHN DOLMAYAN
Torpedo Comics
Las Vegas, NV

WALTER DURAJLIJA
Big B Comics
Hamilton, ONT
Canada

KEN DYBER
Cloud 9 Comics
Portland, OR

TOMIS ERB
Comic Verification
Authority
Brooklyn, NY

CONRAD ESCHENBERG
Collector/Dealer
Cold Spring, NY

MICHAEL EURY
Author
Concord, NC

RICHARD EVANS
Bedrock City Comics
Houston, TX

D'ARCY FARRELL
Pendragon Comics
Toronto, ONT Canada

BILL FIDYK
Collector
Annapolis, MD

PAUL FIGURA
Tenth Planet Comics
and Games
Oak Lawn, IL

JOSEPH FIORE
ComicWiz.com
Toronto, ONT Canada

STEPHEN FISHLER
Metropolis
Collectibles, Inc.
New York, NY

DAN FOGEL
Hippy Comix, Inc.
Cleveland, OH

BRAD FOSTER
SharpComics.com
Plainfield, IL

DAN GALLO
Dealer/Comic Art Con
Westchester Co., NY

**STEPHEN H.
GENTNER**
Golden Age Specialist
Portland, OR

STEVE GEPPI
Diamond Int.
Galleries
Timonium, MD

DOUG GILLOCK
ComicLink
Portland, ME

MICHAEL GOLDMAN
Motor City Comics
Farmington Hills, MI

TOM GORDON III
Collector/Dealer
Westminster, MD

JAMIE GRAHAM
Graham Crackers
Chicago, IL

DANIEL GREENHALGH
Showcase
New England
Northford, CT

ERIC J. GROVES
Dealer/Collector
Oklahoma City, OK

GARY GUZZO
Atomic Studios
Boothbay Harbor, ME

JOHN HAINES
Dealer/Collector
Kirtland, OH

JIM HALPERIN
Heritage Comics
Auctions
Dallas, TX

JASON HAMLIN
Dealer
Richmond, VA

MARK HASPEL
Finalizer/
Pedigree Specialist
CGC

JEF HINDS
Jef Hinds Comics
Madison, WI

**GREG HOLLAND,
Ph.D.**
Collector
Alexander, AR

JOHN HONE
Collector
Silver Spring, MD

STEVEN HOUSTON
Torpedo Comics
Las Vegas, NV

BILL HUGHES
Dealer/Collector
Flower Mound, TX

ROB HUGHES
Arch Angels
Pacific Beach, CA

ED JASTER
Heritage Comics
Auctions
Dallas, TX

NICK KATRADIS
Collector
Tenafly, NJ

BRIAN KETTERER
Collector
Baltimore, MD

DENNIS KEUM
Fantasy Comics
Goldens Bridge, NY

IVAN KOCMAREK
Comics Historian
Hamilton, ON

MICHAEL KRONENBERG
Historian/Designer
Chapel Hill, NC

BEN LICHTENSTEIN
Zapp Comics
Wayne, NJ

STEPHEN LIPSON
Comics Historian
Mississauga, ON

PAUL LITCH
Primary Grader
CGC

DOUG MABRY
The Great Escape
Madison, TN

TOMMY MALETTA
Best Comics
International
New Hyde Park, NY

JOE MANNARINO
All Star Auctions
Ridgewood, NJ

NADIA MANNARINO
All Star Auctions
Ridgewood, NJ

BRIAN MARCUS
Cavalier Comics
Wise, VA

WILL MASON
GetCashForComics.com
New York

HARRY MATETSKY
Collector
Middletown, NJ

DAVE MATTEINI
Collector
Mineola, NY

JON McCLURE
Comics Historian,
Writer
Portland, OR

TODD McDEVITT
New Dimension Comics
Cranberry Township,
PA

MIKE McKENZIE
Alternate Worlds
Cockeysville, MD

ANDY McMAHON
Duncanville Bookstore
Duncanville, TX

PETER MEROLO
Collector
Sedona, AZ

**JOHN JACKSON
MILLER**
Historian, Writer
Scandinavia, WI

STEVE MORTENSEN
Miracle Comics
Santa Clara, CA

MICHAEL NAIMAN
Silver Age Specialist
Chapel Hill, NC

MARC NATHAN
Cards, Comics &
Collectibles
Reisterstown, MD

JOSHUA NATHANSON
ComicLink
Portland, ME

MATT NELSON
President, CCS
Sarasota, FL

TOM NELSON
Top Notch Comics
Yankton, SD

JAMIE NEWBOLD
Southern California
Comics
San Diego, CA

CHARLIE NOVINSKIE
Silver Age Specialist
Lake Havasu City, AZ

VINCE OLIVA
Grader
CGC, LLC

RICHARD OLSON
Collector/Academician
Poplarville, MS

TERRY O'NEILL
Terry's Comics
Orange, CA

MICHAEL PAVLIC
Purple Gorilla Comics
Calgary, AB Canada

JIM PAYETTE
Golden Age Specialist
Bethlehem, NH

JOHN PETTY
Collector/Historian
Coram, NY

JIM PITTS
Avalon Collectibles
Mountain View, CA

BILL PONSETI
Collector
Newtown Sq., PA

RON PUSSELL
Redbeard's Book Den
Crystal Bay, NV

CATHY RADER
"Offbeat Archives"
Comics & Collectibles
Sioux Falls, SD

JEFF RADER
"Offbeat Archives"
Comics & Collectibles
Sioux Falls, SD

GREG REECE
Greg Reece's
Rare Comics
Ijamsville, MD

STEPHEN RITTER
Worldwide Comics
Fair Oaks Ranch, TX

ROBERT ROGOVIN
Four Color Comics
Scarsdale, NY

MARNIN ROSENBERG
Collectors Assemble
Great Neck, NY

CHUCK ROZANSKI
Mile High Comics
Denver, CO

BEN SAMUELS
Collector
St. Louis, MS

BARRY SANDOVAL
Heritage Comics
Auctions
Dallas, TX

BUDDY SAUNDERS
Lone Star Comics
Arlington, TX

CONAN SAUNDERS
Lone Star Comics
Arlington, TX

MATT SCHIFFMAN
Bronze Age Specialist
Bend, OR

DOUG SCHMELL
Pedigree Comics, Inc.
Wellington, FL

BRIAN SCHUTZER
Sparkle City Comics
Neat Stuff Collectibles
North Bergen, NJ

ALIKA SEKI
Maui Comics and
Collectibles
Waiehu, HI

TODD SHEFFER
Hake's Americana
York, PA

FRANK SIMMONS
Coast to Coast Comics
Rocklin, CA

DOUG SIMPSON
Paradise Comics
Toronto, ONT Canada

ANTHONY SNYDER
Anthony's
Comic Book Art
Leonia, NJ

MARK SQUIREK
Collector
Baltimore, MD

TONY STARKS
Silver Age Specialist
Evansville, IN

WEST STEPHAN
Comic Book
Certification Service
St Petersburg, FL

AL STOLTZ
Basement Comics
Havre de Grace, MD

DOUG SULIPA
"Everything 1960-1996"
Manitoba, Canada

CHRIS SWARTZ
Collector
San Diego, CA

BRIAN TATGE
Motor City Comics
Farmington Hills, MI

MAGGIE THOMPSON
Collector/Historian
Iola, WI

MICHAEL TIERNEY
The Comic Book
Store
Little Rock, AR

TED VAN LIEW
Superworld Comics
Worcester, MA

JOE VERENEAULT
JHV Associates
Woodbury Heights, NJ

JASON VERSAGGI
Collector
Brooklyn, NY

JOSEPH VETERI, ESQ.
Comic Con Art
Springfield, NJ

TODD WARREN
Collector
Fort Washington, PA

BOB WAYNE
DC Comics
New York City, NY

JEFF WEAVER
Victory Comics
Falls Church, VA

LON WEBB
Dark Adventure
Comics
Norcross, GA

RICK WHITELOCK
New Force Comics
Lynn Haven, FL

MIKE WILBUR
Diamond Int.
Galleries
Timonium, MD

MARK WILSON
PGC Mint
Castle Rock, WA

ALEX WINTER
Hake's Americana
York, PA

HARLEY YEE
Dealer/Collector
Detroit, MI

MARK ZAID
EsquireComics.com
Bethesda, MD

VINCENT ZURZOLO, JR.
Metropolis
Collectibles, Inc.
New York, NY

THE
ONLINE MAGAZINE
OF

www.fandomnetwork.com

DISCOVER
WHAT'S GONE BEFORE

www.gemstonepub.com

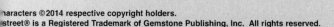

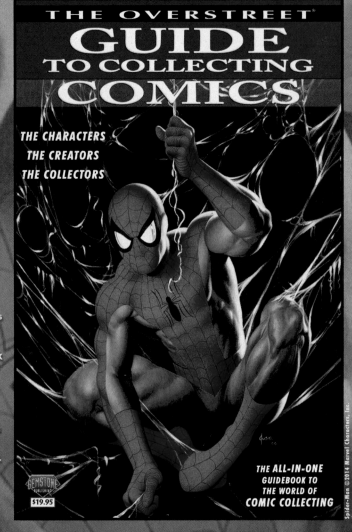

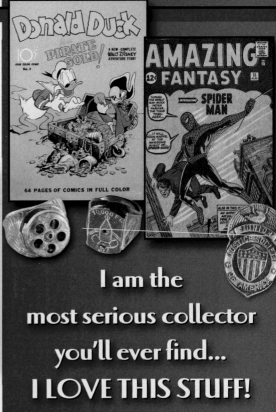